ISLAND GARDENING

ISLAND GARDENING

*A Month-by-Month Guide for
West Coast Gardeners*

RAMONA SOMMER

ORCA BOOK PUBLISHERS

Canadian Cataloguing in Publication Data
Sommer, Ramona, 1941–
  Island gardening
  Includes index.

  ISBN 1-55143-013-4
  1. Gardening–Pacific Coast (B.C.)   2. Gardening–Pacific Coast (Wash.)
3. Gardening–Pacific Coast (Or.)   I. Title.
SB453.3C2S65 1994   635'.09795   C94-910157-5

Cover design by Christine Toller
Interior illustrations by Stuart Duncan
Cover photo by Lynne Milnes

Printed and bound in Canada

Orca Book Publishers
PO Box 5626, Stn B
Victoria, BC Canada
V8R 6S4

Orca Book Publishers
#3028, 1574 Gulf Road
Point Roberts, WA USA
98281

10 9 8 7 6 5 4 3 2 1

This book is dedicated to my children,
Corina, Manuel and Rick,
and to my friends who supported me,
giving me the confidence, patience and
encouragement to keep going despite the obstacles

ACKNOWLEDGEMENTS

Writing this book has been an exciting adventure that wouldn't have been possible without the assistance of many others. Though it would be impossible to name everyone who helped out along the way, I would be remiss if I did not mention a few. First and foremost, I would like to thank my agent, Janet Adams, who first planted the idea in my head to put together a gardening book and who instilled in me the confidence to actually write the book. Thanks also to those working at the various government agencies, libraries, colleges and universities for their tireless efforts in tracking down documents and information on my behalf, and to Judy Southwell of The Development Group for her computer knowledge. Last, but certainly not least, a very sincere thank-you to Tracy Diehl, editor, and all the staff of *The Ladysmith Chemainus Chronicle*, who have assisted in countless ways in keeping the love and interest in gardening alive over the last three years through my weekly garden column, and who wholeheartedly supported my efforts in this book.

TABLE OF CONTENTS

PREFACE

In relation to the rest of Canada the islands off the West Coast of British Columbia and the Lower Mainland are unique in terms of climate. The natural rainforests are, in themselves, beautiful gardens. *Island Gardening* has been organized as a month-by-month guide because the mild, wet winters prevalent on the west coast mean that gardening can truly be a year-round adventure.

This book is written for the amateur gardener. The person who works a 9-to-5 job as a stockbroker, secretary, waitress, truckdriver or nurse, and doesn't want to go through twenty books from other parts of Canada and the United States just to find out when to plant petunias. *Island Gardening* will take readers through gardening month by month and help to strengthen their knowledge in understanding gardening on the West coast.

The reader will find the plants referred to by their common names with botanical names in parenthesis — for example, maple (*Acer*). This will probably disgruntle the experts, but will be beneficial for the amateur, who has no intention of learning every plant by both its Latin (botanical) name and its more common name. Step-by-step procedures for many of the projects can be found throughout the book. You will find the last chapter has been devoted to resource material, including various lists and information for convenient referral.

In thirty years of gardening, the author has made just about every mistake an amateur gardener could possibly make. These mistakes, along with the rewarding successes and her weekly garden column, have made her realize the needs of the amateur gardener. Receiving numerous letters from her readers over the last three years asking WHEN do I plant this or WHEN do I prune has led to this book, with hopes that some of the ideas can be utilized by gardeners from as far south as Oregon and as far north as the Queen Charlottes.

After all, the goal is the same for everyone: the joy, self-satisfaction and happiness of creating beauty through gardening.

JANUARY
The Start of a New Year

JANUARY BRINGS ANOTHER twelve months of the world's greatest hobby—gardening. The weather is usually a mixture of conditions on the islands off the West Coast of British Columbia, from north to south and east to west. Rain can be expected as the norm in most areas. The weather may be clear during the day with temperatures above freezing, and a light frost at night. At other times we have the occasional snowfall, which may last a day or two or even as much as a couple of weeks. Then there are always the years that are a combination of all of the above. December is the month with the most rainfall, November second and January a close third (*see Weather Statistics, page 153*).

January is the month gardeners like to curl up in front of a warm fireplace with their new garden catalogues and become armchair shoppers. January is an excellent time to plan the year's yard and garden work. For your convenience, I have compiled a list of Canadian garden catalogues that will help you (*see page 169*). If you are planning on ordering plants from the United States, be sure to write to one of the following addresses: Agriculture Canada, Plant Health Division, Permit Office, Ottawa, Ontario, K1A OC6; Agriculture Canada, Plant Health and Plant Products, #118-816 Government St., Victoria, BC, V8W 1W9; or Agriculture Canada, Food Production and Plant Inspection Branch, P.O. Box 2527, New Westminster, BC, V3L 5A8.

Ask for their free "Application to Import," which is required for each company you order plants from. You can order seeds from the U.S. catalogues the same way you do from Canadian catalogues, with no need to obtain a permit from Agriculture Canada first. Seeds are considered safe to send to Canada, while plants must be treated with more caution to be sure they are disease free.

January is also a good time to show some compassion for our feathered friends, especially if it has been cold. Birds are exciting to watch and great to have around to help with insects in the garden during the summer months. If the water source is frozen, fresh water can be supplied in a suitable container. There are a variety of bird feeders available on the market, although many talented gardeners would rather build their own. Birdseed is inexpensive and can be supplemented with sunflower seeds, peanut butter, bread crumbs, suet and various grains. Another more permanent way of feeding the birds is to plant shrubs, trees and flowers the birds can winter on, such as the arbutus, fig, persimmon, apple (*malus*), mountain ash, cotoneaster, pyracantha, photinia, Oregon grape, sumac, viburnum, holly and grape.

TREES, SHRUBS & VINES

The possibility of a heavy snowfall is likely during the month of January and can damage limbs of trees and shrubs, especially evergreens. Snow that falls on the coast is high in water content and, therefore, very heavy. Brush or shake snow off trees and shrubs to prevent the branches from breaking. If a freezing rain were to hit while the snow was still on the branches, it could cause a lot of additional damage.

When clearing snow or ice from your walkway or driveway, be careful where you put the snow. Don't shovel it on to the plants along the concrete. You may have used a chemical to make the surface safe and this will kill your plants. Don't use salt to clear the snow and ice. It will damage the surface of your concrete as well as kill plants it comes in contact with.

You may have seen beautiful evergreens standing sentinel at gates, along walkways and next to homes with one or more branches bent down and sticking out like a sore thumb. This is usually from a heavy snowfall that has separated the branch from the rest of the bush with its weight. The branch is seldom broken but is unsightly. Your first thought is to cut it off. If you do, you will leave a large brown spot which may or may not grow over within the next few years, depending upon the species. Instead of cutting the branch off, tie it onto the main stem, drawing it back into its proper position. Place short pieces of hose or an alternative next to the bark to prevent the rope from cutting into the bark of the main stem and branch. Within a season or two, the branch will retain its normal position without being tied.

Fertilize rhododendrons, camellias and azaleas to help replace some of the nutrients lost when blooming. They bloom so profusely, it requires a lot of energy from the plant. These beautiful shrubs have been setting on bud for this spectacular event since completing their blossoming last spring.

You will find some of your plants' soil washed away due to the heavy rains. Top with a layer of soil to protect any roots close to the surface from further washout from rains or exposure to frost.

Spring fever? Try bringing some spring-blooming branches such as forsythia, pussy willow, honeysuckle, winter sweet, quince and cornelian cherry into the warm air of your home and force them to bloom. Place them in a vase of slightly warm water. This will force the buds to swell and bloom within fifteen to twenty days. Be careful when cutting your bouquet not to cut just any branch. Try to do a little pruning while you are at it, since these are spring-flowering shrubs and should not be pruned normally until after they bloom. Cut branches you would usually prune – for instance, the branch pointing towards the centre of the bush instead of up and out, or that unruly branch which never seems to conform to the rest of the bush. What you will actually be doing by bringing them into the warmth of your home is waking them up from their dormant period. This will fool them into believing it is springtime. Wait for a warm day and cut the selected branches back to where they join a main branch, then recut it at the length you want. Place branches directly into the vase of warmish water in a cool room to begin, and in a few days they can gradually be introduced to the warmth of the room where you will display them. Keep the vase of branches away from any direct heat, which will dry out the tender buds before they open. The final step is to wait and enjoy. Forcing branches can be done right up to the time they would normally bloom outdoors. If you don't get to it this month, try it next month if the opportunity arises.

Pruning can begin this month if the days are comfortable

enough to work outside. There is a section on pruning in the next chapter if you require reminders or instructions. If you have any questions about pruning, check with an expert first or hire someone to do the pruning. Poor pruning can ruin the look and health of a tree.

WINTER-BLOOMING SHRUBS

You will often see pussy willow, *Rhododendron mucronulatum*, *Pieris japonica*, *Camellia sasanqua*, *Viburnum tinus* 'Spring Bouquet', Chinese witch hazel (*Hamamelis mollis*), winter heath (*Erica carnea* and *darleyensis*) and winter sweet (*Chimonanthus*) blooming at this time of year, while certain other species such as cotoneaster, firethorn (*Pyracantha*), beauty bush (*Callicarpa*), pernettya, snowberries (*symphoricarpos*), Barberry (*Berberis*), aucuba and holly (*Ilex*) provide colour with berries. Shrubs with brightly coloured or novel features in the winter are varieties of dogwood, willow, *Garrya and hazel (Corylus)*.

PUSSY WILLOW (*Salix caprea, discolour*, and *gracillstyia*) — Willows are natural bog plants, but do well in gardens with plenty of water made available. In order to keep long straight stems with large woolly catkins, either cut back the complete bush every couple of years after it has finished blooming or cut out old wood down to the ground. Either will encourage new growth for catkins next spring, since the woolly catkins are produced on last year's wood. The French pussy willow (*Salix caprea*) is the kind generally sold and used in spring flower arrangements.

RHODODENDRON — The *Rhododendron mucronulatum* is an early, deciduous variety of rhododendron blooming in a bright purple colour on usually bare branches during January and February.

PIERIS JAPONICA (or *Andromeda*) — This is an attractive and neat bush with new growth in a bright red giving the appearance of a poinsettia. The pendulous flower stems are covered with small white bells and are quite attractive in mid-winter or early spring.

CAMELLIA SASANQUA — A large family with a variety of flower forms (double, single, semi-double and anemone) and colours (pink, red, bi-colour, white). This plant has such spectacular blossoms, they are often mistaken for imitations. The camellia loves an acid soil, which is natural to the islands with our large rainfall. Wind and cold winter rains falling on the blossoms turn them brown and cause them to shatter earlier than they would normally, so if you plant an early bloomer, be sure to put it under the eaves or elsewhere where blossoms will be protected from the elements. The camellia is an excellent shrub for a shady or partially shady area.

CHINESE WITCH HAZEL *(Hamamelis mollis)* — The yellow spiderlike winter blossoms are quite showy on bare stems during December and January when so many other plants seem to be at rest, gladly waiting for warmer weather to strut their stuff. Witch hazel is very effective next to a building or in a group planting of evergreen shrubs.

VIBURNUM — The viburnum family is immense, and shows surprising variation. The summer-blooming 'Snowball' is of the viburnum family, as is the northern 'Highbush Cranberry'. 'Spring Bouquet' is a *Viburnum tinus*, but a smaller variety. It will usually maintain a 120- to 180-cm (48- to 60-in) range without becoming too scrubby looking. 'Spring Bouquet' can be pruned to maintain its shape with tiny white flowers forming a miniature bouquet all over the bush from October until March. The plant, although a welcome addition to the winter landscape, is susceptible to powdery mildew (white powdery look on leaves) and is a real "stinker," especially on warm days. I always believed it to smell like highbush cranberries cooking up in the kitchen and wasn't the least bit surprised to learn they were related.

FLOWERS

Early fall cuttings of geranium, fuchsia and marguerite taken in October and protected in a cool area should be ready for potting in 10-cm (4-in) pots. If you have a protected area such as a greenhouse or cold frame, fuchsia baskets can be planted using five plants (four on the outside and one in the middle) per 25-cm (10-in) basket. Some people will use only three plants with much success in obtaining a very full-looking basket, but this all depends on making sure you pinch the plants back a couple of times so they will bush out to fill the pot. Pinching back a fuchsia should be done approximately every four leaves by pinching out the new growth beyond the second set of leaves (four leaves) of each stem. The beginner will not always know when to pinch back and will have a sparse-looking basket with only three plants; but with five plants it will become a full-looking basket even if plants are not always pinched back when required. Fertilize weekly with 20-20-20 when plants are damp from a previous day's watering and pinch back when growth starts. This will strengthen plants and make them bushier. The longer cuttings pinched off can be placed in a rooting medium for future plants. Plants can be pinched back one more time prior to setting bloom (when new growth reaches another four leaves).

Perennials

White English daisies (*Bellis perenis*), primroses, Christmas roses (*Helleborus niger*) and winter pansies are blooming. Early spring-blooming perennials such as delphiniums and canterbury bells will soon start poking up through the ground. Plants such as winter pansies, foxglove and canterbury bells will be referred to as perennials many times throughout the book because in this climate they are treated as perennials. Officially, they are actually annuals or biennials.

Bulbs, Tubers & Corms

Smaller bulbs may be blooming at this time. If not, it won't be long. You seem to notice the crocus before you ever notice the grass-like leaves or stem because the stem of a crocus flower is underground. If you don't have any in your garden, you may want to check into them next fall when the spring-blooming bulbs are available.

Snowdrops (*Galanthus*) bloom this month in the milder areas of the islands, or next month in the colder climates. Although there are several varieties of snowdrops, giant snowdrop (*Galanthus elwesii*) and the common snowdrop (*Galanthus nivalis*) are the varieties we see most often.

Tulips and daffodils will attempt to break through the ground at this time of year. Weather permitting, they will continue growing, but if it is cool, they will grow at a snail's pace until it is warmer. Hill some dirt or mulch over these bulbs at this time of year. There is still going to be frost, or possibly even snow depending on your location, and you risk losing the blossom if they come up too early.

Check your stored tubers and bulbs (begonias, dahlias, gladiolus) to make sure there is no rot or shrivelling. If rot is present, destroy the bulb and check to see if the others are okay. One rotten bulb can spoil the whole lot. If tubers are shrivelled, place them in moist peat moss.

LAWNS

When clearing ice or snow from your sidewalks or driveways, be careful where you pile it. Heavy wet snow in a pile will kill your lawn. Prevent walking on your lawn during the winter. If the lawn is wet and thin, you will sink into it, causing a bumpy lawn, and if the lawn is frozen, you can break the blades. Children and pets are hard to keep from playing on the lawn all the time, but don't worry; you will be able to make corrections in the spring.

PESTS

Insect larvae exposed to any cold freezing weather will have been destroyed. Live insects, however, will have sought protection under leaves, boards, in compost piles, etc., and can be found in their "hang outs" munching away until warmer weather brings out the new, tasty green growth of spring. One way of upsetting their apple cart is to remove the places where they hide — refuse piles, boards, piles of leaves, etc. — and then be ready and waiting for them in the spring.

Some ambitious souls will turn their garden over, if it is not too wet to walk on, while there is still a chance of exposing larvae and other insects to the birds and future frosts.

Dormant oil and lime sulphur spray should be applied once the temperature is over 8°C (45°F) for a few days. Dormant oil and lime sulphur are organic and should not offend organic gardeners. They kill the adults, eggs, larvae and pupae of scale, spider mites and aphids. They can also destroy fungus spores such as black spot and rust on rose canes as well as mildew on lilacs, peach leaf curl, scab on apples, cane spot on raspberries, powdery mildew on fruit, gall wasps and gall mites.

HOUSEPLANTS

Houseplants in winter are quite lazy. Most are in a semi-dormant stage, because of the lack of sun. Keep them clean by washing leaves with soap and water and feed lightly. Fertilizing is not usually necessary because plants should not be pushed to put on new growth during the winter months indoors. Giving them very light fertilizer, such as fish fertilizer (5-1-1), will not hurt. This strength of fertilizer will help to keep the leaves a rich green colour and not give the plant the signal to grow. Never fertilize houseplants when they are dry. Always water the plant first, preferably the day before or earlier in the same day. Fertilizing when the plant is dry will burn the edges of the leaves.

Most houseplants like to drink from below, so have a deep saucer for your houseplants to stand in for an hour or so. Too much overhead watering ruins the foliage unless it is a bromeliad, which often forms a cupped leaf base specifically to hold water.

Set blooming plants on the floor at night during ordinary winter weather so they may have a rest from the overheated rooms of the daytime. It is also a good practise to pull down the shades behind the plants on cold nights, or cover them with newspapers so they will not suffer from drafts. Try to do your watering in the morning and let the foliage dry out before night.

A simple and inexpensive method for watering small pot plants, such as African violets, is to cut off the bottom of a large plastic pop bottle and place it under your pot. The pot uses up what water it needs, leaving the four little recessed wells at the bottom of the deep-dish saucer (our pop bottle bottom) still full of water, creating humidity without the pot actually sitting in water. Plants such as ferns and African violets love it.

If your houseplant is reaching for light and is very tender, it should be moved to a different window. If you had the plant in a north or west window because of the hot sun of summer, you can move it to an east or south window for the overcast days. When the sun starts to warm up in a few months, move the plant back to the north or west windows.

Care of Christmas Plants

POINSETTIA *(Euphorbia pulcherrima)* – The poinsettia, with a little care, can sometimes hold its handsome foliage until June or July. This beautiful plant does not enjoy drafts, overheated rooms or to be kept dry for several days. If your plant has a colourful tin foil wrap on it, punch a hole in the bottom or remove it entirely and place the plant on a saucer or dish to hold water. The plant should be watered when the top of the soil is dry to the touch. Remove any water standing in the saucer. The poinsettia will start to lose its bottom leaves if too wet or too dry. Feed it a water-soluble fertilizer after a few months. Leaves will gradually drop as the plant goes into a dormant stage. Cut plant back to just above a leaf node (joint) and reduce watering. The poinsettia can be placed outside during the summer months and brought in before any frost in the fall. The poinsettia is difficult to bring back into bloom for Christmas. To bring a poinsettia into bloom, place it in a closet or other dark place for fourteen hours a day for a month starting the beginning of October. This may not always work and is not often worth the trouble to most people, as pointsettias can be purchased so inexpensively during the Christmas season.

Poinsettia

CHRISTMAS BEGONIA — The Christmas begonia is an attractive plant with clusters of usually pink flowers above large tender leaves. This plant is difficult to keep for long as a houseplant because of the dry air in a home. If they receive too much moisture, they are susceptible to powdery mildew. Their beauty makes them worth any enjoyment you may receive from them despite their problems. The begonia needs cool evenings to keep blossoming, so place the plant either in a cool room or on the floor to prevent it from drying out from the warmer air. Water when the soil on top is dry to the touch, and fertilize with a water-soluble fertilizer. If you still have a nice plant in the spring, you can plant it outside in a shaded area of the garden or in new soil in a hanging basket to be kept on the shady side of the house.

CHRISTMAS CACTUS (Schlumbergera bridgesii) — The Christmas cactus is a beautiful plant with incredible blossoms. Like other Christmas plants, a Christmas cactus requires full winter sunlight and cool nights. It requires cool temperatures to set buds. Use a regular houseplant fertilizer for feeding it, and keep it moist. To get the Christmas cactus to bloom again at Christmastime, it will have to be given long periods of darkness (a closet is fine) for approximately fourteen hours per day, starting the first week of October. Another way is to keep it cool for the month of October, with no waterings. Once the month is up, you can place the plant in full light and start watering and fertilizing.

CHRYSANTHEMUMS — This long-lasting bloomer is a joy at Christmastime. The mum likes to be cool, so it would be wise to set it on the floor during the evening to keep it away from the warmer air higher up. Chrysanthemums do not enjoy drafts and will need a water-soluble fertilizer, since most are in a soilless growing medium. They should be checked for water every day.

Mums are usually planted with four individual plants to a 20-cm (8-in) pot and three plants to a 15-cm (6-in) pot, making for very crowded quarters. (When I mention pots by size, I am talking about the distance across the top of a pot.) Because of this, they will run out of growing space and dry out rapidly. Blossoms are long lasting and will provide a great deal of enjoyment over the long winter months. Once they have finished blooming, cut the plants back to 8 to 13 cm (3 to 5 in) and continue watering and feed lightly until spring. After any threat of frost, you can remove the plants from the pot, separate them and either pot them up individually, or plant them in your garden with other flowering perennials. Don't be disappointed if, when blooming, they are taller than when you purchased them. Nursery-grown chrysanthemums sold as pot plants are treated with a benign spray to keep them at an attractive and manageable height. Once planted in the garden, the chrysanthemum may grow as high as 45 cm (18 in), depending upon the variety. Be prepared to stake them if they get too tall.

BULBS (Paper whites) — Maintain the water level in the gravel. Once blossoms are finished, the norm is to throw the bulbs away, but I have cut the blossom stem off, continued watering level and then planted them out in the ground once the threat of frost is past. Leaving their leaves intact as long as nature allows provides necessary nutrients to the bulbs. Although normally the bulbs won't bloom the following spring, they should regain enough strength, if fertilized and cared for, to start blooming thereafter.

JERUSALEM CHERRY (Solanum pseudocapsicum) — A nice evergreen shrub with round tomatolike berries. (CAUTION: It has been said the berries may be poisonous, so caution young children not to pick them). Fruit is usually scarlet and yellow. Again, this plant likes full winter sun and cooler evenings.

KALANCHOES (Kalanchoe blossfeidiana) — A succulent that usually blooms in clusters of pinks or reds. Give it as much sunlight as possible; keep it moist and provide cool evening temperatures. This plant is long lasting, and easily kept and brought back into bloom. Although it may be difficult for you to bring the kalanchoe back into bloom at exactly Christmastime, you will enjoy its blooms off and on during the year. A proven method of getting most houseplants to bloom is to shock them. Moving them to a different window may be enough, or completely drying them out may be required.

AZALEAS — The most common varieties of azalea forced for indoor blooming are the 'Belgian Indica' and 'Pericat' varieties. A lovely Christmas plant can sometimes (depending on the variety) be planted outside in your garden once the warmer weather comes. To get the longest period of enjoyment from this prolific bloomer, give them full winter sunlight and cool winter nights. Keep azaleas moist (check them every other day) and give water-soluble fertilizer a month after planting outside. This is necessary to keep the plant blooming successfully. I have had some success planting them outside. The hardiest variety is known as 'Pericat'. Azaleas come in a variety of pinks, shades of orange or salmon, and bi-colours.

CYCLAMEN (*Cyclamen persicum*) — This dainty plant enjoys cool days (18°C/65°F) and cooler nights (10°C/50°F), so it deteriorates rapidly at normal house temperatures. If you start to lose blossoms and leaves, find a cooler place for the plant. If you have it in a cool area and it still starts to deteriorate, it is just going dormant on its own. Don't panic! Place the plant in a cool closet, or somewhere it won't freeze. A couple of months later, take it out and start watering and feeding. This plant can also be planted in a cool area outside after any danger of frost is past. I have treated this plant like a begonia, planting it outside in the shade in late spring and then digging the tubers and storing them in dry peat moss over the winter months.

AMARYLLIS (*Hippeastrum*) — The unbelievable, dramatic explosion of colour from this plant is breathtaking when you see it for the first time. The plant is simple to get into blossom when you first receive it. You will either get one planted and ready to bloom, or a bulb to plant. Planting the bulb is quite simple. Plant in a pot 2 cm (1 in) in diameter wider than the width of the bulb, with a piece of broken pottery over the drain hole to prevent the soil from falling out. Use a sterilized potting soil, leaving at least one-third of the bulb sticking above the surface. The bulb will produce a big flower stalk in a hurry if placed where it receives light from a window. Place a

Amaryllis (Hippeastrum)

saucer beneath the pot and water it when you first plant it, and when the soil is dry thereafter.

Once the amaryllis has set buds, move it away from any heat register so the warm air will not dry out the blossoms. Cut the blossom stalk off when it has completed blooming. Continue to fertilize and water leaves until all danger of frost is past. You can sink the pot in the ground outside in semi-shade or remove it from the pot and plant it at the same level in the ground, to be lifted in August or September.

When you bring the bulb back in, let the bulb dry out and store it for approximately three months. The amaryllis will bloom when taken out of its dormancy. Do this by watering if you want to keep it in its pot or replant it as mentioned above.

This bulb can also be treated like a begonia or gladiolus bulb. If this is your preference, leave the bulb in the ground until fall, dig it up when you dig your other bulbs and store over the winter in the same manner. Replant the amaryllis with your other bulbs outside in the spring.

FEBRUARY
Get Ready, Get Set . . .

FEBRUARY IS THE shortest month and is a good time to get any odd jobs out of the way before you start planting. You can make sure the lawn mower and rototiller are in good working order. Hoes, rakes and shovels can be repaired and sharpened while they are not being used. Rough wooden handles on your tools can be given a light sanding. The handles of these tools are made out of hardwood, so will sand up quite nicely with very little effort. Put linseed oil on an old cloth and rub into the handle to keep the wood from drying out. These tools do not always get put away after every use and are often exposed to the weather.

Pruning of fruit trees, hedges, shrubs, etc., can be started this month. Do you need to construct stakes for grapes or berries? Why wait until you are too busy next month or during the summer to do these necessary chores?

Weatherwise, it is usually quite mild this month, with very few days below freezing over most of the coastal area, and gardeners are starting to feel the itch to get with it. Many gardeners have already started cleaning up outside and have packets of seeds tucked in their jacket pockets just looking for a dry patch of ground to start planting.

TREES, SHRUBS & VINES

Rhododendrons, azaleas, camellias, pieris and heathers would appreciate a light feeding now to help them with their blooming. If they have already bloomed, the light feeding will help gain back some of what they lost putting on such a show for us. These plants are acid (sour) soil lovers and do not want lime put on them. Lime is used to make soil alkaline (sweet). Fertilizers especially for acid-loving plants are available at retail outlets. If you are just top dressing, peat moss will do quite well.

Planting
Fall to late spring is an excellent time on the coast to plant shrubs and trees. The ground seldom freezes more than the surface, and there is no permafrost in this part of Canada. It would be better to wait until there is no frost on the ground, but you can usually plant safely. Prior to planting, there are a number of things you should be aware of:

- Always plant the tree or shrub at the same height it was in the pot. If the tree or shrub is not in a pot and is bare-root, you will see a line on the bark of the tree and a slight colour difference (the bottom being lighter) where the soil line was prior to digging.
- Know whether the tree requires sun or shade.
- How will texture and character of plant relate to neighbouring plants? By placing the plant in the approximate spot it will be planted, you will be able to tell at a glance whether or not the plant will fit in with the character of the surrounding plants. Contrasting foliage, such as needles against leaves, pendulous variety against stiff upright or lazy and sprawling, tends to show off the individual plants.
- The size a plant will be in its mature state. We have all seen the cute little tree planted as a foundation tree in front of a picture window or under power lines. This little tree may grow into a towering giant that blocks all light! The slower-growing evergreens grow approximately 30 cm (12 in) per year in both height and width. The faster-growing trees such as weeping willows, maples, fruit trees, etc., can grow 90 cm (36 in) per year, while the pfitzer juniper grows no higher than 90 to 120 cm (36 to 48 in), with a diameter of 120 to 240 cm (48 to 96 in), depending upon the variety.

Planting trees

- Does plant require acid or alkaline soil?
- Plants should always be wet prior to planting.

Recommended planting steps are:

1. Dig a round hole, separating the topsoil from subsoil (if subsoil exists), approximately 10 to 15 cm (4 to 6 in) wider than potted plant or bare-root plant's root system.
2. Dig hole approximately 15 cm (6 in) deeper than depth of pot, or depth of roots if bare-root. Remove all rocks and debris.
3. Fill hole with water and let most of it soak in.
4. Add 5 cm (2 in) peat moss over the pile of topsoil and mix well. If the tree or shrub requires alkaline soil, a handful of dolomite lime can be mixed in as well. A plant requiring an acid soil could have more peat moss added. You may require more soil if most of your fill looks to be subsoil or of inferior quality. Subsoils may be mixed with topsoil mix if the subsoil is not made up totally of gravel or heavy clay.
5. Once soil has been mixed, place a shovelful or two of mix at the bottom of the hole and work slightly with the shovel point into the bottom of hole, loosening it up to make sure the bottom is not packed.

6. Remove the plant from the pot by laying it on its side and pushing against the pot until the plant comes away freely with a light tug on the actual plant top, damaging neither top nor roots. If the plant is wrapped in burlap, leave burlap attached until it is placed it in the hole. Burlap can stay around roots, but strings will have to be cut and pulled away.

7. Loosen roots with your hand or a fork by scratching the outer surface and bottom of the potted shrub or tree to give the roots a direction. Growing in a pot, once they reach the bottom and sides of a pot they will continue growing in a circle instead of reaching out. It is important that they don't continue growing in this circle. Do not separate the soil from the rootball.

8. Place the plant in the prepared hole and lay a shovel handle or other straight edge across the diameter of the hole to make sure the plant is at the proper depth. This will be at the depth they were growing at previously (*see above*). With bare-root or bagged and burlapped trees, place them in the hole and hold them at the proper depth. Plants have a front and back, so stand back and look at the tree or bush with all sides turned towards you and decide which side should face out.

9. Once the plant is properly placed, fill in half the hole, tamp around it, fill in the remainder of the hole and tamp lightly again.

10. Trees should have a sturdy stake, or even two stakes, placed parallel to the tree trunk, with a wire looped around the tree through a small length of rubber hose (so that the wire will not damage the bark of the tree). This will prevent the young tree from whipping in the wind.

Pruning

Knowing how and when to prune can be difficult for most gardeners. Writing about this subject would take volumes if every type of tree and shrub requiring pruning were included. Most major pruning can be done if you remove the dead, tangled and diseased branches. This is easy to remember, but knowing when, what and how much to prune can be confusing. The best I can do is give you pointers on some of the more important pruning projects, and you can use your own judgment for the rest. An orchardist, botanist or other professional will read and study consistently for each project undertaken. The average gardener may never learn to prune a tree or bush and may never pick up a book to find out how. Either he will hire someone to do it for him, ask a friend or just lop off a branch here and there if it gets in the way of his mowing. So, to make it easier on the average gardener, I am going to mention the general steps of pruning.

A few items about all pruning that you should be aware of before to starting are:

- Tools required for pruning – A small tree is simply pruned with a pair of hand pruners and an understanding of how you want the tree to look when it is older. A larger tree will require long-handled pruners and a pruning saw.

- Proper time for pruning – Generally, the majority of pruning can be done while the plant is dormant during the winter and spring months. Most plants require pruning before sap moves upward and buds swell. There are exceptions, such as conifers, spring-flowering shrubs and birch trees.

- Cuts should be made just above a bud pointing in the direction you wish the branch to grow.

- All cuts over 2 cm (1 in) should be painted with a tar-like substance to prevent rot or diseases from entering the branch through the wound. Trees are more likely to die from bleeding, insects or disease if the wound is not treated.

- Follow the lines of the trunk to make a clean cut, leaving approximately 1 cm (.5 in) to make room for a healing callus. Afterwards, the cut will be flush with the trunk. When removing larger limbs, be sure to make an undercut first; this will let the limb fall free and prevent stripping the bark when you make the top cut.

- Unless you are confident you know what you are doing, it is best to let a professional prune the large tree. They can explain to you what they are doing and you can get pointers for the next time. Make sure the person is a professional and not just someone with a chainsaw and a pickup truck. It would be a shame to have someone prune a twenty-year-old tree incorrectly and either damage the tree or get it growing in the wrong direction.

Properly pruned, a tree can be around for generations. It is better not to prune than prune incorrectly.

ORNAMENTAL TREES — Ornamental trees do not require as much pruning as fruit trees. Occasionally, older trees need a reduction in height or a little shaping or thinning. Remove the limb close to the trunk if the limb is being completely removed, or next to a crotch if it is not. If these rules are ignored, the symmetry of the tree is spoiled and the real purpose of pruning, to admit proper light, is defeated. One rule of thumb when deciding which branches to take off the bottom of a young tree is to consider whether you will be mowing under it. The bottom branches on a deciduous tree will die off because they do not receive enough light. A coniferous tree is tapered to a fine point on top and, therefore, bottom branches are able to have light and will usually grow the full length of the main trunk.

Trees grow from the inside out and not from the bottom up. Therefore, if a branch is only 120 cm (48 in) off the ground while the tree is young, it will still be only 120 cm (48 in) off the ground when the tree is 25 m (80 ft) tall. As the young deciduous shade tree gradually grows over your head, you will want to be able to walk or mow under it. These branches should be removed as the tree grows if they do not normally die at a young age.

SHRUBS — This also is the time to prune late summer and berry-producing shrubs. Remove all deadwood and some of the oldest wood from shrubs as close to the ground as possible. Otherwise, remove the old wood to where new growth starts. Shrubs should have leaves on all stems from ground level to the top. If branches are bare at the bottom, they are probably older. These branches can be cut back to no more than 90 cm (36 in) high to force new branches to grow out from the base and cover the unsightly stubs. Shrubs can be topped to reduce height and may need to be thinned. Thinning in itself will often take care of height reduction. Buddleia and hardy fuchsia can be cut to ground level in the spring. These are summer-flowering shrubs (see Shrub List, page 160) which bloom on this year's wood.

Prune other shrubs after spring flowering. Wait until after they bloom or you will forfeit any blossoms forming at this time on the branches. Spring-blooming shrubs bloom on last year's wood.

The best time to prune your shrubs is directly after they bloom. If a shrub blooms in late summer or the fall, early spring pruning is the best, since, as mentioned above, they produce blossom on this year's wood. This does not mean that you can't prune these shrubs at other times; it only means you may forfeit blossom if you do.

Vines

WISTERIA — Wisterias require a severe pruning to keep them under control, as they are rampant growers. Pruning also encourages blossoms.

In February, prune all lateral growth to within two or three buds of their source (the main branches). Train main branches, tying or attaching as you go in the direction you want the plant to take. All new lateral growth can be taken back in August to six or eight buds from their source. My system is to prune often during the summer growing period instead of the normal February and August pruning by cutting back all lateral growth 10 to 15 cm (4 to 6 in) from the main stem several times. I find it works into my schedule more easily, as I have climbing roses and espaliers that are trimmed the same way.

CLEMATIS — Large flowering clematis blooming during the summer can be pruned back to within 30 cm (12 in) of the ground during the winter.

Large flowering clematis blooming twice a year can be pruned back lightly after spring blooming. Old wood can be cut out to promote new growth.

Small flowering varieties bloom in the spring and can be pruned after blooming to keep under control. Old wood can be cut out to promote new growth.

Clematis of all varieties can grow for many years without being pruned, but because they are such ambitious growers, pruning will eventually be required.

Fruit and Berries

FRUIT TREES — Prune fruit trees from now until the buds swell. The idea of pruning is to open the tree up. All branches require their own space and should not encroach on the other branches. Young branches should have one-third of their new growth cut back. This will shorten the branches, eliminating the weaker ends. The branches remaining must be strong enough to hold the weight of the fruit, and open enough to allow air circulation. The following steps apply to all fruit trees:

1. Always cut to a bud pointing in the direction in which the branch will grow. Cut with a slight slant away from the bud. The lowest part of the slant should be on the opposite side of the branch and just above or even with the bud.

Incorrect   *Correct*

2. Prune all branches that are growing straight up or straight down, are crossing over one another or are dead or diseased.

3. Cut all water shoots and suckers from the tree and remove small branches crowding or shading other branches needing light. Water shoots are the branches that look extremely healthy, but obviously do not belong because they grow straight up no matter where they are on the tree.

4. Never cut off more than one-third of the fruit tree in any one year. If a large amount needs to be pruned, do it over a couple of seasons.

5. Learn the difference between the larger and rounder fruit buds and the small, flat growth buds. If you have trouble with this, check the new growth. Fruit buds are formed on the older wood, never on the new season's wood. The buds you see on new growth are growth buds.

6. Winter pruning promotes growth, while summer pruning promotes fruit.

7. When purchasing a fruit tree, it will probably be three to four years old. A one-year-old tree is one single stem (whip). A two-year-old tree has grown several branches (laterals) off the whip. The three-year-old tree has grown side shoots off the previous laterals, and the previous laterals (now main branches) have grown up to 60 cm (24 in). The four-year-old tree has grown side shoots from the laterals, the previous lateral has grown longer and the main branches have grown 60 cm (24 in).

8. Parts of a tree are:

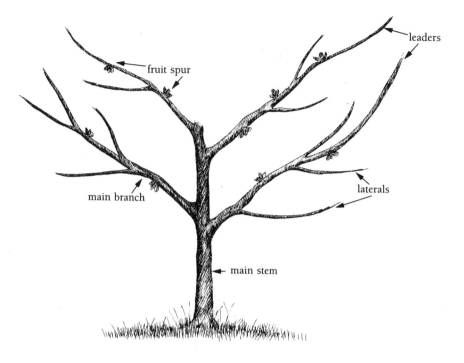

- *Leaders* — main shoot of a branch.
- *Fruit spur* — short fat fruit-producing spurs off laterals and branches of prior years.
- *Main branch* — branches selected from first year's growth to become a permanent part of the framework.
- *Laterals* – side shoots from a branch.
- *Main stem* — first year's growth (trunk).
9. Try to maintain adult tree to approximately 3 m (9 ft) high and 3 m (9 ft) wide. If the tree is allowed to become taller, it is difficult to prune and pick fruit.

I will attempt to explain the pruning of the young tree (three years old) because, pruned properly when the tree is young, you will have fewer problems with the tree in years to come. Trees allowed to grow without pruning are very susceptible to disease, overcrowding and heavy fruit loads, and the tree will eventually become too tall to harvest easily. *(Refer to the above illustration for explanation of terms.)*

1. Cut back the main stem to a branch within 120 cm (48 in) of the ground, leaving four or five evenly spaced branches to be-

come main branches.

2. Cut all laterals coming off the main branches one-third of their new growth to an outward facing bud. If any are closer than 45 cm (18 in), cut them back to four buds from their base.

3. At this point, it would pay to have a permanent marking system to mark your main branches with one colour, your new laterals with another colour. I see no reason to mark the short laterals, but if you do, mark them with a different colour. (I use spray paint, and only one spot of the colour on each branch, near the base).

4. Each year thereafter, maintain this same type of pruning.
   • The main branches will always be the main branches, and one-third of the new growth on the new leader will be cut back to an outward facing bud. No other branches should be allowed to grow from the main stem. All other branches should be cut off flush with the (main stem) trunk of the tree.
   • Main laterals should be kept approximately 45 cm (18 in) apart, other laterals should be cut down to four buds from their base.
   • Every few years laterals may have to be cut off to let other laterals take their place. This is a type of renewal.

If you let side shoots grow on laterals, and never cut back the leaders by one-third, you will soon have the jungle mentioned earlier.

You may never prune your tree and still have an abundant supply of fruit, but this is for those of you who would like to learn some of the basics. I prune other people's trees as I have described above, but when pruning my own fruit trees, I am more strict. I cut all main branches and the leader back by one-third, and all laterals off those main branches are cut back to approximately 40 cm (16 in). Side shoots from the laterals are cut back to four buds. That's it, plain and simple. No confusion and plenty of space for each branch. The tree is attractive and open with plenty of fruit, and the symmetry of the tree is excellent with this system. Branches are kept short and strong, all branches have their own space with lots of sunlight and air circulation, and the tree height is maintained at an easy-to-reach level.

During the summer months, as you get to know how your tree grows and what you want and where, you will be able to rub out buds or nip off branches that do not belong. This will save a lot of pruning time in the winter months.

Older, well-established trees usually need little pruning. Occasionally an older limb should be removed when it is being crowded by younger, more vigorous wood. Be sure to work the entire tree during pruning. Cut out large centre branches. This will enable sunlight to get to all parts. On tall trees, you can cut back the tallest branches to a lateral. One sure rule to remember is to never remove more than one-third of the tree at one time. This encourages water sprouts.

A method called "pollarding" fruit trees has been practised for years and, thank heavens, is finally on its way out. Pollarding is when all branches of an older tree are cut back to only a few main branches. The following spring, hundreds of upright branches (water shoots) grow to replace the wood cut. Water shoots, unless properly pruned and cared for, become a tangled mess when their branches cross over each other. A water shoot is like another tree taking off and growing up. It is their laterals that will eventually produce fruit. Can you imagine hundreds of them growing up from one tree? It would result in total chaos.

You can topwork fruit trees, including flowering crabs, peaches and plums, by thinning their tops. All lateral branches should point outwards and upwards, not straight up, straight down, across another branch or toward the trunk.

FILBERTS — Prune filberts as a bush, keeping as many branches as possible for heavy production. The filbert bush should be kept young, so cut out a few older branches each year to keep new ones always coming in.

GRAPES — Now is also a good time to do the grape pruning. The fruit is borne near the beginning of shoots that will have developed from last year's growth. In order to keep the strength of the plant from going into foliage instead of fruit, you must trim away the oldest wood, leaving only principal stems. Each of these old stems should retain four to six canes that grew last year. Last year's canes must be cut back to ten or fewer buds each. There are many who grow their grapes as an attractive vine and do not wish to prune. You will still get grapes, but not as many. The grapevine can take severe pruning and should be pruned heavily the first two years to develop a strong trunk and root growth.

RASPBERRIES and BLACKBERRIES — Cut out old canes that bore fruit last year. They will not bear again. You can cut down the tops to about 150 cm (60 in) and tie to whatever support you have available for them. Many varieties, especially of blackberries, can become ramblers, making it very inconvenient to pick or take care of them. Berries respond well to a feeding with a general fertilizer such as 4-10-10.

GOOSEBERRIES —Keep the centre free of branches to allow the air to circulate and to expose branches to the sun. If you have the type of gooseberry bush that tends to spread, prune the branches back to an upward (or inside) bud, and if you have an upright variety of gooseberry, do just the opposite. Prune to an outside bud, forcing the plant to fan out more. On a young bush, choose three or four shoots and cut them back about three-quarters of their length to a bud. Cut out all other shoots. If it is an older bush, select eight or so fine branches and cut them back halfway to a bud. Cut back all other branches to within one bud of the main stem. From then on, to maintain growth, cut back leaders halfway and laterals to within three or four buds of the main stem. Always prune out old, dead and diseased wood.

CURRANTS —When you first plant currants, you should prune all branches back to four outside buds, enabling the plant to thicken up and fan outwards. From then on, shorten new growth on the leaders by one-third to one-half, and laterals to one bud from their bases to form spurs. You can cut out any dead wood, diseased wood or branches ruining the shape of the bush. Keep the centre removed to allow air circulation and sun to get to all the branches.

BLUEBERRIES —Blueberries do not require pruning for the first three years. After three years, you should prune back three or four of the oldest canes down to a good shoot close to soil level. Blueberries produce on last year's wood, so the older shoots are not going to produce and will promote new growth by being cut back or by being cut out altogether.

FLOWERS

About the middle of the month, the geraniums, fuchsias, impatiens and pelargoniums, at present wintering in a cool place, can be brought into a sunny location, such as a window, greenhouse or cold frame, to be watered and fed to encourage new growth. Once they start growing, you may want to take cuttings (*see Steps for Taking Cuttings, page 130*).

Be sure any seeds you have received or have left over from the previous year are stored in a container where they will stay dry.

They should be stored in a cool place, either in the garage or in the vegetable bin of your refrigerator. The warm room of a home will generally cause them to dry out or lose their strength.

Perennials

Don't be surprised by any warm weather we get on the west coast this month. Chances are, there will be more cold days to come, which could damage your plants if you pull the protective mulch away from them. Remember, it is not the tops of the plants you are protecting with the mulch, it is the root and crown system.

To renew pampas grass, cut the clump off 30 to 45 cm (12 to 18 in) above the ground and vigorous new growth will develop. Pampas grass is an ornamental grass and you are just cutting the lawn (so to speak). An easy way is to tie a rope around the clump about 1 m (3 ft) up and use long-handled hedge clippers to cut it straight across or an electric hedge trimmer, which makes cutting easier.

Perennials (including rhubarb) are starting to break through the ground now and would benefit from a top dressing of sterilized manure or all-purpose fertilizer. I say sterilized manure because manure straight from the manure pile could possibly have weed seed in it and may still be too fresh. If you do not want to buy steer manure from a garden centre, then by all means use old manure from your barn, but be aware of the weed seed possibility.

Primrose (primulas), delphinium and Shasta daisy needing to be divided can be done now, if the ground is not frozen, by lifting them and using a knife to cut them apart. Replant the smaller pieces in rich soil and fertilize with an all-pupose fertilizer such as 6-8-6 or 4-10-10.

Blooming this month are the winter pansy, primrose (primula), Christmas rose (*Helleborus niger*) and Algerian iris (*Iris unguicularis*).

Annuals

The last week of February is the time to start seeds that take a long time to germinate (geraniums, lobelia, ageratum, verbena, petunia, pentstemon, scabiosa, etc.) in a sunny window, greenhouse or cold frame. Read directions on the back of seed packages if you plan on starting your own this year instead of purchasing bedding plants. For the novice gardener, I would suggest trying to plant your own but it is easier to buy the bedding plants from a garden centre or retail outlet until you become successful at raising plants from seed indoors.

Bulbs, Tubers & Corms

TUBEROUS BEGONIA — If you have tuberous begonias stored from last year's growing season, check them now. If they have started their small spears of growth from the concave top of the tuber, you will be able to plant them indoors to get a jump on the season.

They may be grown from seed planted in a greenhouse in January. For the amateur, it is far better to purchase tubers or wait until later and buy the already started tuber. Considering they last for years, these are quite inexpensive. Begonia tubers may be planted directly out of doors after all danger of frost is past, but a much longer blooming period can be obtained from a start indoors. Unless the tubers show signs of growth when received, it may be confusing as to which is the top. It is essential that they be planted top side up. The bottom of a begonia tuber is rounded. The top of the tuber is concave. By now, there should be small green or red shoots appearing.

The best way to start tuberous begonias is in trays of fine peat moss. First dampen the peat, then place the bottom sides of the tubers in little depressions in the peat, 8 cm (3 in) apart. Firm them down so only a little of the tuber remains out of the soil.

Water must be poured on the peat only. If any drops fall into the top of the tuber, they should be soaked out with cloth or paper towel. Roots will form on the bottom, sides and top of a begonia tuber. Once grown, they are rather top-heavy and many people will plant the bulb completely under the soil. One reason not to plant the entire tuber underground is because the stems of a tuberous begonia are very tender and susceptible to stem rot. Unless you are very good at knowing when to water and how to care for plants that tend to suffer from stem rot, it is safest to plant only the lower half of the tuber, keeping the top dry.

The tray should be placed in a warm spot (15 to 26°C/60 to 80°F). Light is not necessary until the little pink sprouts begin to show. Then the plants need a sunny window and a uniform temperature that is 6 to 10°C (10 to 15°F) cooler. If it is too warm after growth starts, they will grow too fast and the peat will dry out. Putting planted tubers directly into the light will force the tubers to grow on top instead of shoot a strong root mass. The tuber will not be able to do both successfully.

When the tuber has four leaves, it can be planted in a more permanent pot until the middle of May, when it can be planted outdoors. Crowding of the roots makes for a better plant. As stated before, it can become quite top-heavy, and with the tuber barely in the soil, their roots are very important for stability. Stakes may be required for uprights. Pinch out new growth tips to promote bushier plants once the plant has four leaves.

The blossoming season will be more successful if female flowers are kept picked off. You will be able to tell the female flowers by the seed pod directly behind the blossom. There are two of them, one on each side of the large male flower, which is usually double and quite fancy. The female flower, although very beautiful, is usually single, and lesser than the male.

LAWNS

Lawns can be aerated (poking holes down into the lawn) and top-dressed with a mixture of topsoil and peat moss. The top dressing will fall into the holes and help loosen up a tight compact lawn. This is good for heavy traffic areas and lawns planted in a tight, compact clay-type soil.

Apply dolomite lime to lawns at the rate prescribed on the package. Be careful not to place the lime on the roots of acid-loving plants such as rhododendrons, evergreens, arbutus, dogwood, magnolia, etc. Over time, these plants will die if exposed to limed (sweet or alkaline) soil.

If required, moss control can be applied to eradicate moss in your lawn at the rate prescribed on the package. A healthy lawn will have trouble growing moss, so the best way to prevent moss is to maintain a healthy lawn.

GARDENS

Radishes, early peas, broad beans, spinach, parsley and early lettuce can be planted outside. At the beginning of the month, lettuce, leeks, onions, radishes, Brussels sprouts, early cauliflower and cabbage can be sown indoors or in cold frames, as can herbs such as thyme, oregano and marjoram. If you like taking risks, try planting out a few early potatoes.

Jerusalem artichokes are best planted in rows like potatoes, 90 cm (36 in) apart. Feed well and cultivate. They spread prolifically.

I prefer planting my garden later in the year because I don't like taking too many chances. It is your choice. Unless there is an extremely warm spring, I don't feel you will get a jump on the season by planting early. In fact, you may have to replant. The list previously mentioned is for those who would like to start early. In reality, you have until mid-May to get your garden in the ground and still have enough time for it to produce.

The islands off the west coast have a short season for growing tomatoes, so pick varieties that mature even in cool climates. 'Tiny Tim', 'Fireball', 'Golden Delight', 'Early Girl', 'Extra 'Early', Early Salad' and 'Subarctic' perform well in this area. It is always fun, though, to try some of the warmer-climate varieties. Hot caps should be used for the first two weeks to get a good start. If hot caps aren't available, you can use the tops of clear plastic pop bottles or plastic milk jugs with the bottoms cut out of them. With the large plastic pop bottles, cut the bottom off at the line and use the bottoms as saucers for houseplants. Leave the lid on when using as hot caps for tomatoes, squash, cucumbers, etc., and remove only on hot days. Remove the lid, or make a hole in the hot cap and help the tomato adjust to the air outside prior to completely removing the hot cap/bottle. Make sure all danger of frost is gone prior to removing. If cool weather persists, you can keep the hot cap/bottle on until it is completely full of plant. The plants will be quite tender when you do remove the protection, so it is best done in the evening or on an overcast day to prevent the leaves from drying out in the bright sun or from a warm wind.

Strawberry plants are usually good for only two years. Their crop then starts to cut back. Take some of your runners and start a new bed if you have the room or have not already done so, but leave your old plants to produce until the runners have become established, in another year. Keep the runners off the new plants and keep the weeds away from them the first year. A good mulching helps keep down the weeds. This will also keep your berries clean once they start to set on. The proper thing to do is to keep the young plants from producing in the first year.

To tell whether or not new strawberry plants are old, look at the roots. If the plant has black roots, it is older and will not produce much. A good producing plant should have white or light-coloured roots.

Remember, do not cover the crown. Always make sure the new leaves are out in the open. There is a brown skin just down from the leaves. Plant approximately halfway up this.

PESTS

Check your shrubs and fruit trees for anything foreign such as insects or disease and, if unsure, check at your local nursery prior to treating it. A word of caution, though. When you take a possibly diseased branch or a branch with insects on it to your nursery for identification and suggestions on treatment, be sure you have it securely stored in a plastic bag or other container. Or have someone knowledgeable come out to your car to look at the problem. Do not walk into a nursery with an infected leaf or branch. Its plants are subject to infection by your plant. I have seen people walk into a nursery with infected plants and lay them on the counter or toss them into the wastebasket.

Trees, vines and shrubs should be sprayed with dormant oil and lime sulphur to destroy any insect eggs that may have survived the winter before the buds start to swell – around mid-March. Spray with lime sulphur and dormant oil mixes when temperatures are below 5°C (40°F), and when there is little or no wind. Don't use lime sulphur on apricots. Be careful spraying lime sulphur next to your house or a fence that is white or light in colour, because it will usually stain. Check at a retail outlet and read all instructions on the package before using. Lime sulphur and dormant oil are not chemicals. They are natural substances and do the job quite effectively. But, like all sprays, you should use caution and always read instructions carefully.

HOUSEPLANTS

Now that winter is on its way out, houseplants should be prepared for their growing season. Wash the leaves with slightly warm water, using a sponge. Turn your plant weekly to keep it symmetrical. It will always grow towards any light. Hanging baskets with a swivel hook make this an easier practise than those on a stationary hook. Give houseplants a light dose of fertilizer if they have started to show new growth. Do not try to force them into growth with fertilizer. Wait until they start on their own.

When your poinsettia has finished blooming and becomes ragged-looking, put it out of sight in a cool room until spring and water enough to keep it alive. Since most greenhouse-raised pot plants are planted in an almost total peat medium, they are either very wet or very dry, so you will have to keep checking on them. The peaty mix they are in will have to be replaced with a sterilized potting mix, or they can be planted out in the garden when the weather warms up. Before planting out, they should be severely pruned.

Freesias can be repotted and placed in a cool area, such as your garage, when flowering is over. I planted mine in the ground one fall and was able to enjoy them the following year in my garden, since I found them too difficult to maintain at home without the greenhouse atmosphere.

MARCH
Be Patient

NOW THAT THE first warm days have arrived, you may be tempted to start planting, working the ground, removing mulches, etc. Although it wouldn't hurt to loosen the mulch around spring-blooming plants, to let the air circulate, don't be in a rush to start working the wet ground. There are many other ways in which to use all the pent-up energy caused by a long rainy season on the coast.

You should empty your compost bin now to make room for a new season of composting. If you plan on keeping it going for a while longer, fork it over. If you have the two- or three-bin system, place the material currently on the top in one bin on the bottom of another bin. How rapidly it becomes compost depends a great deal upon keeping it moist and stirring it frequently. If it has been exposed to the winter rains, chances are the top portion is quite wet. Forking it over helps to circulate this moisture, and the wet material will start to rot by putting it on the bottom where it can start composting. Compost piles should not have a foul smell, and as long as they continue to be turned and watered properly, they will be clean. I find that a long broom handle with a nail driven through the end works well for turning the small compost piles within bins. For bins, I use the large heavy rubber or synthetic garbage cans, and place 2-cm (1-in) holes every 15 cm (6 in) in completely around it for proper air circulation. Four or five holes are also placed in the bottom for drainage. This is easily done with a little time and a strong-bladed butcher knife. During heavy rains I place the top on the garbage can so the compost won't get too wet; the rest of the time, the top can stay off. This system works equally well for apartment dwellers, and can be moved easily to the garden site for dumping or wherever you will be using the newly composted soil.

March is quite unpredictable, to say the least. Bear in mind that any suggestions I give are dependent upon the weather and your location. What you can do in one part of the islands this month you may not be able to do until next month in other parts. You will have to use your own judgment.

TREES, SHRUBS & VINES

Buds on the trees are starting to swell, catkins are in full bloom on pussy willows. Birches, maples and hazelnuts have tassels of blossoms hanging down from their branches. Forsythia, in some more protected areas, are now starting to bloom while the less protected are holding back for the signal to open their blossoms. Varieties of rhododendron, lily-of-the-valley shrub (*Pieris*), winter daphne (*Daphne odora*), broom, quince, star magnolia (*Magnolia stellata*), *Magnolia soulangeana*, *Magnolia denudata*, flowering cherry, flowering plum, winter jasmine and *Camellia japonica* are showing off the particular genetics that give them the strength to bloom their beautiful and welcome blossoms while the weather is so uncertain. Once these plants have finished their blooming, give them a good feeding and, for those that require pruning, this can be done at this time. Deadhead blossoms from shrubs such as rhododendron and camellia once they have completed their blossoming. It would also be beneficial to pick up spent blossoms that have dropped to the ground, as they will attract insects and encourage fungal diseases.

The fall and winter heathers have been taking turns blooming all through the winter months and the later varieties are still at it. It is a treat to have these dainty fern-like plants bloom during the winter months. There are quite a few varieties and a selection of these can keep blossoms going from fall to spring.

Move or plant any shrubs as early as you can work the ground. Plant them at the same level they were originally. Now is the easiest time to plant hedges, grapes, evergreens, dormant roses, etc.

Dig the hole and have the necessary equipment prior to buying a plant from a nursery. This way, when you get home, you will be able to plant and water your new addition right away. Plants can stay in their pots for a considerable time, but if this happens, be sure to care for them. If it is an outdoors plant, then keep it outside. Don't put it undercover in a garage or basement while you wait to plant it. Let the new plant get accustomed to where you will be planting it. Water plants when the soil is dry on top. If your plant has little beads scattered around on the soil, don't panic. This is a slow-release fertilizer used by nurseries and should be left with the plant.

Prune your hedge once it starts showing some spring growth. Be sure to cut the top narrower than the bottom so sunlight will be able to reach the entire surface. Without sun, the bottom branches will start to lose their needles or leaves, making gaping holes and leaving only bare trunks.

If the winter has been particularly rough, with lots of snow and frost, some of your more tender shrubs may be dead-looking, with burnt leaves. Don't remove these trees or bushes yet. Give them a chance to renew their leaves. We are not used to this kind of winter, and neither are our plants. Even the toughest of plants may have its leaves and the tips of its branches frozen, but with luck, new leaves will replace those that have died.

If you have one of the hardier palm trees growing in your yard, and all the fronds have been destroyed by a colder-than-usual winter, give it awhile to see if new fronds start coming back. The most tried variety of palm for the warmer parts of Vancouver Island is the Chinese windmill palm (*Trachycarpus fortunei*). They can usually withstand -5°C (24°F) without dying. If you do attempt to grow palms, it is quite a heartbreak to lose one. So give them a chance. For anyone interested in trying palms, if you have had success with rhododendrons and azaleas, you will find a palm enjoys the same type of care.

A good suggestion for those who grow palms is to have some system of protecting them over the winter. Many people build removable shelters around their palms to help carry them through the harder winters.

FLOWERS

Start the fuchsias, geraniums and marguerites you brought in last winter now if you haven't already done so. Prune tops to the extent necessary (remember, last year's fuchsia stems will not produce blossoms, so keep them short), and take them out of their present containers. Give them fresh soil, using a good potting mixture. You can dump your old soil on the compost pile. Place drainage material, consisting of clean gravel or broken pots, in the bottom of each pot or container to prevent the roots from sitting in water and soil from washing out the bottom.

Water them well when replanting, and keep them moist to promote good growth. Feed the plants regularly with a well-balanced fertilizer. A good fertilizer to use until your plants start to set on bud is 20-20-20. If your fertilizer is high only in the first number (nitrogen), it will promote excellent green growth but do little for the roots. By giving a fertilizer equal in all three numbers, you are telling all parts of the plant to start growing, not just the roots or the tops.

Cuttings taken last month from the more tender perennials listed above (fuchsia, geranium, marguerite, etc.) should be ready to pot up. Using a fork or similar tool, lift it gently and check to see that it has a good root growth prior to planting. The roots are very tender and will break off if you just pull the cutting out of the rooting medium.

California 'Gold Medal'

Roses

The rose is the elegant beauty of the flower world, often signifying romance and used in songs and legends. The rose dates back to the 1700s. Finding a variety or colour you like is not difficult. Some roses are heavily scented, some are perfectly formed. Many have both qualities. Colours vary from snow white to deep red and from yellow to almost blue. There are various classes of roses.

CLIMBING ROSE — The climbing rose can be found with either the picture-perfect single hybrid tea look or clusters similar to a flori-bunda. The climber can bloom continuously or a couple of times a year. Climbing roses are used in home and public gardens and require a fence, trellis or arbour for support.

FLORIBUNDA — Floribundas can be continuous clusters of single, semi-double or double flowers in a wide range of colours. Perfect for the home garden.

GRANDIFLORA — Grandiflora is a tall, vigorous bush with hybrid tea-like flowers in huge clusters. Grandifloras are good for cut flowers and make nice specimen plants.

HYBRID TEA — The most popular of all roses, the hybrid tea is used in flower arrangements by florists around the world, sold by gar-den nurseries and supermarkets. This beautiful flower, with its long stem and single pointed bud, is the elite of the flower world. The hybrid tea blooms intermittently all summer long. Some varieties are more susceptible to black spot and powdery mildew in our damp climate than others. Check with your local nursery or read about the particular variety in a book specifically written for this area prior to purchasing. You will find many beautiful hybrid teas that are resistant to these types of problems.

MINIATURE ROSE — This tiny rose has impeccably shaped miniature blossoms in perfect proportion to the plant size, with the same variety of colour and progression as the larger roses. An ideal specimen for the border of a rose bed, individual plantings or for pot culture.

POLYANTHA — A small plant with clusters of small and intermittent but perfectly formed flowers. The polyantha is perfect for pot culture.

ROSA RUGOSA — An ideal shrub rose for the coastal area. Famous for its large rose hips, used by many as an excellent source of vitamin C. The rugosa has more of an open bloom and is quite prolific with blos-soms during the summer. The rugosas I am familiar with are highly scented, along the same lines as the wild rose, and are easily cared for.

SHRUB ROSES — This is the hardier variety of rose and is usually seen in hedge form, although it is quite beautiful as a specimen plant. Other varieties of roses need winter protection in colder areas; the shrub rose can withstand more frigid climates. Crossed with wild roses, hence their hardiness, shrub roses can grow as high as 150 cm (60 in) and the same in diameter. Whether or not they lose their leaves in winter and the type of flower depends on genetics. Most varieties will bloom continuously all summer long.

STANDARD — Also called the Tree Rose, the standard is used effectively to accent landscapes with a very formal look. The bare stem, usually 1 m (3 ft) in height, has been grafted and looks very regal with the actual bush growing on top. If grafted with a hybrid tea top, it will be ball shaped. The standard can also be grafted with a climber or rambler to form a weeping (or trailing) variety. Both are beautiful and graceful in a home garden. This plant is very attractive in a large pot on a patio or terrace.

Having a beautiful, healthy rosebush requires work. On the coast, aphids, black spot and powdery mildew are constant problems. Roses should be fertilized with either a special rose fertilizer or an all-purpose fertilizer at least three times a year. The first time is right after pruning, the second during the summer while blooming, and the third a couple of months before frost is expected. Scratch fertilizer into the soil around the plant and water. Standards enjoy a loamy soil and benefit from sterilized steer manure being worked in around them. I like to use the steer manure for the first fertilizing in the spring. This way, they don't grow as rapidly as they would from commercial fertilizers and they enjoy the humus the steer manure provides after nutrients are exhausted. An application of lime sulphur and dormant oil in late winter will help to keep black spot and powdery mildew under control.

Pruning Roses
Hybrid teas produce only on new branches, instigated by pruning. Examine a professionally cared-for rose garden, and you will see leaves from close to the ground to the very tops, as well as numerous flowers. A neglected rose that has not been pruned may be 3.5 m (10 ft) tall, with the bottoms of all branches naked of any leaves for 1 m (3 ft) or more and one flower or cluster of flowers on each branch tip.

Pruning opens them up, renews their growth, encourages blossoms and looks smart. By opening them up and keeping the centres cut from the bush varieties, the air is able to circulate, helping to fight off fungus diseases such as black spot and powdery mildew.

There are general principles that apply to all varieties of roses when pruning:

1. Cut away all weak growth and dead, damaged and diseased wood to the base, a crotch or an outward bud.
2. Cut away all inward growing branches, or branches crossing over another branch, to their base.

3. Keep the centres of your bushes free of branches to provide good air circulation within the plant.

Suggestions for pruning individual varieties of roses:

HYBRID TEAS — Hybrid teas require a moderate pruning to promote new growth. Blossoms are formed on new growth. Cut branches back to an outward facing bud approximately four buds from the base of the plant or approximately 20 cm (8 in) from the ground in the spring once the red growth starts. Do not leave stubs above a bud. These will die and may attract disease. Fertilize your rosebush with either a rose fertilizer, all-purpose fertilizer or sterilized manure, and work into the soil lightly prior to watering.

FLORIBUNDAS — Older shoots are cut back hard to within four buds of the base. Shoots two years old or younger are cut back approximately one-half.

TREE ROSES — Shape each plant to maintain the rounded head of blossoms for tree roses with the more favoured hybrid tea graft. When pruning a standard with the graft of a climbing rose, maintain the original main stems and keep side shoots off these main stems approximately four to six leaf nodes in length after blooming. Main stems can be rejuvenated as years progress by letting some of the new growth take the place of older stems.

CLIMBING ROSES — Climbing roses need pruning in the spring only to shape them. Most climbing roses produce blossoms on old wood. Climbers can be pruned after they bloom. Remove older canes at the ground to promote new growth. Lightly tie canes to a trellis, fence, etc., to keep them under control. Side shoots can be cut off if they interfere with the design. Laterals should be cut back to four leaf nodes after blooming.

RAMBLER — The rambler produces blossoms on this year's growth. Prune off all canes that have produced. Because they are such prolific growers, I keep all lateral branches (side shoots growing off main branches) cut back to four buds. This has to be checked several times a year to keep up, but pays off in the long run. In this manner of pruning, the main branches are covered in small clumps of leaves and blossoms that look like bouquets tied to the branches.

Perennials

Perennials that need to be transplanted in the spring are plants that bloomed the previous fall. This can be done as soon as the ground is dry enough to be readily handled. Perennials growing in clumps, such as iris, daisy, phlox, delphinium and others, bloom best when divided every few years. If the plants bloom in the spring or early in the year, you can divide them in the fall. You can divide them now, but their blossoms will be fewer in the spring. St. John's wort (*Hypericum calycinum*) is a ground cover that can become quite invasive if left untrimmed. This plant develops a woody stem, making it difficult to trim down easily without pruning sheers if left to grow without the yearly pruning. If planted on smooth ground, this hardy little plant can be mowed over once every spring, encouraging young new green shoots to come up and bloom the most incredible yellow blossoms. (Mother Nature really outdid herself when she came up with this one.) If you cannot mow due to obstacles, pruning will have to be done by hand. It is preferrable to keep it as a ground cover instead of as a small shrub, which can take over if left to grow at will.

When planting perennials, consider colour, size and texture combinations in your flower beds and borders. Place the plants that become taller at maturity in the background, the medium plants in the middle and plants short when mature in front, along with trailing plants. Succession of bloom should also be considered. This way you will have bloom all summer long (*see Perennial List, page 164*). Each month, I will list common names of some of the perennials in colour for that month. This will aid those of you who would like to expand or plan your perennial flower bed. In bloom this month are wallflower, primrose, bergenia, saxifrage, aubretia, perennial alyssum, pasque flower and bleeding heart. Try using some of these early bloomers in a cut bouquet for the house. A few stems of bleeding hearts and forsythia with half a dozen white or pink tulips really brings spring into the home.

Wallflowers and primroses are a welcome sight with their colourful blossoms. Wallflowers have such a strong sweet scent, I am amazed they are not more popular. One drawback is that they reseed themselves and, if not kept in check, soon turn into a weed that will literally take over your garden. You just have to shut your eyes, grab a handful and pull them out if they are taking over. The trick is to keep them deadheaded once they have finished blooming. Don't let them go to seed. They will grow out of the cracks of sidewalks or out of any rock with half an inch of soil on it.

Provide stakes or twigs to support taller perennials such as delphinium, Oriental poppy and Shasta daisy, so that the stems will stay tall and straight with their heavy blossoms instead of falling over on other plants or in the dirt. I have found the round metal tapered towers used for tomato plants ideal. They're not expensive and can be stacked and stored easily from year to year. You will find numerous alternatives on the market for this purpose, or you can make one to suit your needs. A very simple and effective idea is to stick several dead twigs in the area where the plant will grow. They will support the plant as it grows and eventually be hidden from sight by the leaves of the plant.

Annuals

The winter pansy has produced blossom all season and is still putting on a cheerful show. If you remember to keep the dead blossoms picked off to keep seed pods from producing, these colourful little faces will produce right on through the summer. Here they can be treated as biennials or even perennials.

If you start your own annual seeds indoors, or would like to try it for the first time, you can start marigolds, ageratum, cosmos, petunias, etc.

Bedding plants are showing up in the garden centres at this time of year. They will be there for awhile so I caution anyone without a greenhouse or cold frame about buying them and expecting to be able to plant them out. We may have an excellent spring and no more frosts or cold rains, but is it worth taking the chance? This could be quite expensive if you have to go back and replace them. There are plants, however, which like the cold weather, such as primrose or polyanthus, wallflower, pansy, snapdragon, English daisy, dianthus and forget-me-not, but if you're thinking petunia, fuchsia, lobelia or geranium, be warned! Most of these plants, subjected to the cool air of March nights and possible cold rains or even a late frost, will not recover once they have been damaged. All islands off the west coast can expect frost until mid-April, on the average.

Bedding plants purchased now should be kept in a protected area where they will get plenty of light and continued watering and feeding.

If the weather is ahead of the norm, you may be wondering why the local garden centres have a scant supply of bedding plants. The reason is that there is no factual way of knowing what the season will bring as far as weather goes in every location. Nurseries have set certain days for their planting. In this part of Canada, Mother's Day is the target date. Greenhouses have the correct temperature, correct moisture and the required staff to bring those plants along in perfect condition for that target date. There are always early plants grown for hanging baskets. For those wanting to buy plants for their greenhouses or cold frames early in the season, this is what you will find on the shelves at your local garden centre. Most bedding plants are just too small to be put out for sale at this time of the year. Most wholesalers growing bedding plants do not want to put them out until they start to show colour (buds or blossoms forming). Be patient, because the large bulk of bedding plants is yet to come.

Sweet pea seeds can be planted out, but need deep, well-enriched soil and good drainage. Provide something for them to climb on if they are the climbing variety. Most people plant them near a fence. Since I have already professed to being a lazy gardener and not one to plant ahead, I plant a small amount of sweet pea seeds in March, a small amount in April and the remaining seeds in May. By mid-June, you can't tell which seeds were planted two weeks ago or two months ago. The ones planted in April have larger blossoms and stronger plants, even though they were seed from the same packet. Too early, it's too cold; too late, it's too warm. You be the judge. Usually trial-and-error helps here, as does experience.

Another hardy annual that you can plant out is the calendula. This faithful little annual usually reseeds itself and comes up as a volunteer. You can transplant these volunteers wherever you need the colour. They will bloom until frost if you can keep the blossoms deadheaded. Because they are such prolific bloomers, and seem to be able to bloom well and produce seed at the same time, they usually get away from us.

When cleaning up your flower beds, look carefully for volunteer seedlings that have survived from last year's annuals. Seedlings such as the calendulas just mentioned, nasturtiums, snapdragons and petunias, to name a few, can be transplanted to a more permanent location.

Bulbs, Tubers & Corms

If the weather has been decent during the winter, the daffodils are in bloom. Snowdrops, bluebells and crocuses are finishing their blast of beauty. When the spring is warm, these bulbs last a short time. This doesn't happen often, and who is going to complain about a warm spring? It is a little frustrating for the large bulb growers on the island, since their tulips and daffodils are supposed to be at a tight bud stage for the Easter season. There are times when they will bloom too early.

Snowdrops

The idea of our having bulbs ready this time of year can be a little disconcerting to the rest of Canada, since the islands and the Lower Mainland are a good month or two ahead. We do enjoy our springs in this part of the world. By the end of the month, even the northern areas of the islands are boasting about their bulbs blooming. For those of you living in apartments, there are always garden centres selling pots of bulbs in bloom or you can plant your own in the fall. Nothing beats the fragrant scent of hyacinths or daffodils after a long winter whether you live in Yellowknife, Whitehorse, Toronto, Winnipeg or here on the coast.

Summer-flowering bulbs such as begonias, cannas and dahlias can be set in pots containing damp peat moss. If the cannas require dividing, do so prior to planting. Dahlias should be planted in damp peat moss, whereas begonia tubers are just pushed down into the peat moss. I prefer planting dahlias and cannas outside when the time comes, while begonias seem to do better by this special type of planting. Indoor directions for getting a jump on the season are for those who enjoy this form of gardening. Glads can be planted outside now, but instead of planting them all at one time, why not plant a few now, and succession plant every two weeks during spring to keep them coming on during the summer? Set a stake with every glad bulb you put in and make sure you know the top from the bottom. There should be a strong spike-like sprout coming out of the top. If not, look at the bottom; you will see either a flat or slightly concave bottom where last year's bulb was attached. A new bulb forms every year along with numerous bulblets. These tiny fellows can be separated and planted in a protected row somewhere out of the way. Dig in the fall as with mature bulbs. It will take approximately three years for the tiny bulb to become large enough to bloom. I like to keep a row in the vegetable garden for nursing immature bulbs such as daffodil, tulip and gladiolus to blossom stage, and also use it to start certain plants from seed. My vegetable garden is always the most fertile piece of ground on my property.

LAWNS

For the already established lawn, there are certain early spring chores that help make your lawn more beautiful, healthier, and something you can be proud of.

Care for the Spring Lawn

CLEAN-UP — For the existing lawn, clean up any debris accumulated over the winter, such as leaves, branches, papers, toys, dog-doo, etc.

THATCH — Thatching your lawn is not a chore required every single year, but it should be done every three or four years, either by purchasing a thatching rake or renting a thatcher. Thatching is a heavy raking job which goes deep to remove a lot of the moss and dead grass and helps to revitalize the lawn. If a power thatcher is used, be prepared for a messy but very thorough job. Power thatching will make a remarkable difference in a thick or packed lawn.

AERATING — If your lawn is sparse-growing and very hard, especially in the heavy-traffic areas, the next step would be to aerate it. This is done with a four-pronged fork or a special aerating tool to put small holes 13 cm (5 in) into the soil. This helps the fertilizers and water get down to the roots where they are needed. I have even driven large nails, about six to eight inches long, into boards, strapped them to my kids' feet (nail points down, of course), and let them walk around on the lawn. Your lawn will love it and so do the kids!

FERTILIZE/WATER — If the weather is mild and temperatures are above 15°C (60°F), you can fertilize your lawn with an all-purpose fertilizer or one especially suited for lawns. This fertilizer will have a larger second number (phosphate) to encourage root growth. A fertilizer with a large first number (nitrogen) to encourage top growth can be applied later in the spring. Use a good turf starter such as 10-20-5. This fertilizer will provide nutrients to your lawn for approximately two months. The numbers on this fertilizer give the lawn enough food for the blades (10) to keep them a rich green and with the larger second number (20), it will have plenty of nutrients going into the root section to help establish a strong foundation for your lawn plants.

Dolomite lime can be applied to the lawn at this time. Lawn grasses like an alkaline soil *(see pH Scale, page 176)*. With all the winter rains we have, most nutrients have been leached from the soil, leaving a lower pH reading. Plants requiring an alkaline soil will have a yellow (chlorotic) look about them if they are in an acid soil. You will notice the difference in the colour of your lawn once lime has been added and given a chance to take hold. Use only the required amount on your lawns, as lime seems to encourage weeds, which also like a sweeter (more alkaline) soil.

Be careful when liming under acid-loving trees such as fir, cedar and arbutus. The lime will cause a slow painful death to these beautiful monarchs of the coastal area. Acid-loving plants never do well when planted in the middle of a lawn because of the fertilizer requirements of both types being so different. They fare better when planted on the edge where fertilizers can also be kept separate.

After you have fertilized and limed, you should give the lawn a heavy watering. Any top dressing of fertilizer and/or lime will go into the holes and become accessible to the roots.

PLANT — Fill in low areas with topsoil and reseed now if you didn't in the fall. Spring is a good time to plant, while rains and cool weather are around to help it get a good start.

ROLL — Rolling is another one of those jobs not required yearly, but is beneficial to the lawn if it can be done every three or four years. Fill a roller, which can be rented if you don't own one, half full of water and roll over your lawn, when it is dry, to flatten out any raised areas. Rolling your lawn while it is wet will compact the soil and do more harm than good. The reason for rolling your lawn is to firm it up. During the winter, the ground seems to heave a little. The most obvious reason would be from frost, but we never seem to get much frost. Our main reason here is people walking or playing on it when it is wet.

MOWING — When mowing your lawn, keep it short until the end of spring. Once the warmer time of year comes, usually in June, let the lawn grow to a longer length of about 8 cm (3 in). The deeper grass will shade the weeds and prevent them from seeding. The longer grass will also shade the grass roots, enabling them to survive the summer heat. Mow frequently over the summer and let the grass clippings fall back into the grass to replace fertilizer and act as a mulch. If there is too much time between cuttings and clippings are too long, they will lie on the lawn and suffocate it. They will have to be raked off and placed in a compost pile.

Problems With Your Lawn

CRABGRASS — Crabgrass can be quite a problem in many lawns. This rampant grower is an annual and should die out if it freezes enough during the winter, but this is not always the case here on the islands. Crabgrass can be dug by hand if it isn't too bad, or you can use chemical controls, available at your local garden centre or hardware store. Chemicals for treating crabgrass are included in certain lawn fertilizers and will fertilize your lawn while killing the crabgrass. Read directions carefully when applying this or any other herbicide.

MOSS — Moss is a sure sign that the soil is poor and not a sign that it is either acid or alkaline. A good supply of food and moisture will make the grass grow more thickly, crowding out the moss. If you have a moss problem in your lawn, rake as much up as you can with a thatching rake and give the soil a treatment of dolomite lime. Dolomite lime does not kill the moss, but it will help your lawn to become healthier, crowding out the moss. There are also iron sulphate formulas on the market to rid the lawn of moss.

If you have a continuous problem of moss under trees and shrubs, it would be ideal to plant an acid-loving ground cover such as ivy.

WEEDS — The best cure for ridding a lawn of weeds is to maintain a healthy lawn. Many weeds are annuals and will die after repeated mowings. Others will die as the lawn gets stronger and healthier. Weeds are broad-leaved plants and can be killed with the application of a weed killer. Lawn fertilizer can be put on later in the season when the days are warmer, or you can spot-kill weeds with a herbicide. Weeds that pose the most problems are dandelions and plantains. Plantains are shallow-rooted and can be cut out by hand with a weeder, but dandelions have a long root and can be very difficult to rid by hand. To rid your lawn of weeds by hand, you will have to stay with it and continue to fertilize, so it will help crowd out this type of plant.

PESTS — Most lawns are pest-free. The most serious pests are grubs, in the form of beetle grubs, cutworms or leather jackets, which are all larvae for various insects. Early spring is the best time to rid your lawn of grubs, since they are most active then, although summer and fall eradication is also effective. One of the only ways to rid your lawn of grubs is by chemical means, which can be effective for one to five years depending upon the type of chemical used. Diazinon requires application yearly, while chlordane dust is effective for up to five years. The chemical is sprayed or dusted on and watered in. Children and pets should stay off the sprayed area until the blades of grass are dry from the watering.

To find out whether or not you have a problem, dig up a small square of lawn. Carefully go through the soil and count the number of grubs you find. If you find one, two or none, don't concern yourself with control as yet. But if you have ten or twenty in this small area, consider spraying. When you see grubs of any sort while digging in a flower bed, garden or yard, destroy them. Grubs feed on the roots of plants.

I discourage the use of chemical controls on lawns because of children and pets, and because pesticides will kill all insects, including the helpful earthworm. If you are in danger of losing your lawn, then use a chemical control, but follow directions carefully.

Planting a New Lawn
Throughout this book I stress the importance of preparation, but nowhere is it as important as when planting a new lawn. Your lawn is the first thing people see when looking at your home, and a well-planned and cared-for lawn can be enjoyed for a long time. Upkeep is easier if the lawn was started off properly; it could cost a fortune over the years to correct errors. If the original plan is too expensive, then do it one part at a time.

Many professionals will tell you that the best time to start a lawn is in the fall, as weeds have less chance of surviving with the cooler weather. I have seen well-prepared lawns planted in the fall destroyed by heavy rains because the young grass is not thick enough to hold the topsoil in place. There is also the chance the weather may be too cold for the grass to really take hold until spring. Hopefully, if you plant in the fall, the weather will stay warm enough for the grass to gain a solid foothold and there will be no problem. You will have to decide.

When purchasing seed, use a variety with a mixture of grass seeds in it. The reason for the mixture is to provide a green lawn all year round. Some grass seeds produce grass that turns brown in the hot weather, while others survive the hot, dry summers and quickly respond after a thorough watering. With many areas now imposing water restrictions during the hottest months, your lawn will benefit from the mixture of grass types and recover more easily in the fall. Suggestions for planting a new lawn are as follows:

1. Topsoil – Grass does not grow well on clay or hard-packed soil. In our climate, lawns receive too much water in the winter and this causes them to pack down. Be sure your lawn drains well to prevent water from standing on top of it. This may involve placing drain tiles through the area to keep water moving away.
2. If you are making a lawn from soil used to excavate a basement, it is best to place a layer of sand and humus (peat, old manure, compost, straw, etc.) and work it into the subsoil prior to placing a layer of topsoil on it. The soil left over from excavation is not ideal to use for a lawn. The ideal conditions are 8 cm (3 in) of good topsoil and 15 cm (6 in) of a soil that drains well beneath it.
3. Prior to planting, remove all weeds and make sure the lawn is level by filling in any depressions. Stake out the area you wish to seed for the lawn and be sure to slope it away from the house.
4. After the soil is prepared, rake the area smooth and roll firm with a heavy roller while it is still dry. The roller can be rented from a garden centre or equipment rental business.
5. The next step is to spread seed mixture by hand or with a seeder. Be sure you seed on a calm day. The wind can blow the light seed, causing irregularity in your seeding. Sow one-half of the seed lengthwise and the rest across the width, going over the area to be planted twice.
6. Rake in the seed lightly and again roll the lawn smooth with a roller.
7. Water lightly and keep the surface of the newly planted lawn moist until the lawn is long enough to be cut.

There is no need to fertilize at this time, since lawn seed requires moisture and warmth to germinate. I work dolomite lime, an all-purpose fertilizer and peat moss into the topsoil and leave it for a day or two prior to seeding. It is totally up to you. Either way, the idea is to build a good base for your lawn prior to seeding.

GARDENS

Soil on Vancouver Island usually remains wet well into spring. Don't be in a hurry to get your vegetable garden planted, or to work the soil, if you are a novice gardener. Working the soil when it is too wet will damage the structure of the soil and it will not break up well. Watch for periods of drying weather occurring alternately with rains for the next several weeks. Work the soil after a few days' respite from the rain.

If this is your first attempt at gardening, be sure the area you use is not situated under any trees and receives at least six hours of sunlight during the daytime. Clear all rocks, weeds and grass from the area you wish to use and then dig and double-dig or rototill as deep as possible. Eight to ten inches of good rich topsoil is sufficient.

If your soil is light and not clay or gravelly, you could add an all-purpose fertilizer (6-8-6) and peat moss into the second dig or tilling. The peat moss is added for humus content, which will break down in the soil and help to keep it light. If your soil is clay and packs easily, you should add sand as well as the above ingredients to your soil. You will still have a good garden in a clay soil; it is just harder to work. Add dolomite lime to your garden (except where you plant potatoes) to neutralize the acid. Combining animal fertilizer such as steer manure and dolomite lime at the same time creates a chemical reaction that results in nitrogen being used up more rapidly than normal. Even if the garden was limed last year, it has leached out over the winter months with all the rain.

When selecting vegetables for your first garden, stick to the basics. Don't try anything difficult. Easy vegetables from seed are peas, lettuce, beets, green or wax beans, corn (plant at least four rows), onions, cucumbers, squash, carrots and radishes. Easy vegetables from plants are peppers, tomatoes, cucumbers and squash.

If this is your first garden, don't try to out-guess the weather and get in early crops. You have until the last week of May to get the garden in and still have it produce well. Concentrate on getting your garden site prepared first. The plants mentioned above need protection from cool weather.

The earliest cool-weather crops to be planted outside are those of the cabbage family. If you want to get a jump on the weather, broad beans, lettuce, radishes, peas, carrots, green onions, spinach, beets and chard can be started, but be ready to protect them. Sowing seeds in wet, cold soil produces poor results — the seeds may even rot first. If it has been a cool spring, you can always start these crops in a cold frame or sunny window in your home.

PESTS

Dormant spraying can still be done before shrubs and trees begin to bloom. Once the blossoms are open, spraying is taboo because you may kill the bees, and without the bees, you will have no pollination. Once the buds begin to swell, the strength of the spray will have to be cut down to prevent injury to the buds. Do not spray in close proximity to a light-coloured house or fence because of possible spotting. It may also discolour brick or stucco.

Plants subject to powdery mildew or other fungus diseases, such as the rose, phlox, delphinium, laurel and peony, will benefit from a dusting of a fungicide. Prior to using any fungicide, insecticide or other chemical, please read directions on the package and store unused portions in clearly marked containers in a cool, safe place out of the reach of children and pets.

Watch for slugs and aphids to start making their entrance. Try to get in the habit of destroying these characters every time you see one. It is hard for most people to pick up a slug and the only other alternative, if you don't want to scatter slug bait, is to step on them. They will do a lot of damage if you don't destroy them. I don't like to scatter slug bait in my yard, but I have a system that seems to work for me. I place a small amount of slug bait in the bottom of an ice cream pail and as I walk in the garden and find slugs, I put the slug in the ice cream pail with the slug bait. Other solutions are the shallow dish of beer where the slug crawls in and drowns (my dog always drank the beer), another is to pick up the slugs you find under boards or leaves and put them in a bucket of water, where they will drown.

With aphids, because of their multiplication rate (they would put rabbits to shame), you must keep on top of the situation (*see Aphids, page 102*).

HOUSEPLANTS

Your houseplants should be feeling the bright rays of sun by now and are probably starting to grow more. Start feeding them regularly to help them on their way.

If you have a very large plant that needs repotting because it has outgrown its present pot, be sure you know what you're doing first. Large plants such as a rubber tree or schefflera are trees in their native climates. The larger the pot, the larger the plant. Anything larger than a 10-cm (4-in) pot can produce a larger-than-life plant. Don't repot a plant into a large pot just because it fits in with your decor. You can set the plant, pot and all, in the large pot, then invert another pot under it. This will bring the rim of your plant up to the height it would be if planted in the larger pot. Fill the empty space around the smaller pot with decorative wood chips or gravel. It will fit in with your decor, and you can still keep it under control.

Houseplants do best when root-bound. An alternative to transplanting then into larger pots is to shear off some of the roots and repot them in pots of the same size, adding houseplant soil to take up the area of trimmed off roots.

Plants such as African violets do not enjoy being transplanted because they do not like their roots disturbed. If your African violet is extremely pot-bound, separate the plants in the pot, if you find you have more than one crown, and pot each plant in a 10-cm (4-in) pot with new soil, then water. (When I talk about pot size, I am referring to the distance across the top of a pot and, in some instances, the number on the bottom of the plastic grower pots, not the size or height of a plant.) Violets love a rich soil and usually bloom for approximately four months and then rest four months. Do any repotting or dividing when the plant is in its dormant state. The blooming stage is quite a strain on the plant without adding the strain of disturbing the roots.

APRIL
Spring has Sprung!

SPRING HAS SPRUNG! The three most wonderful words in the English language. The deciduous trees are shooting out new leaves and colour is springing up everywhere.

April can be a glorious month on the west coast of British Columbia, even though it is wet. Interspered with the rain showers are days of wonderful sunshine. This is a great time to be in the garden. Spring fever is a wonderful feeling to a gardener. By watching Mother Nature awaken from a long winter, you can follow her lead when it comes to making your plans for the garden and yard.

Place still-coarse compost on the bottom of the pile as a foundation for a fresh start. New additions to the compost pile can be layered with soil on top of the compost.

Preparation

If you accomplish one thing this year, let it be preparation. I have mentioned before the importance of preparation and can't stress enough its importance prior to any job, whether it is the vegetable garden, flower bed, planting a tree or shrub, or your lawn. One good thing about preparation is it only has to be done once. From then on, after the soil has been prepared properly, the only job will be to loosen it up in the spring or before planting and add fertilizers or mulch, peat moss and compost. It is easy to blame failures on the weather or poor seed. This is fine, but unless you prepare the soil properly, you are going to have problems, no matter how much time you spend in the garden.

Remove all weeds, dig your soil deep, remove rocks bigger than a pea, and pay attention to the soil. If your soil is gravelly and most rocks are bigger than a pea, you have some work to do. It may sound like a lot of work, but your best bet is to remove the gravel by straining (or sifting) the soil through a screen and saving what soil you can. Have a wheelbarrow alongside to fill with the gravel. The excess gravel can be used on a driveway or to fill a hole. If the rocks are larger, use them for a rock garden or place them at the bottom of a backyard pond or stream. Either way, dig a shovel length deep and replace the gravel and rock with a good humus-type topsoil. A gravel-based soil may have good drainage, but it is difficult to work. There are times when there is no alternative but to dig a hole several feet deep and place all gravel or rocks in the bottom and then back fill the hole with soil. This will provide excellent drainage, but the gravel will be below shovel and rototiller depth. If soil is on the clay side, add sand and humus (peat moss, compost, grass cuttings, etc.), and fertilizer (all-purpose is fine, 6-8-6 or 4-7-7). If the soil seems light and easily worked, you can still add peat moss, but sand is not necessary. Now you can dig or rototill it again and rake it over. This will produce a fine bed for your lawn, flower bed, that special tree, bush or garden.

If you have moved to a place where the plants are already established and doing poorly, look at the soil. You can't feasibly remove every plant to do your preparations, but you can prepare around these plants. You will just have to be more careful as you dig or hoe around each plant. Loosen the soil, remove weeds and rocks, add peat moss (sand if needed) and fertilizer. Work the soil until everything is worked in wherever there are unplanted areas. Rake over and you are ready to plant. Over time, you may also want to replant some of the less fortunate plants growing in the poor conditions.

If you are a busy person, look for shortcuts such as using a slow-release fertilizer in your flower bed, around your trees and shrubs and in your vegetable garden. Slow-release fertilizers are well balanced and coated with urea-formaldehyde, which breaks down slowly in the soil and lasts from three to nine months, depending upon the type and purpose. This variety of fertilizer is often triggered by the temperature. This is one way to save the time and expense spent fertilizing. Use mulches to keep down the weeds, which will save on weeding and watering time. But, if you want a nice-looking garden, you will not be able to get away from proper preparation.

With the soil prepared, you will notice the difference the first year. There will be less wondering what went wrong with the weather, the seed or the garden centre where you purchased your plants. Preparation won't solve all your problems, but it will take out some of the guesswork.

TREES, SHRUBS & VINES

Fruit trees, both ornamental and producing varieties, are in full blossom. Flowering cherries are at the top of the list as far as popularity and beauty go. The earlier varieties of flowering cherry are: pink bell-shaped flowers in clusters — Creeper, TaiwanTaiwan flowering cherry (*Prunus campanulata*); pink buds and semi-double blossoms — Mt. Fuji (*Prunus shirotae*); pink buds and double white flowers — Autumunalis (*Prunus subhirtella*); red buds and single flowers — Whitcombii (*Prunus subhirtella* 'Rosea'); single light pink to nearly white — Yoshino (*Prunus* 'Yae-shidara-higan').

Although there are many blossoms on most fruit trees, fruit production will depend on whether the trees have been pollinated. If they are early-blooming varieties of fruit, such as the transparent apple and most apricots, check to see if there are any bees around your trees. If not, they may not have been pollinated. While the tree is in full blossom, if possible, shake it gently. Although not a surefire solution, this will cause some of the blossoms to brush against each other or pollen to fall onto another blossom. Another way of ensuring pollination is to cut off a small branch with blossoms and brush the cut branch of blossoms against blossoms still on the tree in a gentle sweeping motion. I have tried the latter method with a small transparent apple blooming too early in the season. I touched a small branch of blossoms against only one branch of the main tree. This particular branch was the only branch bearing fruit that year. Another method is to take a small paintbrush and touch it gently to each blossom, spreading the pollen this way. This sounds tedious, but unless the bees are out, this may be the only way to have fruit.

Trees and shrubs should be fertilized now. Apply fertilizer out to the drip line of the branches by drilling holes in the soil approx-

imately 36 cm (15 in) deep every couple of feet. This can be done
with a punch bar, crow bar or an auger. Place about half a cup of
fertilizer such as 10-10-10 or 12-4-4 in the holes and water well.
You can place the soil back in the holes or fill with peat moss. A
useful rule of thumb is to judge the roots of a plant by the top
growing above ground. If the branches of a tree expand horizon-
tally to 6 m (20 ft), then so do the roots. This may not be true in
all cases, but it is a useful generalisation when fertilizing.

This is a good time to apply mulch to your shrubs and trees to
help them retain moisture. We are all used to the damage done
during the months of June, July and August if there are water restrictions. Start now by helping your plants through a hot season.
Good mulches are compost materials such as grass clippings,
leaves, bark, large chunks of peat moss, wood chips, etc. Do not
use grass clippings on your plants as a mulch if the lawn has been
sprayed or treated with a weed killer. The weed killer is in your
blades of grass and will damage the plants you mulch.

Lilacs are blooming at the present time. What a treat they are
to have in any garden. Quince and forsythia are winding down
with varieties of spirea blooming. Pruning can start on these spring
bloomers after they finish blooming. If your lilac blossoms are far
over your head and out of reach, leaving you with several large bare
woody stems to look at all year and no way of reaching the blossoms
for a bouquet in your house, I would suggest you take the plant back
to 1 m (3 ft) from the ground. The plant will shoot new branches
from these old trunks, and although you will risk losing next year's
blossom, the following year you will have blossoms at eye level and
the fragrance where you can enjoy it. Don't be afraid to trim these
shrubs to keep them under control. I have literally trimmed mock
orange, honeysuckle, kolkwitzia, deutzia, heather, althea, spirea,
lilac, forsythia and most varieties of verbena to within 15 cm (6 in)
of the ground to have them come up the following year with double the branches and with some blossoming. What have you got to
lose? What good are the bushes if you can't enjoy them and if you
have to climb a ladder to smell or pick the blossoms?

When using dolomite lime or any other garden lime on your
lawn and plants, be sure you know which plants enjoy a sweeter
soil. People wonder why the beautiful arbutus or dogwood tree in
the middle of their lawn is dying or becoming so unsightly. They
water it, they fertilize it, but yet it still dies to the point where removal
becomes a necessity, yet the lawn is rich green and lush from this

excellent care. If you are unsure which plants like sour (acid) soil and which plants like sweet soil (alkaline soil requiring garden lime to neutralize the acid), check at the nursery when you purchase the plants.

Possibly, this will help. All plants growing naturally, such as arbutus, cedar, pine, dogwood, spruce and fir, require acid soil; evergreen plants (with a few exceptions such as larch (*Larix*), maple, oak and deciduous azalea), require acid soil (i.e. azalea, camellia, spruce, pine, fir, arbutus, laurel, rhododendron, juniper). Those that lose their leaves (deciduous), most garden vegetables, annual flowers, perennial flowers, shrubs, etc., require a slightly acid or more sweet soil (i.e. lilac, mock orange, petunia, gladiolus, strawberry, carrots, etc.) *(see pH Scale, page 176)*.

With the large native maples just coming into bloom now, and buds starting to swell on the large oak trees, you can start your early planting outdoors. Birds more common in the warm weather have started to arrive, telling us it is time to start.

Now is a good time to check shrubs and trees planted by propagating or seed last fall. If they are well rooted, you can plant them where they will grow, and by fall they will become well established. If they are still small plants, mark them or plant into pots and set them where they will not be overlooked for watering. Unless they start to drop leaves prematurely or become yellowish, these young plants shouldn't require any fertilizing for a few years. It depends on the soil they have been planted in.

This is a good time to plant any woody stock purchased from a nursery. Deciduous trees and bushes should be planted before their leaves start. This goes for fruit trees as well *(see Planting, page 14)*.

Camellia, rhododendron, azalea, heather, wisteria, broom, red flowering current, forsythia, fruit trees, lilac and quince are blooming. A few varieties, such as camellia and heather, have been taking turns blooming since fall.

When planting camellias, place the plants under the eaves of the house to keep rain from falling on their remarkable blossoms. Once cold rain or water from the sprinkler hits their blossoms, they turn brown.

FLOWERS

When new red growth appears on your hybrid tea roses, you can do your spring pruning if you have not already done so (see *Pruning Roses, page 36*).

Perennials

Cut back dead stalks on perennials and clean up around plants to prevent slugs and other insects from harbouring under the clutter of dead growth from last year. You will find the new leaves of most spring blooming varieties already coming up.

Disbud (remove all buds but the top centremost) early-blooming perennials such as peonies and carnations as soon as you can. If you have a lot of buds forming on a stem, and leave the terminal bud only on each stem if you want large specimen blossoms. To make bushier stands of perennials such as carnations, cut them back halfway. They will double up and bush out. Stake the taller variety of carnations. Carnations can become messy if not staked.

Columbine

Delphiniums are a favourite perennial of many gardeners. The delphinium doesn't like a hot, dry area. It enjoys being relatively cool

Primrose

and moist. Except for the hottest months of summer, our conditions are ideal for this tall beautiful bloomer. They like being planted in full sun and watered regularly. Left to struggle through a hot summer with very little water, the plant weakens, and although it will flower, the flowers do not last as long as they would normally and the plant tries to go to seed earlier than usual. Feed them well and remember to stake them to keep the sheer weight of their blossoms or a wind from blowing them over.

Perennials for colour this month are wallflower, aubretia, saxifrage, bishop's-cap, candytuft, columbine, polyanthus, alyssum (perennial variety), Lenten rose (*Helleborus orientalis*), bergenia, lungwort (*Pulmonaria*), bloodroot (*Sanguinaria canadensis*) and bleeding heart.

Annuals
Our weather is mild this time of year, but still too cool to do our main gardening. There is a chance of frost even into May. The bedding plants are out in mass for purchase. All gardeners will attempt to do their planting even though the days can be too cool. The more experienced gardeners will place black plastic down to warm the cold soil to get a jump on the season.

When you do purchase your bedding plants or take plants from your greenhouse or cold frame, harden them off first by taking them out a little bit each day and exposing them to the weather outside. After you plant the annuals, pinch back the tops of plants such as petunias, mimulus, periwinkle, nemesia, pansies, nicotiana, four o' clock, zinnias, stock, torrenia and snapdragons. You will get two stems for every one you pinch back, making for twice as many flowers and stronger, bushier plants.

If you like to sow annuals outside, nice ones to start with are pansies, calendula, snapdragons, marigolds, zinnias, twinkle phlox, sweet alyssum, poppies, larkspur, portulaca and nasturtiums. Prepare your soil first by working it deeply and fertilizing with an all-purpose fertilizer (6-8-6, 4-10-10, etc.) or my favourite, a slow-release fertilizer requiring one application per season. If you have compost, you could work some in. The bedding plants should be wet when you plant them. Never plant a dry plant, whether it is an annual or a large tree. The best way to make sure a plant is well watered after you plant is to fill the hole with water prior to planting. If this is not done, be sure to water thoroughly after planting.

When you plant your annual, or any plant from a pot, loosen the roots, which are usually in a mass. Don't loosen to the point of losing all the soil, but enough to send the roots going in directions other than a square or circle.

Bulbs, Tubers & Corms
The hardy early bulbs, corms and tubers of daffodils, hyacinths, species irises and tulips are putting on quite a display right now. When bulbs finish their blooming, do not remove the tops. You

can remove the dead flowers and seed heads but the tops will gradually die back as the bulb itself absorbs nutrients from the leaves. When the leaves have finally turned brown a month or two down the line, you can give them a slight tug and they will come up easily. If they are unsightly, you can fold them over carefully in a bunch and put a tie around them until the time comes to remove them. I have seen tops of clustered daffodils braided together to keep them out of the way in professional gardens. Your bulbs need this food to produce large flowers next year. All bulbs and tubers should have their tops left on until they die back naturally, to replenish the bulb or tuber.

During the summer months, bulbs are dormant and may be replanted, thinned out or placed in another location. If this is done prior to the leaves dying, heel them in or plant them with the leaves attached. Do not set them to dry out while they still have green leaves.

Spring-flowering bulbs (crocus, tulip, daffodil, hyacinth, etc.) with insufficient blooms or no blooms at all on otherwise healthy bulbs should be checked and then replanted once the tops die back. The bulbs are possibly crowded and need to be divided and fertilized with either bulb fertilizer or an all-purpose fertilizer. A good fall fertilizer for bulbs is bone meal.

Daffodil and tulip bulbs should be planted deep, usually three times their height. Shallow planting encourages rapid multiplication, whereas deep planting encourages larger bulbs and blossoms and the bulbs do not multiply as rapidly. If you were to watch professional gardeners plant a large number of bulbs in a park or for exhibit in commercial gardens, you would be shocked to see how much preparation and the depth used to plant these bulbs. They replant their bulbs every fall and dig them up every spring. This gives them the uniformity required in their plantings. Those of us planting home gardens will usually leave them in until the flowers start to get smaller. Planted in mass, bulbs can be very labour intensive.

Dahlias and cannas should be divided and planted out now. Fertilize with steer manure and super phosphate. You can divide dahlias by splitting down the stem between tubers with a knife. A part of the stem should be attached to each piece of tuber, since the plant grows from the crown and not the tuber. Plant dahlia tubers in the sun, 10 to 13 cm (4 to 5 in) deep, with a stake in place nearest the stem where the plant will be coming out. The stake is to attach the plant to as it grows and, of course, to mark the spot where the tuber has been planted until it starts to grow, to prevent it from being disturbed.

Cannas can be divided in large sections, leaving several buds on each. Plant the canna in full sun, 10 to 13 cm (4 to 5 in) deep and approximately 45 to 60 cm (18 to 24 in) apart.

LAWNS

Mow your lawn short to allow the sun to reach the crowns of the grass to stimulate new growth. Again, a reminder to thatch your lawn once it starts growing well, and treat for any insects or disease. Don't feel as though you have to thatch and aerate every year. When I mention thatching, rolling, aerating and fertilizing throughout the book, I am suggesting times when it would be beneficial, although it may not always be possible because of cost and time constraints . Your lawn would appreciate this treatment, but it will not die from lack of it. If you can, fertilize your lawn now with a good lawn fertilizer and roll it when it is dry. It also wouldn't hurt to top-dress with a sprinkling of topsoil mixed with bone meal. This can be done two or three times a year. Bone meal is a slow acting fertilizer excellent for roots of plants with a high (22%) content of phosphorus.

GARDENS

The last weekend in May has always been a safe time for planting sensitive plants such as cucumber, squash and tomato outside. If you are going to plant now, be prepared for cold evenings, possibly even frost. Have something close at hand to cover your tender plants. With a little luck, we may have a mild spring with no more frost. Every year and every area is different. Some areas on the coast will be a month ahead, while others are a month behind.

Fertilize perennial plants such as berry bushes, strawberries, asparagus, rhubarb and grapes if you have not already done so. Keep weeds away from these plants because they will need all their energy to produce for you. They don't want to share the energy they do have with weeds. Be careful when weeding with a hoe around these plants. They have very shallow root systems. Also, tie up your grapes, raspberries and blackberries.

The garden can be started by planting cool-weather crops such as cabbage, cauliflower, broccoli, peas, radishes, onions, spinach, beets, lettuce, early potatoes (Warba) and carrots. A good suggestion for stretching out the pea season is to pick three different varieties from the seed racks with different lengths of time to production. Try to make them within the same height range or else stake to the height of the tallest-growing variety. Mix them all together before planting and then plant at the same time. They will germinate and grow at staggered intervals, producing at the three different times for approximately a two- or three-week stretch. This gives six or nine crops to a row instead of one or two. This is a different form of succession planting. You can do this with many different types of vegetables. When planting beets, remember that each seed is made up of many seeds clustered together producing several plants per seed, so plant sparingly. Thin out to your liking, whether it is young beets, beets for canning, beet tops or all three.

Gardens for the Beginner
If this is your first attempt at gardening and you are not sure how or where to start, here are the basic elements to consider:

LOCATION — Location is very important when planting a garden. Choose a place with sunshine most of the day and good drainage, not too near trees and shrubs that will cast shade or take food and water from your flowers and vegetables.

SOIL — Soil type should be high on the list of priorities. Dig a shovelful of soil out of the place you plan to garden, and look at it. Is it sticky? Does it crumble when it's moist? Does it have a nice dark brown colour?

A good, old-fashioned test is to put a cup of soil in a pint jar and add water to fill the jar. Stir it so it's muddy and mixed up, then let it settle until the water clears. It might take a day or two. You can see by the layers just how much clay, sandy material and humus (dead plant material) there is in your garden area. How wide are the bands? There should be three bands visible. At the bottom you will see the heavier band, which will include sand and rocks, the middle band will be fine clay, and the top band will be the humus layer. A balanced soil will show an even, or close to even, proportion of all three. The humus is the darkest band. The wider the humus layer, the richer your soil is likely to be. Lots of humus means the soil is "light" so roots can grow easily. This is an easy way to see what your garden needs.

SIZE — The size of your garden should be determined prior to any further preparation. Stake the area you plan to cultivate. Stay small the first year with room for possible expansion. It would be wise to decide whether you will be using a rototiller or hoeing by hand. If your decision is to use a rototiller, you should allow room between rows for the machine, and therefore plan a larger garden plot.

PREPARATION — A previously used garden plot is probably already in good condition. A virgin plot will require work to get it in shape for growing your garden. This does not mean you cannot use it the first year; it just means production from the garden may not be as successful as you would like. Each year becomes better.

Prior to digging, spread dolomite lime over the area you will be preparing, except where potatoes are to be planted (potatoes do not like freshly limed soil). You can spend the warmer days of March, April and first few weeks of May preparing the soil when the ground is dry.

Do not work the soil if it is wet. Working wet soil causes solid clods to form which dry like concrete. The time to start is when the soil is easily worked. You can test it by squeezing a handful. If it molds together but doesn't crumble too easily, it is in ideal condition. If it forms into a tight, sticky mass, wait awhile to work the soil and go about other jobs. Nothing is to be gained, not even time, when soil is worked too early or when it is wet.

Once the soil can be worked, dig or rototill the area deeply. Remove all the dirt possible from the clumps you dig up by breaking clods with a shovel, by hand or using the back of a rake. Shake as much soil out of the clods as possible. Remove all rocks larger than a pea and other debris such as sticks and twigs from your garden site.

If the soil is clay in appearance and texture, add sand and peat moss to the soil and work in. An all-purpose fertilizer should be applied at the rate specified on the package. A slow-release fertilizer can be placed on the garden in place of the all-purpose fertilizer and you would not have to fertilize again during the season. All-purpose fertilizer is sufficient, but will need to be reapplied throughout the season.

Rake the garden soil smooth once you have completed the above procedures.

PLANTING — When planting your first garden, you should start the first year with the easier varieties to grow. Keep track of the varieties you choose and mark the ones you like, so next year your selection will be easier. A starter list with suggested varieties and requirements follows:

BEANS, BUSH GREEN ('Tendercrop', 'Blue Lake', 'Bush Kentucky Wonder') — Plant beans 5 cm (2 in) deep, 10 cm (4 in) apart in rows 60 cm (24 in) apart. Plant beans the last week of April or first part of May when the soil is warm. Successive plantings can be made every two weeks until June.

BEANS, BUSH YELLOW ('Gold Crop', 'Cherokee') — (see Beans, Bush Green)

BEANS, POLE ('Kentucky Wonder', 'Blue Lake') — (see Beans, Bush Green). Pole beans require trellises or poles to climb approximately 1.8 m (6 ft) high.

BEETS ('Ruby Queen', 'Detroit Dark Red') — Plant beets 2.5 cm (1 in) deep, 7.5 cm (3 in) apart in rows 30 cm (24 in) apart. Successive plantings can be made every two weeks until June. Thin seedlings to 13 cm (5 in) apart when either tops or small beets are large enough to use. Plant in early spring when the soil is dry enough to work.

BROCCOLI ('Green Comet' hybrid, 'Premium Crop' hybrid) — Plant broccoli plants 45 cm (18 in) apart in rows 60 cm (24 in) apart in early spring. Seed sowed can be transplanted to a permanent location once the plants are large enough to handle. Broccoli can also be planted in mid-summer for a fall crop. Bend large leaves over the green head to protect from hot summer sun.

BRUSSELS SPROUTS ('Long Island', 'Jade Cross' hybrid) — Plant Brussels sprouts 60 cm (24 in) apart in rows 60 cm (24 in) apart. Seeds can be planted at the end of March, while plants can be put out the end of April or early May. When harvesting, pick bottom heads first and remove bottom leaves. Brussels sprouts improve with taste after a light frost.

CABBAGE, EARLY GREEN ('Earliana', 'Early Jersey Wakefield', 'Emerald Cross' hybrid) — Plant cabbage 30 cm (12 in) apart in rows 45 cm (18 in) apart. Succession plantings from seeds can be made using numerous varieties (see Cabbage, Late Green for varieties) from March until August. Plants can be planted in late summer for fall harvest.

CABBAGE, LATE GREEN ('Danish Ballhead', 'Penn State Ballhead') — (see Cabbage, Early Green)

CABBAGE, RED ('Red Acre', 'Mammoth Red Rock') —(see Cabbage, Early Green)

CARROTS ('Nantes Coreless', 'Royal Chantenay') —Plant carrots 1 cm (.5 inch) deep in rows 30 cm (12 in) apart. Thin carrots to 10 cm (4 in) apart when those thinned are large enough to use. Succession planting can be made every two or three weeks from March to July. Carrots store well over winter.

CAULIFLOWER ('Snow King', 'Snowball') —(see Broccoli)

CORN, EARLY ('Sunny Vee', 'Seneca 60', 'Golden Beauty') —Plant corn 25 to 30 cm (10 to 12 in) apart, 2.5 cm (1 inch) deep in rows 60 to 90 cm (24 to 36 in) apart in blocks of at least four rows to ensure pollination. Plant succession crops (see Corn, Mid- and Main Season for varieties) every two weeks until June if you have the space. Harvest corn when the tassel turns brown.

CORN, MID-SEASON ('Goldenvee', 'Sunburst Improved', 'Yukon') —(see Corn, Early)

CORN, MAIN SEASON ('Seneca Chief', 'Lancer', 'Golden Jubilee') — (see Corn, Early)

CUCUMBERS, SLICING ('Marketmore' hybrid, 'Spacemaster') —Plant in well-fertilized holes or small mounds 120 cm (48 in) apart with three or four seeds in each hole or mound. Pinch off the tip after five leaves develop. Cucumbers require warm soil and protection the first few weeks after planting. Protection can be either cloche, hot cap, plastic milk jug or large pop bottle with the bottom cut out. A successful planting can be achieved from either seeds or plants and a cucumber plant requires heavy feeding and water. Cucumbers can be grown on a trellis or fence to save space.

LETTUCE, COS OR ROMAINE ('Parris Island') —Plant lettuce 1 cm (.5 in) deep in rows 30 cm (12 in) apart. Thin leaf lettuce as you use it to 8 cm (3 in) apart. Heads should be thinned to 30 cm (12 in) apart. Lettuce does not like hot weather. Successive plantings can be made every two weeks after March until June and later in the fall during September and October.

LETTUCE, BUTTERHEAD ('Bibb', 'Buttercrunch') —(see Lettuce, Cos or Romaine)

LETTUCE, HEAD ('Great Lakes', 'Rosa') —(see Lettuce, Cos or Romaine)

LETTUCE, LEAF ('Salad Bowl', 'Green Ice', 'Ruby') —(see Lettuce, Cos or Romaine)

ONIONS, GREEN BUNCHING ('White Lisbon', 'White Globe') — Plant seed 1 cm (.5 inch) deep in rows 30 cm (12 in) apart. Thin as you use them to 8 cm (3 in) apart. Onions can be planted early spring, March to May.

ONIONS, FALL STORING ('Early Yellow', 'Yellow Globe', 'Sweet Spanish') — Plant by sets (small bulb onions stored over winter to continue their season when planted in spring) 15 cm (6 in) apart in rows 30 cm (12 in) apart. Press onion set into the soil until only the tips are showing.

PEAS, EARLY BUSH ('Laxton' varieties, 'Alaska', 'Little Marvel', 'Wando') — Peas can be planted 5 cm (2 in) deep, 5 cm (2 in) apart in rows 45 cm (18 in) apart. Even the earlier bush peas require some support to keep plants from falling over on the ground. Plant successive plantings from March to June. If space is a problem, plant both Early Bush and later varieties in the same row with a trellis for support, and when one is complete, the later variety will continue on.

PEAS, SUGAR ('Sweet Pod', 'Oregon Sugar Pod') — (see Peas, Early Bush)

PEAS, LATER VARIETIES ('Fordhook Wonder', 'Green Arrow', 'Tall Telephone') — (see Peas, Early Bush). Later varieties require support for climbing. Tall Telephone can reach heights of 120 cm (48 in).

PEPPERS, SWEET GREEN ('Bell Boy', 'California Wonder') — Plant peppers 30 cm (12 in) apart in rows 30 cm (12 in) apart. Peppers require a warm soil. Protect from cold with cloche, hot caps, plastic milk bottles or large plastic pop bottles with bottoms cut out for the first two or three weeks. Peppers are best planted in late May.

POTATOES, EARLY ('Warba', 'Norland', 'Yukon Gold') — Plant potato sets 10 cm (4 in) deep, 30 cm (12 in) apart in rows 76 cm (30 in) apart. Potatoes can be planted early, after any frost, April to June. Early variety can be used as soon as potatoes are large enough to suit your purpose. Instead of digging the plant, you can reach under through the soil and take a few potatoes from the vine, then recover with the soil, leaving the remaining potatoes on the plant to continue maturing. Do not plant in freshly limed soil. Lime encourages scab on potatoes, and potatoes like a more acid soil than other vegetables. Hill soil up the stems of plants during the growing season as potatoes mature to prevent sun from turning tops of potatoes green. Potatoes form along the stem, so the more stem that is buried, the more potatoes you will have.

POTATOES, LATE ('Netted Gem', 'Red Pontiac', 'Norgold Russett', 'Kennebec') — *(see Potatoes, Early)*. Late potatoes are ready to dig after tops die and before any frost. Dry potatoes for storage in the sun for a short time. Do not store wet potatoes.

RADISHES ('Cherry Belle', 'White Icicle', 'Sparkler') — Plant radishes 1 cm (.5 inch) deep in rows 15 cm (6 in) apart. Thin radishes as you use them to 5 cm (2 in) apart. Radishes can be succession planted every two weeks from March to June. Radishes require watering regularly to prevent them from becoming bitter. Radishes do not like the summer sun.

SPINACH ('Bloomsdale Long Standing', 'Vienna') — Spinach should be planted 2 cm (1 in) deep in rows 30 cm (12 in) apart. Thin to 10 cm (4 in) as you use it. Remove a few leaves from each plant at a time instead of removing the complete plant after main plants are established. Spinach does not like hot sun and can be planted from mid-March to the end of June in succession plantings, then again in the fall from August to October.

SQUASH, PUMPKIN ('Connecticut Field', 'Cinderella', 'Small Sugar') — Plant in well-fertilized hills or holes 120 cm (48 in) apart. Plant six or seven seeds per hill or hole and thin to three or four. Squash love heat, fertilizer and regular watering. Protect plant with cloche, hot caps, plastic milk bottles, or large plastic pop bottles with bottoms cut out for the first few weeks. Winter squash can be stored over winter in a cool area once vines have died from light frost in the fall.

SQUASH, SUMMER ('Seneca Prolific Zucchini', 'Zucchini Elite', 'Golden Summer Crookneck', 'Scallopini') — Plant in well fertilized hills or holes 90 cm (36 in) apart in rows 120 cm (48 in) apart (two or three plants are usually plenty for a family). Plant six or seven seeds per hill and thin to three or four. Squash love heat, fertilizing and being watered regularly. Protect plant with cloche, hot caps, plastic milk bottles or large plastic pop bottles with bottoms cut out for the first few weeks. Summer squash does not store well over winter. It should be eaten soon after picking, canned or frozen.

SQUASH, WINTER ('Bush Acorn Table King', 'Gold Nugget', 'Blue Hubbard', 'Table Queen', 'Waltham Butternut') — *(see Squash, Pumpkin)*

TOMATOES, STANDARD ('Better Boy', 'Big Boy', 'Fireball', 'Early Wonder', 'Early Girl') — Plant tomatoes 45 cm (18 in) apart in rows 45 cm (18 in) apart. Warm soil is required for tomatoes, and so is some form of support or staking. Tomatoes can be started from either seeds or plants. Plants require deep planting up to the first set of leaves. Tomatoes are heavy feeders and require regular watering. Protection is required in the form of a cloche, hot cap, plastic milk bottle or large plastic pop bottle with bottoms cut out for the first few weeks. Do not plant out until late April or May, depending upon the weather.

Remove side shoots as they sprout up between leaf and main stem and pinch tops of tomato plants off during August to enable plant to ripen fruit already on vine instead of making more. This will allow all energy to go towards ripening the tomatoes left on the plant before winter.

TOMATOES, CHERRY ('Tiny Tim', 'Small Fry', 'Pixie', 'Sweet 100's') — *(see Tomatoes, Standard)*. Some varieties of cherry tomatoes ('Sweet 100's') can grow extremely tall (to 2 m/6 ft) and will require adequate staking.

To mark your rows, use string tied to stakes at each side of the garden and pull taut between them. With the string just off the ground, you will be able to bring the edge of the hoe under it and make a straight ditch in the soil. The depth of the ditch will be determined by the seed you are planting.

If a rototiller is used, the width between rows will have to be adjusted accordingly. You should also allow room to walk between the rows for weeding and picking. Be sure to label each row so that you will know what is planted there and the variety. Many gardeners place the empty seed packet on a stake at the end of each row. When doing this, open the seed packet at the bottom instead of the top so the name stays intact. Of course, the rain usually makes short work of the seed packet before too long, but it can be placed in a plastic sandwich bag and stapled to the stake.

All these things must be considered prior to actually planting your garden. After you have planted a few gardens, you will be able to recognize the plants as they break through the soil and it will not be necessary to mark your rows.

A first-time gardener does not always know a weed from a plant purposely planted. The ones in the straight line, of course, are the purposely planted seedlings. This does not always work because when the carrots break through the ground, they look like grass to a beginner and panic strikes, the hoe comes out and, a month later, we are complaining because the carrots didn't come up. On the back side of most brands of seeds is a picture of what the newly germinated seedling looks like. This will help the beginner. The dates of germination on the back of a seed package are estimates. Do not expect these dates to be exact.

A helpful way to identify your rows is to plant radish seeds in the same row as your slower seeds, such as green onions and asparagus. The radishes grow quickly and by the time you're ready to pull them, you will see your other companion plant growing. You can always weed close to the plants and pull the weeds you are certain of. Those of you lucky enough to have asparagus plants already established are looking for those spears coming up through the ground now. This is one time when the weeds that require hoeing can be left in the ground, because if you can't pull them out root and all, any hoeing will sever asparagus spears growing up through the soil.

Water your garden after you have planted, and then water thoroughly once a week. Don't rely on summer rainfalls to water your garden sufficiently.

Garden crops should be rotated and planted in different locations every year to produce better results and control insects and disease. The most important plant family to rotate yearly is the cabbage family (cabbage, cauliflower, Brussels sprouts, broccoli). Clubroot is a soil-borne disease affecting the cabbage family and can be prevented by using lime in soil and by rotating crops. Other reasons for crop rotation are that each type of plant takes certain elements from the soil (i.e.: peas and beans leave the soil with more nitrogenous nutrients) and plants can also extract nutrients from different levels depending upon their root depth. By crop rotating you can prevent many of these problems and keep your garden healthier.

Perennial Garden Plants

Perennial garden plants are very important in most gardens. Once you have planted them, and as long as you take care of them, there will be no need to replace them.

ASPARAGUS ('Martha Washington', 'Viking') — Plant asparagus 20 cm (8 in) deep, 30 cm (12 in) apart in rows 45 cm (18 in) apart. Asparagus plants are heavy feeders requiring spring and fall feedings. Plants will usually be two years old when purchased. Plant with roots spread over small mound in bottom of 20 cm (8 in)-deep trench. Place soil over crown and fill over more as the plant grows. Do not harvest for one or two years or until the young shoots are large enough.

If planting by seed, plant in place. Do not pick for three years. Cut off the foliage when the tops turn yellow in the fall. Female plants having berries at maturity are not heavy producers and should be replaced with non-fruiting male plants.

CURRANTS ('Rovada' [red]) — Currants should be planted 120 cm (48 in) apart in either spring or fall. Prune to shape and keep old wood pruned out to rejuvenate.

GOOSEBERRIES ('Poorman' [red], 'Dawning' [green]) — (see Currants)

GRAPES ('Himrod' [yellow], 'Fredonia' [black], 'Golden Muscat' [yellow], 'Concord' [blue], 'Catawba' [red]) — Grape plants require a trellis, arbour or fence to climb. Prune vine back to two buds the first year to develop heavy root system. Grapes like heat, regular waterings and heavy fertilizing and produce larger quantities of fruit if more than one variety is planted.

RASPBERRIES, EVERBLOOMING ('September', 'Fall Red') — Plant raspberries 90 cm (36 in) apart in rows 180 cm (72 in) apart. Prune bushes to 150 cm (60 in) and attach to a support. Once a raspberry cane produces, cut it out at ground level. It will not produce a second time. New shoots will come up to replace the ones that have been removed. Everbearing varieties should not be pruned until fall or winter.

RASPBERRIES, JUNE BEARING ('Red Latham' [red], 'Cumberland' [black]) — (see *Raspberries, Everblooming*)

RHUBARB ('Victoria', 'Canada' [red]) — Plant the rhubarb root early in the season 90 cm (36 in) apart. Rhubarb is a heavy feeder and can be harvested the second or third year after planting. Cut off seed stalks as they form. When harvesting rhubarb, do not pull more than half of the stalks from any one plant at one time. CAUTION: Rhubarb leaves are poisonous.

STRAWBERRIES, JUNE BEARING ('Blakemore, Surecrop') — Plant strawberries 45 cm (18 in) apart in rows 60 cm (24 in) apart. Do not cover the crown when planting. Strawberries can be planted in either spring or fall. Keep runners off the first year, but encourage the following years and transplant for replacement plants thereafter.

STRAWBERRIES, EVERBEARING ('Ozark Beauty', 'Ogalalla') — (*see Strawberries, June Bearing*)

PESTS

If you are in an area where your fruit trees and ornamentals have not yet blossomed, there is still time to apply dormant oil and lime sulphur for eradication of insects.

Check your plants often for insects and keep piles of debris picked up. Slugs spend their days hiding under this type of material. The only way to stay on top of pests such as slugs, aphids and scale is to check your plants constantly. Look under the leaves, check stems and pay attention to obvious insect bites on your plant leaves.

HOUSEPLANTS

Caring for Your Easter Plant

With Easter coming up, most people will be receiving plants as gifts. Below, you will find tips for caring for the various plants you may have inherited.

HYDRANGEA — These large-leaved beauties with their massive heads of florets can dry out fast in your home. Be prepared to water twice a day to keep the large leaves or large bunches of blossoms from wilting. They will break down quickly if allowed to wilt. Most are planted in a 15-cm (6-in) pot, which is much too small for a long period of time. Keep the plant in a bright room without placing it in direct sunlight. If the blossoms are pink or white, you want to keep the soil alkaline by adding a fertilizer of 5-10-5 or similar each month. A blue hydrangea can be kept healthy and blue by adding an acidic fertilizer or by using ammonium sulfate monthly. Once the weather stays above freezing, you can plant the hydrangea outside in your garden and grow it as a permanent plant. Cared for properly, it may bloom again for you at its normal time in the late summer. If not, you always have next year.

EASTER LILY — This beautiful scented lily is a perennial forced to bloom at Easter. You can plant it in your flower bed when it finishes. While it is in the house, keep it moist and in a sunny place. Once it finishes blooming, the leaves will gradually turn yellow from the base up and appear dead. Plant the bulb outside in a flower bed, approximately 15 cm (6 in) deep. You will be rewarded each year with this beautiful fragrant bulb.

FORCED BULBS — Give these plants a bright spot in your home while they are in blossom. They should be kept as cool as possible. Many people throw them away when they finish blooming, but I plant them outside and the next year they are up and trying to bloom. The first year after planting may have sparse blooms but they will recover and prove a welcome asset to the garden.

GARDENIAS — These plants are difficult to grow, even in greenhouses, so do not be disappointed if you lose one or two. The plant is beautiful, the scent of the blossoms is overwhelming and well worth the effort. The gardenia likes to be warmer than most houseplants, around 24°C (76°F) with cool nights (approximately 10°C/18°F cooler). It likes an acid soil and to be kept moist to prevent buds dropping and leaves turning yellow. During the summer months keep the plant humid. Possibly set on a tray of gravel with water in the gravel at all times. Do not let the pot sit in water, however. A lot of gardenia growers place their plants in plastic bags to maintain the humidity required.

Easter lily

GLOXINIAS — These attractive plants do well in a home and require the same temperature as we do. Bright light is needed and they must be kept moist. If the blossoms fall prematurely, it is usually due to too much moisture or a lack of humidity.

MAY
Garden Planting Time

OUR WEATHER CAN be rather cool and wet at times during May, which is good for the newly planted trees, shrubs, flowers and garden. As long as it is not too cool, our plants can get off to a strong start without a hot sun beating down on them. I always like to plant on an overcast or light rainy day. The plants never seem to wilt as they can do on a hot day.

TREES, SHRUBS & VINES

Tidy up the spring-flowering shrubs by pruning and removing spent blossoms. Plants such as camellia, rhododendron and lilac can become cluttered if their dead blossoms are left on the bushes. After flowering, the plant will automatically set seeds, which take strength away from the bush. This can be prevented by deadheading. Shrubs have a segment just below the blossom that you can use to separate the blossom from the shrub. This is to protect blossoms already starting for next year. This is the time to prune the shrub. If you do it prior to deadheading, you may remove most of the dead blossoms. Be aware of next year's blossoms forming in the leaf axil below.

If you live close to the ocean and find it difficult to grow a variety of different plants because of the salt air, consider planting a hedge or windbreak, where your view is not disrupted. You can then attempt to plant on the landward side of this windbreak. It is done on the Atlantic coast quite successfully and has been done on the Pacific coast as well.

Deadheading rhododendrons

Trees and shrubs can be easily planted in the springtime. When adding a permanent fixture like this to your garden, make sure all conditions are right. Take the time to prepare the area where the plant is to grow for life. A tree in the right location and properly grown can enhance the beauty and value of your property. A tree improperly planted or placed incorrectly can have just the opposite effect. Some large trees, such as maples or willows, can damage the foundation or driveway if they are planted too close to the house. A tiny spruce planted in front of a window as part of your foundation planting could sprout to a huge height, obscuring the view and damaging the foundation and, possibly, the roof. A hedge planted too close to the property line will eventually be in the way of people walking on the sidewalk if it is not strictly pruned. The same goes for deodora planted under power lines. Power lines are approximately 6 m (20 ft) above the ground; the deodora can grow to 12 m (40 ft) high. Make allowances for the adult size of your plant prior to planting *(see Planting Trees, page 14)*.

FLOWERS

Fuchsia baskets already blooming were started in January from last year's cuttings in the nurseries. Unless they are deadheaded as their blooms expire, they will set seed pods and stop blooming about mid-summer, placing all their energy into producing seeds.

This is the first month of the year when roses are freely blooming. Be sure to feed these heavy bloomers often and check for mildew or black spot. Mildew is recognizable by the white dusty look on leaves. Black spot is just that: a black spot on the leaves. It is a very contagious fungal disease. Pick off infected leaves (more will grow back), making sure none are left on the ground, and destroy them. You will find the infected leaves almost fall into your hand when you go to pick them. Don't panic if all the leaves have black spots and need to be removed. New leaves will grow back within a week or two. If necessary, a fungicide will need to be used to control black spot and powdery mildew. Read directions and storage requirements prior to using.

When a rose finishes blooming, or if you are picking roses for a bouquet, cut the blossom off down to an outward facing bud at a place where there are five individual leaves on a main leaf stem. You will notice that, close to the flower, there are only three individual leaves. If you want to keep a symmetrical look to your hybrid tea bushes, cut back to shape as you go. The place where the last blossom was picked off will shoot a branch that will quickly grow 25 cm (10 in) while it forms a bud. By cutting back when deadheading or picking a bouquet, it is easier to keep the bush under control and healthy. Blossoms are only on new branches, so don't be afraid to cut them back a little each time.

Often, the best way to produce more blossom on plants or to make them bush out is to pinch them back. Some plants, however, should not be pinched back. There are some plants with only one blossom per year. They shoot out long blades instead of leaves and are usually bulbs or rhizomes. Pinching them back will destroy any hope of their blooming. Plants such as iris, daffodil, tulip, crocus, lily, gladiolus, amaryllis, yucca, daylily and red-hot poker should not be pinched back.

Perennials

Why not grow your own perennials from seed this year? Use a place either in your garden or with your flowers where you can leave these seedlings to grow until fall, when they can be replanted to a more permanent position. Some are quite slow to germinate but well worth the wait when you compare the cost of a single plant at the retail outlets. Easy perennials to grow in the springtime are:

flax	delphinium
columbine	lupine
carnation	balloonflower
Oriental poppy	Chinese lantern
coneflower	coral bells

Shasta daisy	leopard's-bane
sea holly	gaillardia
geum	hollyhock
painted daisy	sweet pea
red-hot poker	'Basket of Gold' alyssum

Propagating Perennials

Perennials can be started from a parent plant by dividing the existing plant and planting the starts in their permanent location. When the foliage indicates a dormant condition, dig up a good root of each perennial.

Perennials easily propagated by division:

Shasta daisy	lily-of-the-valley
lady's-mantle (*Alchemilla*)	Michaelmas daisy (*Aster*)
astilbe	bergenia
balloonflower	iris
centaurea	coneflower (*Rudbeckia*)
coreopsis	coral bells
cynoglossum	delphinium
daylily	pinks (*Dianthus*)
sea holly	gaillardia
geum	globeflower
sunflower (*Helianthus*)	hosta
peony	Oriental poppy
painted daisy	red-hot poker
viola	yucca
chrysanthemum	

Basal Cutting

With most perennials' growth stopping or slowing down during the summer months, now is a good time to begin to propagate from root cuttings (basal cutting) to provide more of your favourite perennials. Cut the long roots of the chosen perennials into 2-cm (1-in) pieces and plant them where the soil is a mixture of sand and rich loam. Keep the area fairly moist and soon tiny leaves will shoot up. The new plants will be ready for permanent quarters in your garden by spring. You only have to buy one plant and use it to take your starts from. Following is a list of plants for basal cutting:

bleeding heart	baby's breath
Chinese lantern	globe thistle
delphinium	sea holly

gaillardia   flax (*Linum*)
viola   Oriental poppy
yucca

You can now see what you need in the way of perennial replacement since any perennials surviving the winter are well on their way. Small plants purchased at this time will become large, blooming plants by fall, or at the latest, by next spring. Most will last for years, so care should be taken when planting them. Plant taller varieties, such as delphinium and hollyhock, toward the back of the bed, the medium-height perennials in the middle and shorter perennials in front along with ground cover, annuals, etc. (*see Perennial List, page 164*).

The flowering stalks of iris can be cut freely without injury to the plants if care is taken to leave plenty of foliage for the promotion of subsequent growth. The same applies to peonies and, later on, the gladiolus plantings. Remove faded blossoms of perennials as they appear. This will prevent the plant from forming seeds and it will continue blooming. By pinching back roses, shrubs, perennials and annuals, you are doing the plant and yourself a favour. These plants will double their blossom, and it will keep the plant in shape.

Suggested varieties of perennials blooming for this month are:

bleeding heart	iris	gaillardia
columbine	daylily	lily-of-the-valley
carpet bugle	moss pinks	snow-in-summer
rock speedwell	peony	goldentuft
coral bells	geum	ajuga
spurge	delphinium	trillium
woolly lamb's ear	poppy	rock rose
dianthus	vinca minor	blue poppy

Annuals

When planting flower beds and borders, consider colour and texture combinations. Place the taller plants in the background, medium plants in the middle and short plants in front, along with trailing plants. Succession of bloom should also be considered. This way you will have bloom all summer long. Annuals, continually deadheaded, will bloom the entire season and are used to bring instant colour to your garden while perennial plants are taking their turns. This is why annuals are mainly used for hanging baskets and container gardening to provide continual colour.

Bachelor's button, zinnia, marigold, four o' clock and other mid-size to tall annuals also are favourites to plant in a vegetable garden. Do not feel you must plant only vegetables in the vegetable garden. Plants such as marigolds are often planted in vegetable gardens because they discourage certain types of bugs, which are harmful to the vegetables, from entering the garden.

Petunias, unless deadheaded, will become long single stems of seed pods. For every bit of pruning you do on these plants, two new stems will start to grow, producing twice as many blossoms, so don't be afraid to cut back leggy growth. All annuals will bloom longer if they are clipped. Planting time is going full steam ahead by now with the warmer weather upon us. To transplant seedlings from a flat or pot into the open ground, carefully loosen the rootlets, which have formed a mass at the bottom of their soil ball, so they will take up food and water. To prevent shock and drying out from the sun or wind, it is best to plant these tender young plants when it is cloudy or even late in the afternoon, giving them the cool evening and following morning to adjust to any transplanting shock. To ensure a stocky growth, remove the central bud at the top of the plant when it is 15 cm (6 in) tall. Calendula, ageratum, snapdragon, stock, marigold, Drummond phlox, alyssum and petunia all need such treatment. The poppy, aster and nicotiana are best left alone. Always be ready to place some newspapers or some other cover over your more tender plants just in case of a light frost.

Hanging Baskets/Containers
Retail outlets have a selection of bedding plants for hanging baskets on display, so, with a good chance of the weather holding out, it is a good time to put together some hanging baskets or patio pots. Hanging baskets and container plants are planted in the same way. The only difference is the centre plant for containers can be of a taller variety than in a hanging basket because of the support wires in a basket. The hanging plant is usually within 60 cm (24 in) of the roof overhang and the centre plant should be comfortably below it. Suggested steps for planting hanging baskets and container gardening are as follows:

SOIL should be new potting soil with a small amount of fertilizer and a handful of vermiculite per pot or basket. If using last year's soil, rejuvenate it by mixing half and half with new soil and vermiculite for water retention. If your fuchsia saved from last year is growing well in last year's pot and last year's soil, rejuvenate by adding some new soil on top. If not, you will have to fertilize more often. The soil from last year will be leached of most nutrients due to the large amount of watering needed for a hanging basket. If the hanging basket or container is placed in a hot area or in direct sunlight, place a couple of layers of newspaper or a sponge in the bottom of the pot or basket prior to putting soil in to hold moisture. This is not necessary for plants like the begonia, fuchsia or impatien, which should be in full or partial shade.

PLANTS should be selected by picking those with strong compact growth. The leaves should be a rich green and not be yellowing or reaching for light. Prior to planting any bedding plant, make sure the soil is damp. Bedding plants put in with dry soil, which will fall away from the tiny hair roots of the plant, will most often die once planted. In a crowded hanging basket only the strong will survive, so make sure all the plants have a chance.

Select three levels of plants: hanging (lobelia, fuchsia, petunia, ivy, ivy geranium, etc.); mid-size uprights (small varieties of marigold, upright petunia, schizanthus, dianthus, salvia, etc.); and a larger stronger variety, usually in a 10-cm (4-in) pot (geranium, marguerite, large blooming mid-size marigold, dracena, etc.), so it cannot be overgrown by the more aggressive side plants. Pots or containers using plants of one variety such as begonia, fuchsia, petunia, marigold and marguerite are attractive favourites using five plants per 25-cm (10-in) basket or pot and six plants per 30-cm (12-in) basket or pot.

Hanging basket

POT size is a personal choice. I suggest having a pot at least 25 cm (10 in) in diameter. There are many 20-cm (8-in) pots available, but upkeep is difficult during the hotter months of July and August, and the 20-cm (8-in) pot does not have the depth to hold enough soil for the plants to survive a full season. Do not leave the saucer on a hanging basket if it comes with one. The water should be allowed to run free out the bottom. Hangers provided with the baskets are usually three or four strands of strong wire either twisted at the tops to form a loop for hanging or connected to a hook for hanging. Bend all wires approximately 5 cm (2 in) from the ends at the same time and then place in the holes and twist twice (for strength) with the ends of the wires pointing *in* the basket instead of outwards to prevent your being stabbed or scratched.

FERTILIZERS are a definite must to keep your plants growing well. Nurseries fertilize their young growing plants every week with a well-balanced fertilizer such as 20-20-20, and, once the plants are mature and ready to bloom, some nurseries switch to a fertilizer with a larger second and third number, such as 7-15-15, to promote blooming. This feeding program is maintained throughout the growing season. Plants must be wet to feed. Water one day, feed the next. The best fertilizer for the busy gardener is a slow-release such as osmocote 15-15-15. Sprinkle a tablespoon or two (depending on the size of the pot) of slow-release fertilizer across the top of each pot. Once the temperature reaches 20°C (70°F), the fertilizer pellets will slowly release a small amount as needed as long as the pot is watered consistently. Once the basket is planted, if the weather is still cool, tender plants such as cucumber, tomato, fuchsia and begonia may need some protection from the cooler days and evenings. If you don't have a greenhouse or cold frame to place the plant in, using a laundry bag from the clearners, place it over the plant hanger and all, sliding the hanger through the hole in the top of the bag, and let it fall down over the wires. The wires will hold it away from the plants. Tie a knot in the bottom of the bag if it is hanging or tuck it under the pot if the pot is sitting on the ground. Once the weather is warm enough for the plants, usually at the end of May, you can easily pull the plastic bag away and discard it or slip it off the top carefully for next season's use.

Hanging Basket/Container Plant List
One-of-a-kind baskets or containers:

common impatiens (shade)	New Guinea impatiens
petunia	tuberous begonia (shade)*
fibrous begonia	Reiger begonia (shade)
flowering maple (*Abutilon*)	fuchsia (semi-shade)
ivy geranium	verbena

* Leaves should be pointed to outside of basket.

Tall centre plants for mixed baskets:

geranium
marigold (large varieties)

Tall centre plants for containers:

geranium   marguerite
marigold (large varieties)   dracena
cosmos

Mid-range plants for mixed baskets and containers:

dianthus   alyssum
browalia   cineraria
mignonette   mimulus
periwinkle (annual)   African daisy
Virginia stock   torenia
viola   nicotiana
petunia   phlox (annual)
fairy primrose   impatiens
marigold (mid-size)   butterfly flower
coleus

Trailing plants for edge:

petunia (cascade)   nasturtium
nepita   potato vine
ivy   lobelia (trailing)
ivy geranium   portulaca
lotus vine   wandering Jew
verbena   fuchsia (trailing)
creeping Jenny

Baskets and containers are not for flowers alone. Try the following if you are looking for something different or perhaps if you live in an apartment where it is impossible to have a garden:

cucumber ('Pot Luck')
squash (non-vining varieties 'Zucchini', 'Scallop', 'Crook Neck')
strawberries
tomatoes ('Tiny Tim', 'Sweet 100's)
New Zealand spinach
lettuce
herbs (chives, mint, parsley, thyme, rosemary, etc.)

Whatever you try and whatever you do, have fun. I am only offering suggestions. Whether you use my idea or someone else's, be sure to put lots of plants in the pot so you won't have empty spaces. The plants will grow among each other. Enjoy and remember to water weekly and fertilize every two to three weeks if you are not using a slow-release variety. It wouldn't hurt to give one-quarter-strength fertilizer every time you water. Be sure to deadhead all blossoms as they expire. Don't be afraid to pinch back to thicken a plant or keep it in bounds. If using a dracena for a centre plant, this plant is one you do not pinch back.

Bulbs, Tubers & Corms
Tulips and daffodils are becoming shabby-looking, with just foliage and ugly stems left. The foliage must stay with the bulb until it dies back naturally. A professional gardener will dig the bulbs each spring and either heel-in somewhere else out of sight, or, if in a place where other plants will soon cover the unsightly tops of the spring-flowering bulbs, braid or bunch and then tie them off letting them die back naturally. The bulbs need to take the food stored in the leaves to grow and develop next year's blossoms. Annuals planted among the bulb tops will soon hide the tops until they are ready to be separated from the bulb.

Dahlias should be pinched back once they have reached a reasonable height. Even the smaller varieties would benefit from being pinched back a notch. This will enable the plant to grow bushier and shoot up more stems to blossom.

If you are just planting tubers or corms such as dahlia and gladiolus, be sure to put fertilizer in the bottom of the hole. Placing plants directly on fertilizer can burn the tender roots of a plant, so be sure to work the fertilizer into the soil first. Use a specified bulb fertilizer, bone meal or superphosphate. An all-purpose fertilizer will work if you have none of the above and happen to have some left over from your garden. It may not have the recommended proportions for bulbs, but this is the instance where some is better than none. You can work in the special fertilizers around the plant when you are able to get some.

LAWNS

Mowing the lawn fairly short in the spring is beneficial to the grass. By now it should be kept at 8 cm (3 in) high. It makes for a better appearance, shades the crabgrass seed and keeps it from germinating, retards the evaporation of moisture and nitrates by keeping the surface of the soil cool during the weather, and crowds out weeds that flourish in the hot soil.

Apply post-emergent herbicide to kill weeds only if there are more than it is possible to pull by hand. Remember not to put lawn clippings into the compost after adding a herbicide.

GARDENS

If your soil is still too wet to work, chances are your water table is too high. Add more soil, and try to build your planting area up above the present level. Spread an all-purpose fertilizer over the soil prior to planting and work it in to the top level.

When planting vegetables, provide protection for tender plants such as tomatoes, cucumbers, squash, melons, etc. You can get an extra early boost from these plants by placing hot caps over them. On hot days you can remove the lids to let the air circulate. Once the temperature stays above 12°C (54°F), the bottles can be removed, preferably on an overcast day, and stored for next year.

Plants such as broccoli, cabbage and cauliflower like the cool spring weather and will be fine without any protection at all.

Root crops such as potatoes, carrots beets and onions should be planted in single rows, far enough apart to be able to pull soil from between the rows up onto the row containing the crop (radishes, beets, carrots, turnips, potatoes, etc.) so the root crop can be covered during the season. A root crop seems to push its way up as it grows, exposing the top of the edible root to the sunlight. The part exposed to the sun turns dark and, in the case of potatoes, makes them inedible or bitter.

Corn is a fast-growing, voracious feeder. Corn needs cross-pollination, so make sure you plant in blocks, and not just one row. Although one row will grow and look healthy, the ears produced will be small with very few kernels, if any, of corn per cob. Plant at least four or more rows of corn in any one block to ensure pollination of plants from the wind, using plenty of fertilizer and water during the growing season. The corn cob is ready to harvest when the tassel at the top turns brown. Cook as soon after picking as possible, when the sugar content is at its highest.

Potatoes, too, are voracious feeders. Do not plant potatoes in an area just recently limed. Potatoes like soil on the acid side (see pH Scale, page 176). Potatoes are planted from sets, not seeds. There is a variety planted from seed, but it is not very productive. Sets are

small untreated potatoes from last year's crop. Split the potato sets in half or in quarters, making sure there are eyes on each piece you plant. Let the fresh-cut potato sets sit out overnight before planting, to dry and seal the newly cut area.

Having a row of early variety will lengthen your season of potatoes. Early varieties will not store well if left to grow for harvest in the fall. Work your hand through the soil around the plants to check their size to feel if they are ready. They should be big enough to use once the blossoms drop. Remove potatoes by feel and leave the plant in the ground to continue growing and producing.

Rhubarb should be divided every three or four years. If you let the plant continually grow from the same root year after year, you will find the rhubarb stalks getting smaller. Do not let the rhubarb plant go to seed, even if you are not picking it. As you walk by your rhubarb plants during the year, break off any hard stems coming up the middle and drop them in your compost pile.

Tomatoes should have their side shoots removed as they occur, so check the plants often. Don't forget to support the plants as they grow. The side shoots are little branches starting to grow off the main stems on the inside of a leaf node. Leave only the branches shooting from the main stem of the plant. The others will be considerably later than the main plant and will also blossom and try to produce ripe tomatoes, competing with the main plant. If these shoots aren't removed, most of the tomatoes will be very small.

PESTS

Insects have been waiting for tender, newly planted plants to gorge on, so keep an eye out. Walk through your plants daily and check for signs of insects. Learn to differentiate between harmful insects that can cause damage and good insects such as ladybugs, which are beneficial to our gardens. The next step, of course, is to learn how to get rid of the ones capable of destroying or damaging plants. If you must use chemical means, check with your local garden centre or retail outlet and carefully follow the directions on the label. There are usually two or three chemical treatments for each insect or problem you may have, depending upon the plant and time of year. Edible plants such as tomatoes, peas and apples must be washed prior to being eaten. Insecticides do not distinguish between good and bad insects, so use them sparingly and with forethought. Prior to using a spray, all of these things should be taken into consideration. (NOTE: Keep all pesticides, herbicides and fungicides out of the reach of children and, if possible, locked up in a cool, dry area.)

The best control of all for insects or disease is to either destroy the plant, or remove and destroy the insects by hand.

JUNE
New Beauty Every New Day

IF JUNE IS cool, heat-loving and blooming plants will slow down. Bees and other pollinating insects tend to be slower when the weather is cooler. While June is usually warm and balmy (22°C/72°F), the temperature can dip as low as 8°C (48°F). With only a short time to go before the first day of summer, we feel a bit cheated when we have a cold winter and a cool spring. For those with a sundial, the day to set the time is June 15 at exactly 12 o' clock noon. Make sure that when you place it in the garden, the shadow falls directly on noon.

Cultivation is one of the most important chores for June. It is often better than watering. It helps prevent insect problems by exposing different stages of insects to the elements and aids in the fertility of the soil. Work the soil deeply and often and you will find it pays off. Be careful not to injure the plant roots. In the same way that birds will follow a tractor plowing a field, robins and sparrows will make quick work of any insects unearthed.

As mentioned before, mulching is also important. The hot days force plants into bloom earlier, and with flowers, this can be a problem. It is important to remove spent blossoms from annuals and perennials. If the plants are allowed to go to seed, they will stop producing flowers. Unless you deadhead and remove spindly growth, they will not have flowers for the entire summer.

Take care that newly planted materials receive a thorough soaking each week. Soak, do not sprinkle! Mulch plants and wash the leaves. Mulching materials can be grass clippings, bark mulch, hog fuel, straw and leaves. In recent years water restrictions have become a fact of island life. There are numerous ways to help plants through the hottest summer months. A couple of years ago, I experimented with using several layers of newspaper. I put them between the plants to keep the weeds down and retain some of the moisture in the garden. It worked quite successfully.

In the vegetable garden, place a heavy thickness of newspapers between rows and weigh it down with rocks, boards, lawn clippings or other mulch. Make sure they are thoroughly soaked – any wind can set the papers blowing if they aren't kept weighed down.

When landscaping the front of my daughter's home, I placed newspapers down after planting and then placed thick bark mulch over it. This worked for a few months, but it wasn't long before the cat found out and started digging it up. Needless to say, it had to be redone with landscape cloth. But the important thing is it does the job. It was damp under the newspaper whenever I checked. The newspapers hold moisture quite well and, by fall, they will have broken down enough to be worked into the soil.

This year I will put it beneath the plants that like moisture or plants that are hard to keep damp during the hotter days prior to planting. Plants in a hanging basket, strawberry plants, tomato plants, cucumbers, squash and others that have an unquenchable thirst should enjoy the idea.

Composting

For those who have never composted and would like to start, following are a few hints to get started. Adjust these suggestions to fit your own individual way of doing things. In order for it to work successfully, and it can be an eyesore if it doesn't, composting must be easy. Don't make it a job. Composting is both economically and environmentally smart.

Some organic material, such as oak leaves, coffee grounds, pine cones, laurel leaves, rhodo leaves, cedar, etc., is too acidic. Except for coffee grounds, all should be shredded prior to placing them in a compost pile. Wood ash, a popular additive to either compost or directly on the garden, is highly alkaline and will need nitrogen added to it. I have, in the past, had two compost piles going. One was on the acid side and contained the more acid materials layered with dirt. The other was for alkaline plants, and contained grass clippings, vegetable plants from the garden when they were finished producing, vegetable scraps from the kitchen, etc. I must confess that now I put all organic material in one. I just make sure I don't add an enormous amount of one variety of plant such as oak leaves. I try to alternate between acid- and alkaline-producing material along with layers of soil. A handful of fertilizer, either organic or chemical, can be sprinkled over the soil or plant material when available (all-purpose fertilizer is fine for this, as it has a good balance). This is a good way to use up old fertilizer that has been sitting around for years or has become wet and hardened. I keep any excess leaves, grass clippings, etc., piled close by and add them as I go. When cleaning up during the fall, it doesn't take long to fill up a compost bin.

Composting

1. Build a bin for composting. This can be as simple as a large garbage can with holes poked in the sides, a homebuilt one or the elaborate store-bought variety. Compost can even be piled on the ground without a bin. A circle made with wire fencing is excellent and inexpensive. As long as air can circulate on top and the sides, anything goes.
2. Composting is done in layers of vegetable matter and soil. Start with one layer, approximately 30 cm (12 in), of vegetable matter. Water it down, add approximately 8 cm (3 in) of soil (this can be subsoil), water it down, then repeat the process, ending with a soil layer. Build the pile layer by layer as garden and kitchen waste is available until the bin is filled or has reached the desired height. Manure and fertilizers can also be added.

There are commercial additives on the market that will help speed up the process.

3. Keep a depression in the top centre of the pile to catch water.
4. The pile should be kept damp but not soggy; water when necessary.
5. A three-pronged fork or other tool can be used to turn the pile, rotating the bottom to the top, at least once a month. If you happen to have the two- or three-bin system, you can place the top of the compost pile in one bin.
6. If everything goes well, compost can be added to the soil within three to four months in the summer and longer if building during the winter.

Materials used for composting:

grass clippings
weeds (prior to setting seed)
sod
leaves
straw
hedge trimmings*
pine needles
garden scraps (potato tops, lettuce leaves, corn stalks, etc.)
kitchen scraps (vegetable only, no meat)

*Leaves such as oak, laurel, camellia and rhododendron do not break down as easily as other organic matter. Use a composter to grind up leaves and big branches prior to placing on the compost, or run over them several times with a composting lawn mower.

Do not use in your compost:

grass clippings with weed killer
meat scraps
bones
iris and peony plants (because of possible disease)
seaweed (salt water should be washed off first)
weeds going to seed
prolific weeds (wild morning glory, chickweed, etc.)*
diseased plants

*Weeds such as wild morning glory and chickweed are extremely hardy and may not completely die in a compost. Just one tiny piece will start again if placed in your garden. It's not worth the risk.

TREES, SHRUBS & VINES

Trim broom back a little after it has finished blooming. This is a very aggressive plant and most varieties reseed easily. Don't give it a severe cut or one straight across. The plant looks better in a round ball so cut each branch back 3 cm (1 in) or gather all the branches together, hold them tight and give it a straight cut. When the branches are released, they will fall down into position with a neat cut. You may have to touch it up a little.

Now that spring-flowering shrubs have finished blooming, cut out all unnecessary wood to the ground. All hedge trimming should also be done now. A second pruning may be needed in August or September. Frequent trimming of hedges makes a thick green surface growth and avoids unsightly open spots. The open spots are usually made by cutting large wood or having the top wider than the bottom. If you keep trimming back young, new growth, you will thicken out the hedge from fresh new growth. Break or cut all seed pods from rhododendrons, azaleas and lilacs, but be careful because next year's blooming buds are already being formed.

Plan a feeding program for flowering shrubs and trees to develop flower buds for next year. It is not often realized that poor flowering of such plants in the spring is due to improper feeding the summer before. This is the time when spring bloomers are starting to develop next year's blossoms.

Hardy fuchsias and hydrangeas should be blooming soon, while kolkwitzias, weigela and spireas are already blooming. These plants could use a feeding to help them through their blossoming.

Fertilizing
A fertilizing tip: remember to fertilize when planting, in the spring, when the plant blooms and when it finishes blooming. This applies to all plants. Use either all-purpose plant food or the specific fertilizer for each type of plant. Some specific-use fertilizers can be used more generally. For example: rhododendron fertilizer is good for any blooming acid-lovers like camellia, azalea and blue hydrangea, and rose fertilizer is appropriate for any sweet-soil plant with blossoms or fruit like hanging baskets and tomatoes.

How you feed your plants is as important as when you feed them. The essential plant food elements are nitrogen, phosphorus and potassium. Nitrogen promotes vegetative or foliage growth, adds green colour to the plants, and slows flower development and the maturing processes. You need to decide if you want more foliage for certain plants or if the flowering is of the greatest importance.

A good example of an overdose of nitrogen on a broadleaf evergreen is evident by the way it responds. When a plant gets more nitrogen than it needs for proper flowering, the foliage growth is stimulated at the expense of flower bud formation. This results in fewer flower buds next spring.

Phosphorus not only advances seed germination and root development, but also favours early crop maturity and increases and assists flower development.

Potassium is essential for flower bud development and seed formation. Feed a balanced diet during the growing season for a well-balanced plant with flowers and leafiness. Nitrogen for foliage growth, plus phosphorus and potassium for flower, fruit and seed are needed for flowering shrubs. Keep in mind that early flowering shrubs and trees must have their fertilizer for that year's blossoms the summer before they bloom.

One application of fertilizer per season is better than none, but two or three applications spread evenly over the summer months is ideal.

Espaliers
A true work of art like topiary and bonsai, espaliers can be fun but a lot of work with pruning, tying and training. Espaliers are shrubs or trees trained to grow flat against a wall or trellis. Some of the popular plants used for espaliers are:

cotoneaster	firethorn	peach
apple	apricot	pear
camellia	azalea	plum
Photinia	holly	fig
Escallonia	Euonymous	Osmanthus
viburnum	sumac	nectarine

Pick the branches you want to keep and attach them to the wall or trellis. Prune, year round, all growth growing out of bounds. You can also keep the height and width in check this way. If you have a fan espalier climbing a wall with five branches fanned out from the main stem, cut each of the five branches the length you want them and maintain that length. Keep all side branches pruned back to two to four buds from the main stem. Espaliers are very attractive and quite a joy to take care of if you enjoy this type of gardening.

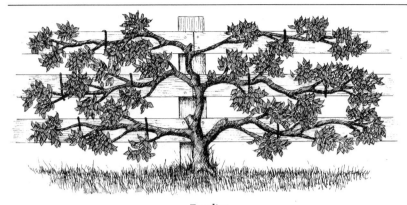

Espalier

FLOWERS

June is a beautiful time for flowers across Canada. All climates are enjoying the fragrant beauty of the gardener's labour.

Watch your roses for suckers from the root stocks. Remove the suckers and pick all leaves with black spot.

Climbing roses should be looked over carefully and any heavy growth should be firmly tied into the proper position. Prune them after blossoming.

I will prune a climbing rose constantly during the year to keep it under control and still seem to have a large amount of blossom. My system is to take four or six long canes and tie them to the trellis or fence and then shorten every lateral shoot coming off each branch to three or four leaf nodules and try to maintain this same length all summer. Roses do tend to run rampant, but this way they are kept under reasonable control.

Edible Flowers

Edible flowers are served in restaurants as garnishes and salads. No matter how they are used, edible flowers add colour to any meal. This is a list of the edible flowers that commonly appear.

nasturtium (flowers and leaves)	geranium petals
dianthus petals	marigold petals
rose petals	Johnny jump-ups
pansy/violet (flower)	dianthus petals
cornflower (bachelor's button)	columbine (flower)
calendula petals	squash blossoms

English primrose (petals, leaves)   dahlia petals
hollyhock (leaves, bud, flower)   portulaca petals

1. CAUTION: Do not think all flowers are safe to eat. Those I have listed were checked and double-checked. Some plants such as foxglove, four o'clock and lily-of-the-valley are poisonous and may even be deadly. If you are unsure or question the use of the plant at all, then by all means, DON'T use it.
2. Be sure flowers used as a meal are free of insects and pesticides of any kind.
3. Pick flowers when at their peak prior to fading.
4. Remove the stem and leaves. Before separating petals, wash and drain flowers just prior to using.

Perennials

Cut down the tops of perennials once they finish blooming. Most perennials try to bloom again later in the summer. Of course, if you would like them to seed and start new plants, let them go to seed.

Flowering perennials for the month of June are:

hollyhock   astilbe
larkspur   foxglove
regale lily   baby's breath
pentstemon   Oriental poppy
Madonna lily   Canterbury bells
Shasta daisy   coral lily
sweet William   Iceland poppy
globeflower   meadow rue
delphinium   daylily
Jacob's ladder   lychnis
iris (*Sibirica*)   iris (*versicolour*)

Annuals

This is a good time to replace annuals damaged by late cold weather. If there are no replacements tucked away in a border somewhere, check the retail nurseries, although it will be difficult to find the same annuals since most are picked over. After the main season of six-pack bedding plants are over, garden centres either purchase or pot their own leftover plants from six-packs and make 10-cm (4-in) potted annuals out of them. These are usually the favourites such as impatiens, petunias, marigolds, dianthus, snapdragons, etc. Be sure to loosen the roots a little and water the plant thoroughly when you put it in your garden.

Bulbs, Tubers & Corms
Spring bulbs should have finished flowering and died down sufficiently for digging and storing, or moving to a new location. If you can pull the tops freely, they are safe to move. A lot of people dig them up and store them until fall. This is not necessary, but if you want to, now is the time to do it.

LAWNS

This is the right time to fertilize the lawn again prior to the hottest summer months. Also apply insecticide, if necessary, for insects in the lawn (chinch bug, sod webworm, cutworm).

If weeds are a problem in your lawn, purchase a fertilizer with weed killer in it. When using this type of product, keep children and pets off the lawn for a couple of days. You will not be able to water your lawn for a week to ten days when you use this type of product and ideally it should not rain after using. This will wash the product off and it won't be able to do its job effectively.

When mowing your lawn, make sure the blade on your lawn mower is sharp. You can do this yourself or have it sharpened professionally. A dull blade frays the tips of the grass and leaves the lawn yellowish-looking a few hours after cutting. Check your blade often and always take care when changing a blade and operating a mower.

When cutting your lawn, you may feel that it still looks rough. Possibly you have cut against the grain. Try different mowing patterns (lengthwise, across or at a 45° angle) and see if one direction is better than another. If you look at the lawn closely prior to mowing, you will see the blades of grass tend to lean in one direction. Mow against this lean for the cleanest cut. The lawn has a "nap" to it, just as corduroy and velvet do.

GARDENS

If your apple trees are dropping fruit, don't panic. This is called the "June drop" and is nature's way of thinning out heavily laden trees. The tree can only supply a certain amount of energy for fruit; if the tree starts neglecting some of the fruit, the stems will close off, weaken and the fruit will fall. Orchardists thin their fruit once it starts to set on to approximately two fruits per cluster. It is better to have nice even-sized fruit than to have a lots of small fruit encouraging insects and disease or possibly damaging the tree with extra weight. Be sure to pick any fruit off the ground and place it in the compost pile. Leaving the fruit on the ground encourages pests and rodents.

Corn, beans, marigolds and zinnias can still be planted with good results. Also, tomatoes, eggplants and peppers can be set out. This is a good time to find bedding plants and vegetable plants on sale to fill in the spots that inevitably open up. These plants will probably be root-bound and in need of nutrients, but they should perk up given time and a good feeding. Buy just a few if you are concerned and plant them out remembering to spread their tight rooting system out a bit prior to planting and water them well. Pinch plants back by half if tall and gangly so they will thicken up. Don't panic about taking off some of the blossoms. Twice as many will appear.

Tall spindly tomato plants can be planted stem and all in the ground up to the more lively-looking tops. Remove all the bottom leaves and leave four or five sets of leaves above the ground. Lay the plants in a shallow trench instead of digging a hole for just the roots. Cover them and water well. You may be surprised in a week or so.

Plant late potatoes, bush beans, carrots, corn, cucumbers, spinach, Swiss chard, radishes, lettuce, beets, turnips and cauliflower still to produce before fall. Asparagus can be planted, but don't expect any asparagus for another three years. Garlic can also be planted, but should be left in the ground over winter.

Pull soil up higher on the plants of potatoes. As potatoes start to develop, they tend to push out of the soil, as do beets and carrots. The portion of the root no longer protected by soil from the sun turns colour and is very bitter to eat. During the summer months, keep piling dirt on these root crops by pulling it from the aisles between the rows.

All asparagus spears showing, although tempting, should be allowed to grow to reestablish, and could use a heavy feeding of sterilized steer manure at this time.

Strawberries should be coming on as established plants by now. The plant will also try to shoot out runners at the same time. Instead of allowing the plant to try to do both at the same time, try to keep the runners off the plant while it is still producing. There is plenty of time after it finishes producing fruit to let the runners grow. The idea is to maintain the strength of the plant. Its habit of shooting out runners is a good way to expand your bed or renew. (Strawberries should be renewed every threee or four years.) Try to have a couple of

rows of new plants growing all the time. A good mulch for strawberries is to put straw quite deeply down the rows tight against the
plants. This way the strawberries can lie on the straw and keep clean.
The plants will also enjoy the coolness with the coming hot months.

Planning on growing one of the large Atlantic mammoth pumpkins this year? Nothing is more jealously guarded in gardening
circles than the secret to growing a giant pumpkin. I will share my
method, even though the largest I have grown is 125 pounds. This
is small compared to the 500-pound monsters they can become.
Plant three or four seeds 5 cm (2 in) deep in a hole of rich soil
(one bag of steer manure worked into and around each hole).
Make three or four holes, so if one fails the other will take. Once
they start to bloom and you're sure you have a female blossom
(you can tell by the small bulge just below the blossom if it's female), go to the next leaf segment and cut the stem off. One
pumpkin per plant and no excess plant. You want all the energy to
go to that pumpkin, not making stems, leaves or anything else.
This is the reason for keeping all the plants in one hole instead of
keeping just one, because sometimes that one pumpkin will not
develop into the beauty you are aiming for.

Some mammoth varieties and their sources are:

ATLANTIC GIANT (517+ pounds) — Stokes Seeds Ltd., 39 James St.,
Box 10, St. Catherines, Ontario L2R 6R6; McFayden, Box 1800,
Brandon, MB R7A 6N4

BIG MOON (200+ pounds) — Geo. W. Park Seed Co., Inc., Cokesbury
Road (Hwy. 254 N), Greenwood, South Carolina 29647-0001, USA

Pumpkins require warmth for growing, so if the summer is
cool and rainy, you will not have any success unless you build a
greenhouse or cloche to cover the plants and provide heat. Usually,
our summers will produce large pumpkins without the cover. Be
sure to feed your plants often no matter what system you use.

Gourds, like squash, require a warm season. Plant gourds at
the end of spring or cover with a hot cap or plastic bottle with the
bottom cut out to keep the soil warm until the plants take hold
and the weather is more stable. Planting around the end of May
should be safe. When planting gourds, place five to ten seeds per
hole. Plant them near a fence or trellis for them to climb, since
they will grow up to 3 m (10 ft) tall. Use a sterilized steer manure
worked into the soil when planting, fertilize several times during
their growing season and water frequently.

PESTS

Fungus diseases are common to certain plants (mahonia, roses, lupine, delphiniums, hollyhocks, begonias, phlox and many others) and the wise gardener is prepared in advance. Have a fungicide or other cure on hand for this purpose. Dust several times each month if necessary to keep this under control. One fungal remedy recommended by many leading horticulturists is to place 15 ml (1 tbsp) of baking soda and 5 ml (1 tsp) of liquid detergent into 4.5 l (1 gal) of water and spray the affected plants regularly. Not only is this inexpensive, it is also environmentally friendly.

To help control aphids, have a spray bottle handy with insecticidal soap or liquid household dish soap. Also, you can spray the plants with a strong jet of water and knock the aphids off the plant. Once knocked to the ground, they cannot get back up to the plant, since not all generations of aphids have wings. They have young with wings when their food source is expired. That next generation of young will have wings to fly to another food source (see Aphids, page 102).

The spittle bug is so called because of the white froth it leaves on plants. If you were to take the froth and smooth it over with your fingers, you would find one or two small insects living inside the froth. They can easily be killed by hand (if you can get up the courage). They are not as dangerous to your plants as aphids because they are not as prolific, but still can cause damage. If you use chemical means, it is usually in dust form, which will dry the froth.

Remember to check roses constantly and remove all infected leaves, both on the plant and on the ground. Do not place infected leaves on the compost pile or you will infect the compost.

HOUSEPLANTS

A recycling method I have used for years, is to take large, clear soft-drink bottles (not the brown ones) and cut the bottoms off at the line below the label. The bottoms can be used for drain pans under indoor 10-cm (4-in) pots. They work especially well with African violets, as the water in the four indentations hold water which slowly evaporates, giving the violets a nice humid environment without the plant actually sitting in water. The top can be used as a hot cap for tender outdoor plants that need protection in the spring.

JULY
Summer's Here!

JULY CAN BE a month of mixed emotions as far as the weather goes, from extremely hot *(see Weather Statistics, page 153)* to the occasional shower. Plants don't know whether to turn it on or turn it off, but July is the hottest month with August a close second. When the days are warm, the corn grows taller, the tomatoes set on and seem to enlarge almost overnight, the zucchini grow more during the hot days and, of course, the annuals bloom more freely.

If it is a normally hot July, be sure to mulch around your plants, as water restrictions are bound to go into effect.

TREES, SHRUBS & VINES

Conifers can be pruned now, if they need it, to maintain good form. With upright conifers, leave only one leader, cutting out other competitors to halfway. With pines, cut back the candle (new growth) by one-third or one-half, depending upon the slope you desire in your tree. Unpruned pines can stretch out, with quite a distance between branches and side shoots. Most short-needled pines are bred for their tall lanky growth with a large spread between branches producing lots of trunk for merchantable timber. These pines are excellent in the home garden, but for the best results, and to encourage a thicker growth, pruning is necessary. When the new growth (candle) is cut back, it will encourage new buds for a couple of inches below the cut. As many as twenty buds may appear. You can see how this will thicken the tree once these all become branches in the next season. Without pruning, there would be one branch with two side shoots. Quite a difference.

If you have seen a shrub or tree you like, I wouldn't suggest planting it at this time of year because of a new plant's water needs. Take down the name and obtain as much information as you can about the plant. This way you will be able to find out if it will work into your landscape theme. Make sure that any plants you plan to buy for your garden will not need a completely different kind of care than your other plants do. Although you can plant this month, or any month for that matter, you may prefer waiting until fall or even spring when the weather is cooler and there are fewer risks to planting.

Some shrubs seldom planted but well worth checking on if you're looking for something different are:

Seldom-Used Shrubs

ALTHEA *(Hibiscus syriacus)* — This is a favourite of mine because of the time it blooms. This is a late summer bloomer with hibiscus-like flowers. It is slow to leaf out but is well worth the effort. This shrub has a wide assortment of flower types and colours so can fit in to any landscape.

WITCH HAZEL *(Hamamelis mollis)* — A sweet-smelling specimen. The naked branches produce yellow spider-like flowers mid-winter. The leaves are a special bonus, especially when they turn a bright yellow in the fall.

SMOKE BUSH *(Cotinus coggygria)* — An attractive specimen alone or in a group planting, it has a rounded form growing to approximately 3 m (9 ft), which can be pruned in spring. Leaves are rounded and flowers appear as wisps of smoke from a distance. Rich soils reduce the autumn colour and encourage leaves at the expense of the attractive flower habit of this bush. One variety, 'Royal Purple', has rich purple leaves that turn to various shades of red in the fall.

HYDRANGEA 'LACECAPS' *(Hydrangea macrophylla* 'Lacecaps') — An unbelievable hydrangea with a flat head and an outer ring of larger flowers and smaller ones in the middle. A dainty hydrangea requiring the same treatment as other hydrangea.

TAMARIX — A large, light and airy shrub forming delicate leaves with tiny pink flowers cascading down, giving the impression of pink smoke or a fragile feather. This shrub is an eye-stopper.

FLOWERS

Check your plants for water twice daily on hot days, especially those in baskets or containers. With baskets and containers, make sure the water runs out of the bottom before you quit watering. Fertilize lightly every time you water container or hanging basket plants and give a full dosage every two weeks to keep them lush and beautiful, unless you are using a slow-release fertilizer.

The fuchsia is probably exhausted from blooming if it was already in bloom when purchased in the spring. Rejuvenate it by cutting all stems that have completed blooming by one-half, and keep seed pods from forming. Most varieties will not bloom as profusely as they did earlier in the year, but they will stay bushy and green, shooting out blossoms as they produce. If the fuchsia was purchased as a cutting, the blooming season will begin now. The plants will go on until the frost kills them if fertilized and watered regularly. Set them in a pan of water to water thoroughly. Some gardeners place a few ice cubes on their plants in the morning before they go to work and the ice cubes gradually melt and water the plant.

To keep both annuals and perennials blooming throughout the season, keep them deadheaded. Plants put as much energy into producing seed as they do blooming. Don't ask your plant to do both. Once seeds start producing, the plant will stop or slow down blossom production.

Petunias and snapdragons are famous for becoming leggy. If this happens to your plants, cut them back to within a few inches of the ground and let them start their blooming all over again. It will only take a couple of weeks until they are in full colour again.

Give your roses a feeding and be sure to deadhead all spent blossoms. To keep the hybrid teas in balance, cut back on the stems to an outward facing five-petalled leaf when you cut flowers or deadhead.

Perennials
Perennials, everyone's favourite "backbone" of the flower border.

Perennial bed example

Unlike the annuals requiring replanting every year, the perennial is a plant you need only purchase once. Easily propagated by root division or seeds *(see Propagation, page 73)*, the perennial is an inexpensive and welcome addition to any garden. Some of the more popular are: iris, peony, Oriental poppy, daylily, bleeding heart, Shasta daisy, delphinium, columbine, lupine, hollyhock and chrysanthemum.

In our climate, perennials can be planted all year long with little or no trouble. Perennials spread, so don't plant too closely to start with. If not kept in check, a perennial border can be like a runaway horse.

Make the perennial bed 1 m (4 ft) to 1.5 m (5 ft) wide and curve it for effect. A bed 1.5 m (5 ft) wide is as large as can be easily worked. Remember, perennials in masses are more showy than those set out in a random fashion, and it doesn't do a bit of harm to repeat the same variety in a perennial bed. Perennials are best planted by height. Plant taller ones such as delphinium, hollyhock, daylily, foxglove, Matilija poppy, yucca, red-hot poker, lupine and bearded iris to the back of the bed, mid-range varieties like Shasta daisy, columbine, Canterbury bells, coral bells, and gaillardia in the middle, and shorter perennials like aubrietia, hepatica, violet, polyanthus, carpet bugle, creeping phlox, snow-in-summer and maiden pink in front *(see Perennial List, page 164)*.

It will take years to get the plants you want and place where you want them, so don't try to do it all at once.

Perennials in bloom this month are:

pink plume poppy	tiger lily	bergamot
bugbane	daylily	sneezeweed
loosestrife	heliopsis	liatris
phlox	globe thistle	penstemon
coral bells	Maltese cross	bellflower
bee balm	butterfly weed	red-hot poker

tunic flower   false dragonhead   Shasta daisy
phlox   coneflower

Dare to be Different

If you enjoy perennials, but would like to try something different to
add to your garden, I suggest you try some of the scarce or newer
varieties of some of the more popular standbys.

PURPLE CONEFLOWER — Purple coneflower has the scientific name
of *Echinacea purpura*. I remember this flower as a child, but I knew
it by the name *Rudbeckia*. All three names should be used when
trying to find this plant.

Daisy-like in appearance, this tall, graceful plant has been
around for two hundred years or more. Before synthetic drugs, it
was used for its medicinal properties. It has been said the rudbeckia will help the body increase its resistance to various viral and
bacterial infections, by activating the body's own defence system.
Placed on a wound, it promotes healing much like the aloe plant.

MATILIJA POPPY (*Romneya coulteri*) — Quite a show stopper, this
spectacular perennial grows to 2.5 m (8 ft) or more and takes easily to being neglected. The 10-cm (4-in) leaves are greyish green,
and flowers with five or six white petals surround a gold centre.
Don't confuse it with a Shasta daisy because of the colour of the
flowers. The petals have the texture and look of an Oriental poppy,
only larger. The Matilija poppy is beautiful for cut arrangements
and can get away from you if not controlled. They like it dry,
blooming in mid-summer, and will do well even in poor soil.
Worth trying if you are interested in something a little different.

BEARDED IRIS — If you're used to seeing iris in purple or yellow, try
the bearded iris. There are over three hundred varieties of the tall
bearded iris in some of the most spectacular colours of any flower.
This is one flower that always has attracted my attention. I have catalogues from companies specializing in the tall bearded iris, and even
though some of them are thirty or more years old, I still enjoy
wandering through them. The colour variety is amazing, with both
standards (upright petals) and falls (down-curved petals) being attractive. Hybridizers of this flower have outdone themselves over
the years and definitely deserve credit for their work. I'm hoping
that one day the bearded iris will be bred to last longer or be able
to bloom at different times during the season so they can be enjoyed for longer.

ORIENTAL POPPY — You may know the large Oriental poppy as a large bright orange poppy. A beautiful plant, it comes in shades of red, pink and orange. This attractive plant is finished blooming about now and plants will go dormant. If you have some that you want to move, mark where they are planted before the plant dies out. Some will come back and bloom in the fall.

DELPHINIUM — This tall, statuesque plant with its bee-like blossoms comes in pink, lavender and white as well as the beautiful variety of blues we see so often in our gardens. There is also a harder-to-come-by yellow variety. Many of the most popular plants have changed considerably in both size and colour. The new colours and varieties of our old standbys are worth investigating.

DAYLILY *(Hemerocallis)* — Flowers for the old-fashioned garden or today's modern garden. These old standbys come in a variety of pink, yellow and red flowers, standing up to 60 cm (24 in) tall in both miniature and standard varieties. Well worth trying some of the new varieties.

CALLA LILY *(Zantedeschia)* — This is one flower I have never planted outside, but I plan to do so in the near future. The calla lily is a stunning sight. The large, shiny, arrow-shaped leaves are almost as beautiful as the flower. The flower is a pastel-coloured or white funnel-like spathe folding around a large yellow spike covered with tiny true flowers. This is a tender rhizome but can winter over in this area. The calla can also be used for ponds. During blooming it enjoys lots of water if grown in the garden bed. A calla lily can be grown in the sun in this climate, but prefers a semi-shaded area.

Annuals

Plant winter pansies from seed now so they will be ready for winter blooming. Winter pansies will bloom all winter, and if kept dead-headed, will bloom throughout the next summer. These pretty little faces are a welcome sight in mid-January. Winter pansies, flowering kale or cabbage and dusty miller make an attractive winter basket providing colour through the winter months.

If you wish for more colour in your flower beds and it's too late to buy the packs of annuals, seeds can still be planted that germinate quickly, such as zinnias, calendula, larkspurs, cosmos (small), gypsophila, snapdragons (small) and nasturtiums. Check some nurseries or grocery stores to see if they have potted up some annuals from their bedding plants, which will put colour in the garden. Wholesale garden centres now pot up all their bedding plants when they start to get root-bound in the little four- and six-packs which are then sold to retail garden centres. You may be lucky enough to find petunias, snapdragons, marigolds, four o'clocks, impatiens, dianthus, fuchsias, fibrous begonias, zinnias and celosia, among others.

Bulbs, Tubers & Corms
The main stems of dahlias should be kept free of side shoots. In larger varieties, a single stalk is the best. Remove half the flower buds. Some sort of adequate support must be provided to prevent storm breakage for taller varieties. If you have cultivated the large dinner plate dahlia to obtain the massive blooms, you will need to disbud the whole stem, leaving only one bud per stem. Leaving the buds on to flower instead of disbudding will make for a beautiful show, but will not produce a large 20-cm (8-in) blossom. Be sure to support these well, as the blossoms can reach a large size at maturity.

If you have some gladiolus bulbs yet to plant, you can still plant them to bloom this fall. Water, fertilize and stake as you plant them. In this area of the country, we have the luxury of having a long growing season. Seldom will we get a killing frost early in the year. Even a light frost will not harm the bulbs. Many years, gladiolus bulbs can be left in the ground to grow up the next year. This is risky and I don't advise it, but it can be done.

LAWNS

Be sure to raise the cut of your lawn this month. July is usually the hottest and driest month. By letting your lawn grow long (around 8 cm/3 in), it will shade the roots and keep them cool. It will also shade weeds and weed grasses that require sun to grow.

Watering the lawn is different than sprinkling the lawn. When you water, give it a thorough soaking. This means watering down to the bottom of the roots. If you are on water restrictions and are only able to water your lawn once a week, it is enough if watered deep enough. If the water restriction prohibits you from watering your lawn at all, deep watering is very beneficial prior to restrictions being put in place. The lawn may turn brown and look dead during a drought, but it will come back once you are allowed to water it again, as the roots are still alive and should return a nice-looking lawn if they went into the drought in good condition.

GARDENS

Plant crops this month for fall production. You can plant cabbage, Brussels sprouts, carrots, cauliflower, kale, beets, lettuce and beans.

The raspberries should be done by now, and canes bearing fruit this spring can be cut down to the ground before it becomes difficult because of new shoots coming up. These canes will not produce again. If you have the everbearing type of raspberry, cut the fruit-bearing canes back once the plant has finished bearing fruit or once winter sets in. Canes that have not been removed from previous year's crops are dead and will easily pull out with a light tug from a gloved hand.

PESTS

You may take all of the preventive measures necessary to keep harmful insects out of the garden, but it will do little good if your neighbour does not consider it a priority. Even though you have invested time and money into the problem of keeping harmful insects from your plants, they can come from your neighbour's yard and do the same damage. You should constantly check your plants for harmful insects or disease.

APHID — Aphids reproduce very rapidly, without having to mate or even move from their places during most of the year. Aphids go through seasonal reproduction cycles.

In the spring, an aphid hatches from an egg. All of the spring hatchings are female and spend all summer producing baby aphids. Baby aphids (nymphs) become mature adults just a few days after birth, and start bearing their own offspring.

If you look closely, you will see a whole aphid family lined up on a stem of your plant. First is the adult female, with the youngest and smallest female nymph immediately behind her. The eldest female nymph is at the end of the line.

Aphids bear three to ten live young each day. They do not leave the stem they were born on and continue to suck the juices from the stem until there is none left unless they are knocked off by a strong jet of water or other means.

When the plant juices are consumed, the youngest generation of aphids gives birth to a new group with wings, and the winged females fly to other juicy plants to start again, continuing the cycle until winter begins.

In the fall, some winged males are born, along with winged females. These females give birth to egg-laying females who, in turn, lay one egg only, in a protected spot. The eggs hibernate until spring, when the cycle begins again.

As you can see, control of these prolific little creatures will be fruitless unless you are as aggressive as they are. This means daily control. Whether you use organic or chemical controls, the trick is to use them every day or so until the aphids are completely gone. Insecticidal soap will destroy the aphids, but persistence is the key to actually keeping them under control.

When using chemical controls, always remember to follow directions carefully.

CABBAGE MOTH — The white butterfly with black spots on the wings flitting around your garden is the cabbage moth. It will lay eggs on your cabbage family (broccoli, cauliflower, Brussels sprouts, cabbage). Once the eggs hatch, the young green caterpillars will feed on the juices of your plants and, since they are green, sometimes wind up on your dinner table. You will be able to identify damage to your plants by the holes in the leaves and the resultant green droppings. The cabbage looper also leaves the same type of damage, but it is striped whereas the cabbage worm is green and fat. Of course, why shouldn't it be? Look at the size of the plants it uses to fill its belly. It has a voracious appetite and can drill holes right into the cabbage. The cabbage worm is hard to find because it is green, but if you see holes in your leaves, you should check around and you will find a cabbage worm or looper. Pick it off by hand, or spray with an insecticide such as rotenone. A better way, and easier on you, is to send the children out catching pretty white butterflies with little black spots on their wings!

AUGUST
Hot! Hot! Hot!

JULY AND AUGUST are the driest months of the year. Sometimes there is no rain at all, or very little. We really find our gardens and yards panting for moisture at this time of the year. Seldom do we have a complete summer of rain and cool weather.

The coast is famous for its beautiful blackberries growing wild wherever the ground has been disturbed for roads, along the fence lines of farmers' fields, housing developments, etc. Left to grow without any cultivation, fertilizing or extra watering, we are blessed with an excellent treat this time of year. Be extra-careful when picking blackberries along railways, as sprays may have been used to kill the aggressive blackberry plant and can be very harmful if ingested. The thorns of the blackberry are more vicious than those of the rose, but like the rose, the end results are well worth the effort.

TREES, SHRUBS & VINES

Azalea, rhododendron, camellia, magnolia and other spring-blooming shrubs and trees will need ample water and feeding now. These plants are forming buds for next year's blossoms. The water must go deep to provide moisture to the entire root system to be of real benefit.

Hedges of all types, evergreens confined to a form (poodle cut, topiary, espalier) and clipped plant should be gone over now, as growth for the season is about to cease and a final clean-up clipping can be done. One of the secrets of success with such plants is to never let them get dishevelled and out of hand. Be careful not to fertilize at this time. This will start new growth which could possibly winter kill if cold times are ahead. If planting evergreens, make sure they have been thoroughly watered before and after planting.

The kiwi (*Actinidia arguta*) should be starting to produce for those growing this hardy variety. If kept cool and picked when firm, fruit should keep for three or four weeks. Recipes for the use of kiwi are becoming more popular every year. Kiwi makes a nice jam or jelly, is excellent eaten fresh and provides a rich green colour in a fruit salad.

Vine Pruning

Vines of all sorts can be pruned at this time. Unproductive wood should be removed from all vines. A few different varieties are pruned as follows:

CLEMATIS – This plant can be a little confusing when trying to figure out when and if to prune. It can best be explained by noting the type you have. Most are deciduous (lose their leaves in fall), and a few varieties are evergreen. All clematis can be pruned after they bloom to keep in check, but there are specific pruning practises for individual varieties. Stems may look dead on deciduous varieties in the spring, but a close look will reveal buds starting at leaf nodules all along the stem as soon as the weather warms.

Large-flowered varieties – If it is a spring-blooming clematis (blooms on last year's wood), a light pruning after blooming is all that is needed. If branches are bare, it can be pruned hard after flowering to rejuvenate. This will usually be an older, out of control plant. If the clematis is a summer blooming variety (blooms on this year's growth), it should be pruned back hard after it blooms to encourage more growth next year. This plant can also be rejuvenated if looking shabby.

Small-flowered varieties – The small-flowered clematis is usually the most fragrant. It is easily cared for and grows quickly into a beautiful blooming, eye-catching vine. Most are flowering on last year's growth and bloom during May and June, requiring pruning to control afterwards.

For those of you wishing to plant more clematis, but hesitating due to the prices at nurseries, I suggest you try propagating from cuttings.

WISTERIA — During the month of February, you should have pruned all lateral side shoots from the main branches back to within 15 or 20 cm (6 or 8 in) of flower buds. During August, shorten lateral growth. This vine (like the grapevine) will survive a severe pruning, so don't be afraid to keep it under control.

VIRGINIA CREEPER *(Parthenocissus)* — The only pruning needed for this popular climber is enough to keep it under control.

HONEYSUCKLE *(Lonicera)* — Like the Virginia creeper, prune as needed to keep under control.

For those of you who would like more vines and have a friend or relative with an attractive vine, try taking cuttings and propagate *(see Propagation, page 73)*. Vines are very easily propagated and, since they are such prolific growers, come into bloom quite quickly.

FLOWERS

Roses like 15 ml (1 tbsp) of epsom salts (Magnesium sulphate) scattered around their perimeter, scratched into the topsoil lightly and watered. You may think I'm crazy, but somewhere, years ago, I heard the idea, tried it and found it very successful. Epsom salts are quite economical when purchased from the drugstore instead of a nursery. One small package lasts a long time and is also helpful for your houseplants. Cut the dosage down to 5 ml (1 tsp) for houseplants.

Don't let the flower garden run down as many people tend to do this time of year, especially with the heat. Keep tall flowers such as gladiolus, delphinium and dahlia staked and cut out all dead stalks. Keep edges trimmed on your flower beds and stir the soil on the surface as a weed preventive and to conserve moisture. Use a mulch to save labour and moisture. Both flower and vegetable gardens tend to look a little dishevelled this time of year, but luckily, so do the weeds. They certainly don't grow as fast as they did during the spring.

Prune ramblers and old-fashioned roses by cutting out all dead and diseased wood and prevent their setting on rose hips unless you are growing them for this reason. Old-fashioned roses have large, marvellous rose hips. Scrape the seeds and fuzz from the inside of a rose hip and then set it to dry for using like raisins in your cooking or for eating fresh or dried. At a time when I had a gas range with just a pilot light in the oven, I would set rose hips, with the seeds removed, to dry and then use them in place of raisins in cookies or cakes. Rose hips can also be ground up and used in carrot cakes or other cake and cookie recipes. Rose hips contain vitamin C and are very healthy for you.

Perennials

ORIENTAL POPPY — Do not mulch Oriental poppies. They prefer hot sun-baked ground when they are resting. Fertilize and cultivate poppies now for next year's enormous blooms.

PEONY — The peony is dormant now and can be divided every three or four years at this time. Leave the main plant and only take part of the root so that you will still have some blossom next year. The peony root you take undoubtedly will either not bloom or you will have second-rate blossoms after transplanting. Peony roots will not bloom if planted too deep or too shallow. The crown should be approximately 5 cm (2 in) deep.

CHRYSANTHEMUM — Chrysanthemums wait for the shorter days to commence setting buds. Expect your fall-blooming mums to begin while the annual marigold starts to slow down for just the opposite reason.

IRIS — Since iris (or "flags" as our grandmothers used to call them) are dormant now, it is a good time to divide and replant crowded plants. Try doing a few each year to keep a continuous show of the blooming bearded iris. The large bearded iris blooms only in the spring and will not bloom again this summer. Leave behind the major portion of the clump if you wish to keep it in the same spot. Separate the outer portions of the rhizome and plant three to a circle, 45 cm (18 in) apart, with the rhizome pointed towards the middle. This will keep the clump growing outwards. New growth comes from the end with the fan of green growth. Destroy any rot back to the strong part of the rhizome, since the rot will continue to get bigger and bigger, destroying the complete plant. "Standards" is the name given to the three petals going upwards, "falls" is the name for the three petals going down towards the ground. The hairy mane on the falls is where the name "bearded" comes from.

When planting iris, leave the top of the rhizome exposed or lightly covered with soil. Next spring you should have a few blossoms, depending on the size of the rhizome.

Perennials in bloom this month are:

Henry lily	mugwort	hollyhock
Speciosum lily	goldenrod	salvia

coneflower	Turk's cap lily	baby's breath
speedwell	seaside aster	chrysanthemum
coreopsis	stokesia	Marguerite
plantain lily	spike gayfeather	heliopsis
chimney bellflower	mugwort	red-hot poker

Annuals

Cut strawflowers (*Helichrysum*) used for winter bouquets before the blossoms are fully open. Dry them in the shade, hanging the head downward in small, uncrowded bunches. In handling, be especially careful not to crack the stems near the blossoms.

Pansy seeds can be planted now for bloom next spring.

Bulbs, Tubers & Corms

Spring-flowering bulbs are beginning to show up in the stores. You have plenty of time to plant bulbs so don't feel that you have to buy right away in order to have beautiful tulips, daffodils and crocuses blooming in the spring. You have until October or November to plant them. I have planted them in December and they still bloomed. Plan what types you would like to plant ahead of time.

Fertilize and disbud the dahlias now. You will have a larger dahlia blossom if you keep the side shoots pinched back. Dahlias make wonderful cut flowers in your home or office, but you should keep the cut blossoms away from windows and doors. They do not like drafts. I have heard that a couple of pennies in the bottom of your vase of water will help the dahlia blossoms hold their petals as cut flowers indoors.

LAWNS

August is the time to go over your lawn, destroying insects and keeping weeds from seeding, as they will weaken the grass. Look carefully for crabgrass to keep it from seeding. If the lawn is in good shape, give it a dressing of light fertilizer on a cool day and a good soaking afterwards, or apply a liquid fertilizer, which is taken up by the roots much more easily. When sprinkling the lawn, do the job thoroughly to wet the ground several inches deep.

This is the ideal time to start a new lawn, since cooler weather will help give grass a good start (*see Lawns, page 42*). If your lawn is already established, reseed thin or bare spots.

GARDENS

The first crop of figs is ready now for those of you graced with such a nice tree. There are a lot of fig trees planted on Vancouver Island as specimen trees, but there never seems to be enough of a good thing. Figs will produce two crops a year in a warmer climate such as the southern United States, one crop in the summer, the other in the late fall. But we do have the pleasure of enjoying one crop of figs from many varieties available at local nurseries.

Pears are excellent on the islands. Be sure to pick pears prior to their ripening. You can tell if a pear is ready to pick by bending it on the stem where it will separate if ready. Do not pull the pear from the tree or handle roughly, as it is very fragile. Wrap

Vegetables

pears individually in paper to prevent bruising and keep them separate while they finish ripening. Store pears in a cool (15°C/60°F) place. Pears picked ripe from the tree will have to be used immediately, as they break down rapidly.

Plant peas, radishes, lettuce and spinach for late September enjoyment. Provide enough moisture to germinate the seeds.

Celery tastes better and is more tender when it is blanched. Blanching can be done by hilling the soil up to the leaves, preventing the sun from getting to the stalks. I prefer putting a collar around them, made of light cardboard such as a milk carton. This works well and keeps the dirt off the stalks.

Cauliflower, unless it is a self-blanching variety, will turn purple if left to the sun. Once the white head starts to form, break the back rib of the large leaves by bending them over the top of the cauliflower head, or tie the tops with a cord to shade the white cauliflower from the sun.

Root crops such as potatoes, beets, carrots and turnips should be hilled to prevent the wind and sun from drying out the tops of the exposed root and turning them green or red. This can make them quite bitter and strong-tasting.

With fall around the bend, plants such as tomatoes, squash and melons are still blossoming and setting on young fruits. These fruits (except for summer squash) will not mature before harvest. To help the fruits already on your plants, pick any blossoms and newly formed fruit from the vines to divert all nutrients and energy to the fruits already on the plant, giving them a chance to complete their growing to harvest size before frost. Any new growth on the tomato, squash or melon itself can be removed for the same reason. If you have trouble picking and destroying those pretty squash blossoms, just remember they are edible, and unless they have been sprayed with insecticides or other chemicals, are very attractive as a garnish on a plate or salad. Potatoes, too, can have their blossoms picked off once they have been on the plant for a week or two to put all strength back into making larger potatoes.

Tomatoes

Tomatoes are easily cared for and, depending on the type you grow, will soon start rewarding you for your time and effort. A few tips on caring for tomatoes will be beneficial to ensure steady production from healthy plants until frost.

You can increase tomato production during the growing season three or four times by seeing all, or nearly all, of the flower buds develop into healthy blooms and then into fruit, by hand pollination or spraying them with a blossom-set chemical, available at retail outlets.

Tomato plants respond to supplementary feeding when blossoms first form. Apply fertilizer in a ring around the root area and water well with a fine mist.

Suckers forming in between leaves and main stems should be cut or pinched off regularly. If left, they will divert water and nutrients from fruiting stems. Removal at a very young stage is easily accomplished by just bending them to the right or left; they will snap off cleanly without out damaging the parent plant.

Tie tomatoes to stakes with soft twine or strips of rag (old t-shirts,

Tomato tower

panty hose, etc.). Always tie knots on the stake —not on the vine. There are excellent, inexpensive tomato towers on the market, or you can build your own for use year after year to keep your plants off the ground. Although staked tomatoes are practically immune to damage by slugs, which are not strong climbers, vines allowed to ramble along the ground may sustain considerable injury from these pests, particularly in damp weather.

Don't smoke when handling tomato vines, since tobacco often carries several viral diseases including spotted wilt, leaf curl and mosaic. Another sensible precaution against spreading disease is to not touch tomato foliage when it is wet.

Most diseases of tomatoes can be treated with fungicides or by picking off damaged or diseased stems and destroying them. If using chemicals, make sure they are specifically for tomatoes —and read directions carefully.

SEPTEMBER
Beginning of the End

SEPTEMBER IS HERE and on the northern islands and at higher altitudes, so is fall. Was your gardening experience worth it? Did you have a good year? Well, guess what? It's not over yet. There is always something to do in the yard and garden. In the southern part of the islands, the weather may still be too warm for you to start some of these projects. Fall clean-up and taking care of your flower beds, vegetable garden, shrubs and trees is very important, and luckily the mosquitoes have gone. Most years on the islands we still have a couple of months of gardening left, but the days are shorter and the bedding plants and vegetables are ready to be replaced or uprooted and placed in the compost heap (*see Composting, page 84*).

TREES, SHRUBS & VINES

If you want to expand but are feeling a little put off by the high cost of plants at nurseries, lift the branches of your shrubs such as cotoneaster, viburnum, oak, laurel, vine maple (and other maple trees as well), and you will see seedlings growing under these shrubs from last year's seed. Make sure the soil is wet before you dig up these small plants, and either plant them in a protected area until they are big enough to fend for themselves (usually one year), or plant them in

a pot and keep the soil watered until the plant is of sufficient size
to hold its own in the garden. It takes approximately two years to
get a seedling to the size sold in 4.5-l (1-gal) pots in the nurseries
(depending on the type of plant), but it is rewarding and fun, not
to mention economical. Trees such as mountain ash, the purple
flowering plum, oak and maple start easily and readily from seed.
Give it a try if you are in for this type of gardening.

Plant seeds or seedlings in the fall. Seeds planted in the fall
will not start growth until spring, so be patient. Be sure to leave
seeds or seedlings outside or in an unheated greenhouse.

If, like most of us, you make your purchase decisions based on
the vibrant spring colours that appear in others' gardens, you may
find yourself neglecting the other seasons' beautiful bloomers.
Come fall, when the mass of maples, beech, oak, sumac and other
plants are in full, fall colour, we want those in our yard, too. The
best bet is to select one or two that bloom each season so there is
something blooming at all times. Don't get carried away with one
season. There is beauty in all of them. Don't forget about winter
(evergreens, rhododendron, camellia, witch hazel, holly, etc.) or
summer (hawthorn and althea).

Summer-flowering shrubs (see Shrub List, page 160) can be
pruned (see Pruning, page 18) if they have completed their blooming. You may have to wait until early spring for some, since they won't
be doing any growing on top during the winter months while they are
dormant.

Hydrangea
The hydrangea is in its prime right now. Here are few tips to ensure
bloom next year and to answer a few questions you may have
about these plants.

Hydrangea does best in full sun, although it will tolerate some
shade. Transplanting, as with most other plants, is more successful
in the spring and fall while the weather is cool.

The potted hydrangea you received at Eastertime was planted out
after the holiday and will grow to a large size within a matter of a few
years, although it will not usually bloom until the following season.

If your hydrangea never blooms, it is probably because of over-
fertilizing or pruning at the wrong time of the year. The reason
dead blossoms are left on the plant over the winter, no matter how
shaggy they appear, is because directly below them, next year's
buds are forming. If the old spent blossoms are removed and there

is a hard winter, the new buds will more than likely freeze. Possibly, when removing the spent blossoms, you have removed too much of the branch, damaging next year's blossoms. When pruning hydrangea, prune after blooming. Flower buds are formed in the fall, and with most varieties on last year's wood. Some common species, such as *Hydrangea paniculata grandiflora*, *Hydrangea peegee* and the 'Hills of Snow', bloom on new wood and may be pruned in the early spring. On a few other types, particulary the common greenhouse or 'French' (*Hydrangea macrophylla*, formerly called *H. opuloides*), the buds originate near the tips of the canes formed the preceding year.

Colour is very important to most growers, and in some hydrangeas, colour of the blossom can be changed by adding certain chemicals to the soil mix. Hydrangeas come in red, pink, blue and white. The red colour can be maintained or enhanced by adding lime or superphosphate to the soil. Aluminum sulfate will keep a hydrangea blue.

To make blue flowers produce pink flowers, the soil should be made neutral or very slightly alkaline by adding of lime. Too much lime will cause mottling of the leaves because of a lack of iron. The lime should be thoroughly mixed with the soil. It is best to lift the plants in the fall, shake off as much soil as possible, and replant in the specially prepared lime soil.

Any corrections to the soil to change or improve the colour of the hydrangea should be done well in advance of blooming.

FLOWERS

It will not be necessary to feed the roses from now on, but they should be checked after every rain for black spot. This is a fungus disease and very contagious among the roses. Remove infected leaves and place in a plastic bag to burn or destroy. Do not place infected leaves on either the compost or on the ground around roses. If roses are fed or pruned now, they will put on new growth which will be too tender for winter weather and will freeze. For those of you who take a great deal of pride in your roses and would not like them to suffer through a hard winter, the best way to protect them from the weather is to put mulch around them before January and pile it up 15 cm (6 in) or so above the crown.

Winter Storage of Tender Plants

GERANIUM (both upright and trailing) — Fall and spring are the times to start geranium, fuchsia, marguerite, tibouchina and other tender plants from cuttings. If you would like more geraniums in your landscape next spring, you can save money on potted plants by taking cuttings of your geraniums now if you have the space to grow them over winter.

On well-developed or already-established geraniums, cut branches back to within 8 cm (3 in) of the main stem without endangering the parent plant. New leaves and shoots will soon appear, and before long the plants will be in full bloom again. Drastic cutting back actually benefits geranium plants that you intend to lift, pot and bring indoors for winter bloom.

Study plants before taking cuttings. Although all stems and branches will eventually root, some root more quickly than others, producing better plants.

Soft and spongy top growth should never be used for cuttings as it is too tender and often rots before rooting. Choose comparatively new branches and stems which have hardened slightly. The leaves should be fully developed, and growing close together. These root more quickly and produce the most compact plants. They may or may not have flower buds set. Cuttings should be 10 to 15 cm (4 to 6 in) long, cut just below a leaf node. Be sure to cut off any stub above a leaf node left on the parent plant, as it will rot.

As you work deeper into the plant, you will find short, woody branches which seem tempting. As a rule, woody cuttings do not root readily. However, if you need these, there is a quick way to root them, simply by removing all except the topmost leaves and standing five to six stems in a glass half-full of water. Always break such woody cuttings flush with the main stem. They are more likely to root at the natural junction of branch and stem than at a hardened leaf node.

Geraniums grown in soil that is overly rich or in partial shade tend to become tall and lanky with large gaps between leaf nodes. Cuttings from such geraniums produce plants that are just as tall and awkward. It is possible to use them, however, if you are willing to pinch the tops back sharply twice as new plants grow.

Some prefer to let cuttings heal after taking them by laying them down on damp sand in heavy shade for two or three hours before planting. During this time the cuts dry off nicely without the cuttings

themselves wilting. This method seems to prevent stem rot and promotes quick rooting. You may also dip the ends in a rooting medium.

The most convenient way to start a large number of cuttings is
to insert them 4 cm (1.5 in) deep in a large tray of damp sand.
Tamp the sand down by hand or with a brick or board. Then, with a
pencil or small stick, poke holes 2 cm (1 in) apart in straight lines.
Insert a cutting into each hole and firm the sand well around its base.
Water the entire tray with a fine spray and place it in the open shade
on the north side of a building. Cover the tray with plastic to maintain high humidity or place in a greenhouse if you have one. If rooted
in individual pots, cover each with an inverted jar or pop bottle. (The
large plastic kind can be used by simply cutting away the bottom at
the visible seam a few inches up from the bottom.)

Within two to three weeks they will be ready to pot up. Over
the winter, keep them indoors or in a greenhouse and water only
when the soil feels dry.

FUCHSIA (both trailing and upright) — Fuchsias will continue
blooming until hit hard by frost. Often, fuchsia baskets can still be
seen blooming at Christmas. Once the plant looks too shabby and
you want to store it, cut it back around the perimeter of the pot on
the sides and cut the new growth off the top. This will leave 10 to
15 cm (4 to 6 in) of plant. Dig a hole in the vegetable garden or
flower bed and place the trimmed plant in the hole. Cover the top
with soil and pile any available leaves over it. You can also place it
under the house, in a crawlspace or in a large box stuffed with
crinkled-up newspapers for insulation. The important thing is to
protect it from freezing. At this time, it doesn't need light. Water
lightly before storing the plant. Some people find the styrofoam
coolers used for summer picnics economical and useful for holding
wintering plants. Once your plants are tucked away inside, these
containers can be stacked upright like boxes.

MARGUERITE — In some winters, this daisy-like flower grows outside
without freezing down. Its survival depends on what kind of protection it gets. On a south-facing wall it will probably survive, but
in an open garden with little or no protection, cut it back to approximately 15 cm (6 in) and repot in fresh soil. Place it in a cool area
until early spring, when it can go into a sunny window. Take cuttings
in the same way as you would with geraniums or fuchsias.

TIBOCHINA — This rare and profuse bloomer is not very popular in
our gardens yet, but after seeing one in action, I am sure they soon

will be. This plant is hard to find so it would be wise to store it for
the winter, as the cool winter weather will kill it. Prune back to
approximately 15 cm (6 in), repot in clean soil and either place it
in a sunny window away from a heat source, or put it in a greenhouse for the winter months. Again, take cuttings as you would a
geranium or fuchsia using a rooting medium.

NEPITA – This plant does not often survive a cool winter, so it is
advisable to take cuttings. It is easy to take cuttings of this plant.
Lay a piece of the plant on the soil and weigh it down with soil or
rooting medium at the leaf node. This will hold it down so it will
take root. Another method is to take a plant that is already growing
in a larger pot and wind all the nepita stems into the pot, touching
the soil with as many leaf nodes as possible. These will root and by
spring, there will be a snarled batch of nepita that you can cut
apart for use in hanging baskets. Keep it in a cool greenhouse or
other area where it won't freeze. You will appreciate this in the spring
when there is none available at the garden centres.

FIBROUS BEGONIA – These little beauties can be wintered over and
cuttings can be taken from them to be rooted for next season. They
can either be kept in a sunny window away from any heat vents or
put in a greenhouse. Either way, you will have shoots to take cuttings from in the spring.

IMPATIENS – This prolific bloomer is also a nice houseplant. Repot
a good specimen in the fall and place it in a sunny window where
the plant will get lots of light. In early spring, you can take cuttings
which easily root in a glass of water or soilless mix.

COLEUS – This South Pacific native was a houseplant long before it
became so popular in the garden. Coleus comes in many colours
and has exotic foliage. This plant can be repotted with clean soil
and brought in to a nice sunny window away from a heat register.
When spring comes, it can be cut back. Cuttings can be easily
rooted in a glass of water or soilless mix.

Perennials

Do not fertilize perennials at this time. Fertilizing the permanent
plants in your garden tells them to grow, and new growth now can
be set back by a frost.

Now is a good time to plant perennials for next year. Perennials can be planted all year, but it is best to plant in spring and fall.
Fall plantings of perennials will establish a strong root growth over

the winter and get them off to a good start in the spring.

Dividing of perennials should be done the same way as with flowering shrubs. Divide and transplant after they finish blooming. Moving and disturbing the roots just prior to blooming will either destroy the blossoms already forming on the plant or minimize their blooming.

If you would like to plant perennials for addition to your garden, seed can be collected from existing perennials or by propagation (*see Propagation, page 73*). Perennials that grow easily from seed are columbine, delphinium, linum, Shasta daisy, poppy, painted daisy and hollyhock, among others. Oriental poppy, iris and bleeding heart start easily from pieces of root or tuber. It is fun, self-satisfying and an inexpensive way to expand your perennial borders (*see Perennial List, page 73*).

Clean up the perennial bed by cutting away dead stems and foliage. Continue watering until rains take over. You will find some perennials continue blooming until close to Christmas.

Perennials blooming this month are:

boltonia	giant daisy	Marguerite
aster (various var.)	monkshood	Chinese lantern
sneezeweed	torchfly	Michaelmas daisy
purple coneflower	stonecrop	red-hot poker
plumbago	chrysanthemum (various var.)	

Annuals

To help revitalize the annuals and keep them blooming for the rest of the season, cut them back to within 2 cm (1 in) or so of the ground, and water thoroughly after giving a light feeding of all-purpose fertilizer. They will start shooting new leaves, thicken up and begin blooming again as long as the weather stays cool.

If you would like to save some seed, do so by marking envelopes for each type of seed you take. Keep them separate and dry. Place the envelopes in plastic baggies and put in the crisper in the bottom of your refrigerator or a cool place in the garage. Some of the seeds will not come true because of the way they were bred. Sometimes in order to get a certain plant, two varieties are crossed and you may wind up with one of those varieties showing up. It's always fun to see what happens when growing your own seed.

Clean up the annuals by pulling out and putting on the compost all the ones that are finished. If you have annuals such as

dianthus, petunia, snapdragon, nasturtium and calendula still looking healthy and with possible blooms, leave them to pull up later
on as they bite the dust. There are times when a petunia, geranium,
marguerite or snapdragon lasts through the winter, blooming up
until Christmas, and starts to grow again in the early spring.

Bulbs, Tubers & Corms

BULB FORCING —Bulb forc-
ing is when you trick a bulb
into blooming when it does
not normally bloom. You will
be able to have tulips, daffodils, crocuses or hyacinths
blooming in the middle of
winter. It can be done with
soil or without soil. I'm going
to walk you through this pro-
cedure step-by-step for bulbs
with soil:

Forced tulips

1. Select bulbs from the gar-
    den centre that have
    "good for forcing" or
    similar words on their
    labels.
2. Plant in September for blossoms in December, and in October
    for January bloom. Our bulbs are blooming outside by March,
    but if you want indoor bloom at this time, plant March-bloom-
    ing bulbs in November.
3. Pots or bulb pans provided should have drainage holes with ei-
    ther a broken piece of pot, gravel or other drainage material
    placed over it to prevent the soil from running out.
4. Use new potting soil for this project. You can add sand and peat
    moss to the soil using three parts soil, one part peat and one
    part sterilized sand, but I find the potting soil available in the
    garden centres sufficient for this project.
5. Place approximately 8 cm (3 in) of soil in the bottom of the pot,
    depending on the size of the pot, and tap a couple of times to set-
    tle the soil. Do not pack it down. Evenly space bulbs on the soil,
    pressing bulbs in slightly so they will stand while you space
    them. Make sure to leave approximately 1 cm (.5 in) between

bulbs so they don't touch and have room to expand while growing. Place tulip bulbs with flat side facing inwards. This is the part of the bulb where the blossom shoots up. This way it will look like a large bouquet with all blossoms springing up in the middle.

6. Place more soil in the pot, leaving just the tips of the first layer exposed. Place another layer of bulbs between the tips of the first layer of bulbs. Again, be careful the bulbs do not touch, spacing as explained in step 5.

7. Fill the pot to within 1 cm (.5 in) of the top of the pot, leaving just tips of upper layer of bulbs exposed. Gently firm the soil down without packing and water thoroughly.

8. Place planted pots in a cool dark area for the time required to form roots. If you are putting them in your garage or shed, you can pack them in a box with either peat moss, styrofoam peanuts or crumpled-up newspaper, so they will stay dark and cool. Styrofoam coolers are ideal for this. Just pack newspapers between the pots. This way the mice can't get into them. You can also plunge them in your garden by digging a trench and placing the pots of bulbs in it. Place sand around and over the pots to keep them clean on top. If you live at a higher elevation where it is colder, put soil and mulch (leaves, straw, etc.) on top of the pots. You will have to mark where you have placed them so they can be found later. Check their progress every few weeks and water if they look dry.

9. Leave pots in the cool area to form roots. Large bulbs such as tulips, hyacinths and daffodils take approximately twelve to fifteen weeks, while smaller bulbs eight to twelve weeks.

10. After the rooting time has expired, or if you want to check them, look at the drain holes. If roots are protruding, the bulbs are ready.

11. Bring pots indoors and place in a cool room, approximately 10 to 15°C (50°F to 60°F), that has some light to start forming tops (roots form in the dark, while tops need light to start adequately). After a few days of the plant adjusting to the indoors, gradually move it into a warmer room with full light. If there are several pots rooting, bring in one or two at a time. The ones left in storage will stay in the rooting stage and you will have successive bloom through the winter.

Bulbs forced without soil are special pre-cooled bulbs or do not need a cooling period. Examples of these bulbs are: Paper white narcissus, Soleil d'Or, Chinese sacred lily and pre-cooled hyacinth. Step-by-step directions for these bulbs are:

1. If using a hyacinth in a glass especially for this purpose, the glass holds only one bulb. It is shaped to prevent the bulb from sitting in water. Only the roots go into the water. Fill the bottom of the glass up to but not touching the bulb. Add water as needed. Place in low light until roots start growing well, then bring out into the light.

2. For paper whites or other bulbs, a small handful of charcoal should be placed in the bottom of the bulb pan to prevent the water from souring.

3. Place clean gravel to within 2 cm (1 in) of the top of the pot.

4. Add water until it is just below the top of the gravel.

5. Set the bulbs on gravel, evenly spaced with the points up, and then fill the pan with gravel to half of the bulbs height to hold them in position. No more water should be added at this time, but the level of water should be maintained.

Hyacinth bulb

6. Place the pot of bulbs in a cool low-light area for approximately three weeks. When the roots become established, expose the bulbs to more light and higher temperature.

When the bulbs are finished, they can be planted out in the garden the following fall, although the blossoms will not be as nice as the first time.

Spring-flowering bulbs

Now is the time to think of those spring-flowering bulbs. If you purchase them early, don't put them in a warm house. Bulbs deteriorate when in a dry area, so leave them in a cool room until you are ready to plant. You can safely plant bulbs in this area right up until Christmas, so don't panic if you haven't planted your bulbs by the end of October or mid-November. They are better planted, no matter when you plant them, than left in a room to wait until next fall. When you plant the bulbs, either mix bone meal with the soil in the bottom of the hole prior to planting, or a bulb fertilizer. If you don't have either of these handy, an all-purpose fertilizer will be better than nothing.

TULIPS — When selecting tulips, it helps to know several things: bloom time, colour, height and the habit or style of bloom. There are fifteen or more different classes of tulips and thousands of varieties, so selecting is no small task. Usually we pick out the ones having the colour we want, disregarding the fact that they may bloom at different times. Tulips of the same colour will sometimes bloom at different times. The reason for this is that the bulbs are sometimes planted at different depths in the soil. This makes sense if you think of a bulb planted 8 cm (3 in) deep taking longer to come out of the ground than one planted 2 cm (1 in) deep. This is why someone invented the bulb planter.

Sometimes you may select tulips graduated in height and blooming in unison for a momentous display. Other times you may want to select kinds that bloom successively, to keep colour coming over a long period. Spring garden colour is what most people expect from tulips, with cut flowers as a secondary purpose.

You will notice specific colours and forms of flowers are described in the catalogues or on retail bulb bins. Bloom succession and heights are indicated on the charts for each variety.

Plant tulip bulbs after soil cools until freeze-up. Set large bulbs 16 cm (7 in) or more deep unless the soil is a heavy clay type (the lighter the soil, the deeper you can plant), and set smaller bulbs such as 'Kaufmanniana' 10 cm (4 in) deep. Space large bulbs 15 cm (6 in) apart. Twelve of a kind make a satisfactory show in a mixed planting. Deep planting lengthens the useful life of the bulb.

Extra-early tulips blooming with snowdrops and crocuses are *Kaufmanniana* hybrids 10 to 20 cm (4 to 8 in) tall.

Early tulips blooming at the same time as scillas, forsythias and redbud are *Fosteriana* hybrids 20 to 50 cm (8 to 20 in) tall; *Greigii* hybrids 20 to 30 cm (8 to 12 in) tall; 'Early Singles' 25 to 40 cm (10 to 16 in) tall; 'Early Doubles' 25 to 35 cm (10 to 14 in) tall. Mid-season tulips blooming at the same time as peach trees and bluebells are the *Darwin* hybrids, 50 to 70 cm (20 to 28 in) tall; 'Mendels' 35 to 55 cm (14 to 22 in) tall; 'Triumphs' 40 to 65 cm (16 to 26 in) tall; and 'Bouquet' (*multiflora*) 45 to 70 cm (18 to 28 in) tall. Late tulips blooming with dogwoods and lilacs are 'Darwin' 55 to 75 cm (22 to 30 in) tall; 'Rembrandt' 50 to 70 cm (20 to 28 in) tall; 'Lily Flowered' 45 to 65 (18 to 26 in) tall; 'Cottage' 40 to 85 cm (16 to 34 in) tall; 'Parrot' 45 to 65 cm (18 to 26 in) tall; and 'Double Late' 45 to 60 cm (18 to 24 in) tall.

DAFFODILS — The daffodil is one of the most popular cut flowers and a favoured bulb in most gardens. The daffodil springs up in the most unusual places on the islands. You will find them growing naturally along the roads in the Victoria area, springing up in pastures across the islands and, of course, planted purposely in our gardens. On the Lower Mainland and in the Victoria area, farmers grow daffodils commercially and supply most of Canada with spring cut flowers. Daffodils are a member of the *Narcissus* family and may also be known as jonquil. The large trumpet bulbs are usually known by the name daffodil, while the shorter trumpets are called narcissus. The jonquil is usually a name given to the smaller variety, but no matter what you call them, they are all exciting additions to your yard or garden. Different varieties are: 'Trumpet Daffodils', 'Cupped Daffodils', 'Double Daffodils', *Triandrus* hybrid daffodils, *Cyclamineus* hybrids, *Tazetta* hybrids, 'Poeticus', 'Small', 'Miniature Daffodils', 'Split', and 'Collar Daffodils'. All varieties are in various colour combinations of white, yellow, cream, orange-red, pink and orange, with some varieties in double and some varieties in clusters of more than one flower per stem.

HYACINTHS — The strong heady fragrance of a hyacinth is unforgettable. Whether a pot flower in your home or planted in your garden, the hyacinth is worthy of every garden. Plant bulbs 15 to 20 cm (6 to 8 in) deep depending upon the texture of your soil. They provide an interesting highlight planted in front of daffodils or tulips. Hyacinths are shorter than most large bulbs and do not make good cut flowers. All are impressive, coming in shades of white, pink and blue. I find hyacinth bulbs quite expensive compared to other spring-flowering bulbs, but worth the expense, especially if you plant them in mass.

MISCELLANEOUS BULBS — There are many spring-flowering bulbs to choose from and experiment with. Try a few of the different varieties. The more exotic the name, the more exotic the flower. You may be pleasantly surprised.

crocus   *Allium*
windflower (*Anemone*)   *Brodiaea*
Freesia   meadow saffron (*Colchicum*)

winter aconite (*Eranthis hyemalis*)   checkered lily (*Frittilaria*)
Watsonia   Dutch iris
African corn lily (*Ixia*)   grape hyacinth (*Muscari*)
star of Bethlehem (*Ornithogalum*)   shamrock (*Oxalis*)
Ranuncules   *Pushkinia scilloides*
snowdrops (*Galanthus*)   bluebell (*Scilla*)
glory-of-the-snow (*Chiondoxa*)   *Triteleia*
camass (*Camassia*)   harlequin flower (*Sparaxis*)
dog tooth violet (*Erythronium*)   lily (*Lilium*)
snowflake (*Leocojum*)   *Sternbergia lutea*

Planting Pots of Bulbs

For those of you who want to plant just pots of bulbs without the worry of forcing, be aware that once the bulb has blossomed for you in the spring, the bulb will be spent. Plant it in the garden and forget about it for a year or two before it will bloom again.

When potting bulbs in pots, it is possible to put a layer of soil, then three or four bulbs, another layer of soil, and then three or four more bulbs if your pot is deep enough. Water well and set outside for spring bloom. This will work with tulips and daffodils. Crocuses and other small bulbs can be planted three times their depth in a pot.

The most beautiful spring hanging basket I ever made was when I took a 25-cm (10-inch) hanging basket, cut 2-cm (1-in) round holes around the outside in two alternate layers (eight to ten holes altogether) and placed a small amount of soil in the bottom to the first layer of holes. I then planted a couple of crocus bulbs pointing out towards the hole. I used spagnum moss to keep the soil from running out of the holes until the roots held it in place. I then went up a little farther until reaching the second row of holes and did the same thing. I put a mass of crocus bulbs on top of this layer and finished it off with dirt. The rain through the winter kept it watered and come spring I was overwhelmed by the number of blossoms. Between blossoms and foliage, there wasn't much pot showing to detract from its beauty.

As the bulbs finish, you can plant annuals in between the leaves and above any planted bulbs if you plan on not using the bulbs. If you want to try and salvage the bulbs, you will have to take them out in the spring, after they bloom, and hill them up somewhere until their tops die away naturally. They will not bloom successfully in the pot a second season.

LAWNS

Keep on cutting the grass as long as it grows vigorously. You can lower the blade your lawn mower with the hottest months behind us. You must be prepared to water abundantly in case the fall rains fail to put in their usual appearance. Don't let your lawn go into the winter dry. Make sure you water deeply so the roots can absorb as much moisture as possible after a hot summer.

Fertilize with winter fertilizer, available at garden centres. If you fertilized with a slow-release fertilizer (contains ureaform nitrogen which releases slowly over a period of months), it is not usually necessary to fertilize again during the season. Slow-release fertilizers for lawns release slowly by moisture and microbial activity. Only small amounts of nitrogen are released, which prevents burning. Rain will leach other types of commercial fertilizers out, so they only last a couple of weeks.

If you wish to plant a new lawn, it is generally agreed that fall is the best time. It will give the lawn cooler weather to start, fewer problem with weeds and plenty of rain to keep it damp (*see Lawns, page 45*).

GARDENS

The majority of gardeners in a mild climate still have it in their minds that they can only plant vegetables in the spring, and once initial gardening is completed in the spring, they stop planting. Planting for fresh vegetables can continue in this climate during the winter. Root crops such as carrots, parsnips and beets can be planted now for harvest over the winter months. Any frost or snow we have will not usually destroy these plants. If it becomes extremely cold you should have a mulch ready to bury them with. You will find the taste of root crops grown in a colder soil over the winter a little different than those grown during the hotter time of the year. They will be fresher and sweeter tasting. You may even prefer winter-grown root crops.

Cabbages, cauliflower, Brussels sprouts and broccoli can be grown through the winter months, but because they are above ground, the outsides may get nipped by a frost. It will not destroy them, however.

Garlic, elephant garlic and leeks can be planted now and will winter over quite well underground without fear of winter kill.

Broad beans, snap beans, lettuce and radishes can be planted at this time and will produce until Christmas, although protection will be required if a cold snap occurs. I have even, at times, had some success planting peas at this time of year! If you plant snap beans, use the bush type instead of the pole variety, and plant in a block instead of a row. This will make it easier to cover if the weather changes.

There is nothing like the experience of eating Christmas dinner fresh from your own garden. Give it a try one year. It can be difficult to find the seed at this time of year, as the garden centres turn back all their seed to the seed companies so they can be stored properly until next year. Prepare ahead and purchase extra seed in the spring for fall planting. Place the seed in the bottom of the refrigerator in a container to prevent humidity from damaging the fragile seed.

If you have supplied all your neighbours and relatives with your excess garden produce and you still have lots more than you will ever use, don't throw it away or leave it in the garden to rot. Find a food bank and distribute it. There are lots of places that would appreciate your donation. Please don't let it go to waste.

Have you pruned your raspberry and blackberry bushes of canes that produced fruit this year? If not, prune down to the base and cut up for the compost pile.

HOUSEPLANTS

It is time to bring in houseplants that spent the summer outside. Spray plants with an insecticidal soap prior to bringing them inside. Insects will spread from one plant to the next and destroy all your houseplants if left untreated. Houseplants that have lived the summer outside must be given time to adjust to the indoors.

OCTOBER
Colourful Trees and Harvest Time

NOW THAT OCTOBER is here and summer is gone, all our gardening mistakes are a thing of the past — but don't think that your work is over. Jot down your mistakes, as well as your successes, while they are still fresh in your mind. It's an excellent habit to get into, making next year's gardening more enjoyable.

Everything suffers from a hot summer. How do we revive it? With water restrictions on when we needed the water the most, we find ourselves with a scorched lawn, burnt-looking flowers and trees to revive. Don't worry. On the west coast, and especially during the fall months, a drenching rainfall is usually not very far off.

The first thing to do after the rainfall is check to see how deep the water from the rains has gone. Although we may endure two or three days of heavy rain, and it seems like a lot, when we check the soil we find it has only wet the surface. In order for rain alone to do our plants any good, it must reach down to the roots. Although moisture is taken in by the leaves, the majority of moisture is taken in by the roots. Large trees, shrubs, perennials and lawns have roots deeper than one or two inches. The first thing to do is thoroughly soak the plants and your lawn at least once before frost, as deep as possible so all roots are soaked.

It's a good time to empty the compost piles to make room for leaves that will soon start to fall.

The October weather is excellent for planting, cleaning up outdoors and any other garden chores you have in mind before the weather turns cold and wet. The time for raking leaves will soon be upon us. Leaves are a source of humus and if you have enough space, by all means, start a compost pile. If you use a heap, it can be held in place by piling strips of sod around the edges, either to form a wall or as weights. Compost must be kept moist and in it you can empty the vacuum cleaner, cleanings from the chimney or fireplace and practically any vegetable matter that will decay. Add some manure, peat moss and/or soil if you want to increase the supply. It usually takes from six months to two years to make a good compost, so have two piles if there is enough room. If you already have a compost bed, fork it over and wet it down frequently if there is no rain.

When leaves start to fall, be sure to rake in the corners of your lawn, where leaves may smother the grass or plants if they get too deep. Heavy leaves such as oak, laurel, rhododendron and some varieties of magnolia do not decay easily, and therefore should be kept separate from others. Feed them through a mulcher, if one is available, or run over them several times with a lawn mower. Maple leaves are an exception, as they tend to deteriorate rapidly. Remember, compost is not a fertilizer. Once the leaves or lawn clippings have lost their green, they are no longer suppliers of nutrients. Although some nutrients may still remain, the main purpose of compost, or humus as it is now called, is to loosen the soil, making it light and more easily worked.

Prior to freezing weather, all garden hoses and in-ground sprinkler systems should be drained. Garden hoses should be taken inside and stored. Water freezing in the lines or hoses will cause them to break.

TREES, SHRUBS & VINES

Cedar trees and other conifers will lose some of their needles after a hot, dry summer. These will not grow back, but rather fall to the ground and contribute to the layer of humus. If this has happened in your yard, it would help to prune new growth lightly next year to force side branches to cover up any gaps made by the loss of needles from a hot summer.

The fall is usually a better time to plant than spring because weather conditions are often more favourable and plants will receive less shock when moved. If their root systems become well established before winter sets in, they will be able to make rapid growth in the spring and will suffer no setback. Most gardeners have more time in the fall to plant than in the spring. Be sure to water all plantings adequately.

Don't let either established plants or newly planted shrubs or perennials go into the winter dry. Even though you see no real growth during the winter months, the roots are still growing. A plant will set roots before the top grows.

Fall Colour

Fall brings the bright, vivid, almost fluorescent colours of certain trees and shrubs. A frost is not needed to supply the beautiful fall colours so evident on Vancouver Island. My favourite is the vine maple (*Acer circinatum*). With several growing close to my home, I have yet to see two identical leaves. Whereas so many trees are all yellow or all red in the fall, the vine maple is shades of red, yellow, green and orange all on one leaf. With hundreds of leaves on a tree, it is overwhelming!

The variegated maple leaves turn yellow, and the red maple leaves gradually dry to a bright chestnut colour before falling to the ground. The large scrub oak leaves turn yellow and dry to a golden brown before falling from the tree.

The rains are usually accompanied by light winds, and the combination will strip the trees quickly. If you plan on taking pictures or collecting any of the leaves, do it before the inevitable rain and wind takes them.

If you are interested in planting fall colour in your garden for the future years, now is the time to take note of the colour available in deciduous trees. Maple (*Acer*) is the most widely known and comes in many varieties, leaf shapes, sizes and colours. Have your nursery go through the maples with you and help you find the right one for your yard or garden. They range from shrub size at maturity to 20 to 26 m (60 to 80 ft) in the more majestic varieties.

Another popular fall colour tree is the oak (*Quercus*), which also comes in many varieties (approximately thirty), with their leaves turning a yellow or orange colour.

Other fall colour trees you may be interested in are: *Ginkgo biloba*, sweet gum (*Liquidambar*), dogwood (*Cornus*), poplar (*Populus*), persimmon, pear, apple (*Malus*), tulip tree (*Liriodendron tulipfera*), Gleditsiahoney locust (*Gleditsia triacanthos*), hawthorn (*Crataegus*), willow (*Salix*), ypress, baldbald cypress (*Taxodium distichum*), mountain ash (*Sorbus aucuparia*), flowering cherry and flowering plum (*Prunus* [deciduous]), beech, larch and sumac (*Rhus*).

Propagating Shrubs & Trees From Seed

One of the most enjoyable fall habits I have adopted is starting plants from seed. Some of the most popular are plants like oak, pine, mountain ash, cotoneaster, laurel, maple, firethorn (*Pyracantha*) and berberis. It's always a challenge. I enjoy taking the seeds from grapes I have eaten or an apple core, pear, japanese quince, peach seeds, walnuts, filberts, etc., and planting them outdoors in a marked pot and waiting for them to grow. I have had success with all of the above without more effort than actually planting them. The most successful have been cotoneaster, maple, firethorn, quince and berberis because of their rapid growth. By fall of the following year, you have 15- to 20-cm (6- to 8-in) plants, healthy enough to be planted out or sold at garage sales. By planting them in a pot and leaving them outside for Mother Nature to water and take care of, only the hardiest survive. I prefer to let Mother Nature take care of the seeds naturally. If the soil gets dry, it won't hurt to water them, although I have never had to water my seedlings until spring.

Propagating Shrubs by Cuttings

I take tip cuttings from laurel, weigela, forsythia, lilac, mock orange, juniper, viburnum, hydrangea, cotoneaster and firethorn and dip them in a rooting hormone prior to sinking them 1 cm (.5 in) or more into a pan of sterile damp sand. By spring, all but the juniper are heavily rooted and ready to plant out in soil in the garden or in pots.

Steps for taking cuttings:

1. You will require a pot or container with drainage holes in the bottom. An ice cream bucket, a tin-foil roasting pan or green seed flats from a garden centre work well for a large number of cuttings. The container should be at least 5 cm (2 in) deep.
2. Fill the container with damp rooting medium made of one of the following:
    *   sterilized sand (my favourite)
    *   equal parts perlite and peat moss
    *   equal parts peat moss and sand

- plain peat moss
- purchased soilless mix

3. Take cuttings from the tips of plants with at least two leaf nodes. The cut should be made just below a leaf node.
4. Remove bottom two leaves from cuttings.

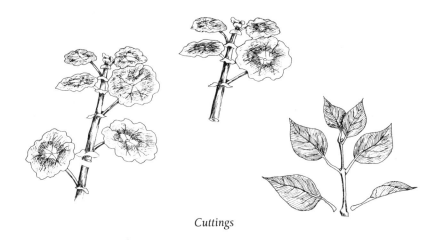

Cuttings

5. Poke several holes in the damp rooting medium with a pencil or stick.
6. Dip cut end in rooting hormone: #1 for softwood cuttings (houseplants, fuchsias, geraniums, etc.); #2 for semi-hard cuttings (laurel, cotoneaster, hydrangea, etc.); and #3 for hardwood cuttings. Shake off the excess.
7. Place one cutting in each hole and press mix gently against stem.
8. If they are indoor cuttings or tender perennial cuttings, place a plastic bag over them. Make sure the plastic does not touch the leaves of the cuttings. A stick may be needed to hold the plastic bag up and away from leaves.
9. Put the pot in a warm, well-lit place until rooted if the cuttings are tender or indoor varieties. If the cutting is an outdoor plant, either place in a cold frame or cool greenhouse, or leave it outside. (I leave mine outside and have had a 90% success rate.)

With the price of plants and shrubs rising season after season, it is nice to be able to save money and get the satisfaction and enjoyment from producing your own seedlings.

FLOWERS

Fall is the time to lift your geraniums. I remember as a child seeing geraniums as houseplants. If you have one that has been doing well outside for the summer, it may be worth taking it in and giving it a chance in a nice sunny window. Introduce it gradually to the warmth indoors.

Cut branches back to within 8 cm (3 in) of the main stem without endangering the parent plant. New leaves and shoots will soon appear and before long the plants will be in full bloom again. Drastic cutting back actually benefits geranium plants you intend to lift, pot and store in a cool place over the winter.

Fuchsia plants are long bloomers. I have seen many blooming into November. They should be cut back prior to any heavy frost. After the plant has completed the majority of its blooming, cut it back to the perimeter of the pot on the sides and take about 15 cm (6 in) off the top. The plant will not bloom next year, so don't expect any miracles. The fuchsia blooms from new growth. Once you have cut the fuchsia back, either bury it in your garden lying on its side and then cover with soil, or place in a cool room where it will not freeze.

If you haven't taken geranium, marguerite or fuchsia cuttings, and still intend to, do it now so they will get a good root setting before they are too difficult to start. As the weather gets cooler, the stems get tougher and sap lowers in the plant, making the chance of success very slim, if not impossible.

Perennials
If you have white mums outside turning purple, and you think that the nursery has sold you a cross-bred mutant, don't worry: cold weather turns white chrysanthemums purple.

Clean up your perennial beds by removing dead leaves and dead blossoms. This will save time in the spring when you want to start your planting. Division and planting of perennials can be carried out this month.

Be sure all plants, including your perennials, are well watered before the winter months in case we have a winter with little rainfall.

A beautiful display of the chrysanthemum family is starting now. If you look closely at the part of the plant nearest the soil, you will see lots of stems which increase every year. These new starts have roots attached wherever they have come in contact with the soil. This is a way of propagating more of your favourite varieties. Separate by either cutting with a sharp knife, scissors or pruning sheers and plant it where you want it to grow. If the start has a tall stem, cut the stem off within an inch or so of the ground. Chrysanthemums are nice in mass plantings. This small start just planted will double or quadruple over the next winter and summer and will become a well-developed blooming plant next fall.

Perennials blooming this month are:

boltonia	giant daisy	lily turf
aster (various var.)	monkshood	pampas grass
sneezeweed	torchfly	mist flower
purple coneflower	stonecrop	red-hot poker
plumbago	chrysanthemum (various var.)	

Annuals

Continue to deadhead annuals, to keep a good show into the fall. Many will continue to bloom until freezing, which could be in November or as late as January.

Bulbs, Tubers & Corms

Grocery stores and nurseries are now fully stocked with fall bulbs. Planting is carried out from now until Christmas in our area. Fertilizing with bone meal and/or bulb fertilizer will help them on their way. Make sure bulbs are planted deep. For large bulbs such as tulips, daffodils and hyacinths, bulbs should be 15 to 20 cm (6 to 8 in) deep. Shallow planting encourages rapid multiplication, whereas deep planting encourages larger bulbs and blossoms.

Easiest of all, you can have paper whites or narcissus brought to bloom indoors in a few weeks just by placing bulbs on a bed of pebbles and water. Be careful not to sit the bulbs in the water. Plan this for Christmas. White paper whites are an excellent accent with a beautiful red poinsettia.

Lilies are a nice addition to the garden and get more beautiful as the years go by. This flower is centuries old and, like the rose, is a very popular plant. Don't be afraid to try it. The lily is a heavy feeder, requiring fertilizing several times during the growing season. Most will reach a height of 60 to 150 cm (36 to 60 in) so be prepared to stake the taller varieties. Plant lilies approximately 15 to 20 cm (6 to 8 in) deep. They like a cool soil with good drainage. This may mean mulching is required during the hotter months.

Make sure your soil has adequate drainage prior to planting.

Many summer-blooming bulbs are not winter hardy here on Vancouver Island and must be lifted and stored indoors during the winter. The way you store them can make a difference in how they perform for you next summer.

Some bulbs like a warm spot and others like it cool and moist. Many plants stored at fairly high temperatures need soil left around their roots or some packing like peat moss or vermiculite to help slow water loss. Handle those with fleshy roots carefully so they remain intact for good growth next year.

Check bulbs, tubers and corms in storage occasionally during the winter to spot rot and other problems, including mice. You may need to sprinkle water on them if storage conditions are extremely dry.

Winter Storage for Tender Bulb & Tubers

GLADIOLUS like a cool storage. Dig after tops die down or just after a frost and cut off the tops. Space in a shallow box in an airy place to dry for about two weeks. Dust with an insecticide-fungicide and store in a dry, cool, dark place. Clean off bulblets and plant separately next spring. Within a few years they will reward your patience with blossoms. A gladiolus may survive our winters, but do not count on it.

DAHLIAS also like cool storage. Dig just before a killing frost or right after the foliage is blackened. Cut off dahlia foliage and dry clumps, with the earth still intact, in the sun for several hours. Place in flats with stems down to drain. Store the clumps in peat moss, sand or vermiculite and examine frequently during the winter. Dahlias can also be stored in a plastic bag filled with dry sand or vermiculite. If roots begin to shrivel, sprinkle or dip into lukewarm water and store again.

CANNAS should be dug, then dried and stored in cool temperatures after a frost has killed the tops. Dig canna roots carefully as damaged roots will rot. Store fairly dry in boxes covered with dry sand or peat moss. The clump of soil can be left around the roots.

TUBEROUS BEGONIAS should be dug when their leaves turn yellow in late summer or early fall and stored in a cool area. Store potted begonia tubers undisturbed in pots. Store dug tubers with soil around them. Clean carefully and store in peat moss. Moisten just often enough to prevent shrivelling.

CALADIUM and ELEPHANT EAR like warm storage. They should be dug when their leaves turn yellow in the fall or after frost has killed the tops. Leave the soil around them and store packed in peat moss or dry sand in a dry area.

GLORIOSA LILIES are dug after tops die down or just after a frost. The Gloriosa lily likes warm storage in sand, peat moss, sawdust or vermiculite. Do not let them sprout. If they begin to sprout, move them to a cooler place such as the refrigerator.

LAWNS

Fertilize lawns now for winter. Keep leaves raked up and place in a compost pile or pile around bottoms of shrubs and trees. They can smother your lawn if left on it. Be sure to get in the corners and tight places when raking.

GARDENS

A green manure crop (rye seed) can be planted now to grow through the winter. The crop can be dug or rototilled into the garden in spring to add nutrients to the soil.

If you have planted a late crop of vegetables such as lettuce, beets, carrots, parsnips and members of the cabbage family, you are able to benefit from crisp, sweet vegetables even after any early light frosts.

Harvest Time
Storing your harvest is the grand finale to all the hard work you have put into your garden during the year. Some plants, such as cabbage, carrots, beets, turnips, parsnips, leeks and garlic, are fine left in the garden during the colder winter months. Place a mulch of leaves or straw over them if you are concerned a cold winter may be on the way.

ONIONS – Bend tops of onions over once outside leaves turn yellow. This will also make for larger onions. Do not let onions go to seed unless you are collecting seed. A few onions can usually provide enough seed for a family. Onions you have curing outside should be brought in or placed under cover on a sundeck or garage where they can keep dry.

GARLIC – Garlic planted last year can be harvested this fall when the leaves dry and after blooming. Either sever tops or braid tops together. I place them in a mesh bag after severing tops, and store them in my garage until I am ready to use them.

POTATOES —Once the tops have died or frozen on potatoes, they can be dug. If the days are sunny, potatoes can be left out for a day to cure (air dry), but if it is raining, they should be spread out on newspapers or straw in a protected area before storing in a cool, dry place. Leaving newly dug potatoes out in the hot sun will cause them to turn green and bitter.

PUMPKINS and WINTER SQUASH —Winter squash used for making deserts or for baking in the oven keep several months if cured properly. Harvest them before a frost and leave a portion of the stem on when cutting from the vine. Handle carefully, because bruised ones will not keep. If kept in a warm place for the first ten days, they will keep better. Then store them in a cool, dry place. Place several newspapers or cardboard under them for padding if placed on a concrete floor.

TOMATOES —Tomato plants have green unripe fruits on at this time of the year. Gather them before a frost, leaving some stem on if possible. Place in single layers in flat boxes, cover with newspaper and store in a cool, dry area. Check frequently and remove any signs of decay. Entire vines can be pulled up and hung by the root in the basement or garage and the fruit remaining on the plant will ripen. Tomatoes ripen faster at 18 to 20°C (65 to 70°F) and slow down with cooler temperatures. Remember, tomatoes ripen from the inside out, and the longer you can keep them on the vine, the more flavour they will have. Ripened tomatoes left on the vine will not keep long. Either use immediately or can them.

ROOT CROPS (beets, carrots, turnips, parsnips, etc.) —These vegetables can be left in the ground over winter, but if you want to dig and store them, remove the tops and place in moist sand, peat moss or in plastic bags with holes in them for ventilation. Be careful when removing the tops from beets. Always leave a bit of the the top attached to the beet because they will "bleed" if cut too closely. When cooked, they will be a very pale red or even pink because the colour has bled from the top.

HOUSEPLANTS

Place Christmas cactus and poinsettia in the dark for fourteen hours a day or in a cool area for several weeks to get them to bloom at Christmastime.

NOVEMBER
Putting Everything to Bed

NOVEMBER – I CAN'T believe it has come so quickly. Just because the days are shorter and there is less light, don't think that all activity in the garden has ceased. With the winter rains, the last leaves are falling, geese are flying south and the winds are blowing. Mother Nature is preparing for winter and so should we. This is the time for protecting our tender plants or losing them altogether. In colder climates than ours, the fall would have come and gone and winter would be tightening its grip. Gardeners would have worried about protecting their plants two and maybe even three months ago.

Start a new compost with this year's leaves and plant tops cleaned from your garden or flower beds. Use last year's remaining compost on your garden or flower bed. If you don't want to start or care for a compost, rake the leaves up and pile them around tender plants for winter protection or on the garden to be worked in next spring. One way is to dig a hole in the garden and place the leaves in it and cover with soil. Another way is to pile it evenly on the garden area. You can pile a 15- to 20-cm (6- to 8-in) layer of leaves onto the garden and then rototill or work it in next spring. This will slowly turn to compost over the winter and become excellent humus for your garden.

Caring for tools and storing them when not in use will prove beneficial. Clean, sharp tools are easier to use than those which have been neglected. Replacing these tools is becoming more and more expensive.

Proper care should be taken to thoroughly clean all soil off the tools after each use, then dry and wipe the blade with a soft, oiled cloth and hang on a rack especially prepared for each tool. Replace broken handles on tools between now and spring and replace the tools that are beyond repair.

Weathered wooden handles should be lightly sanded and wiped down with linseed oil to prevent them from drying up and splitting.

Blades of tools such as hoes, shovels and clippers can be cleaned off and sunk blade-depth into a barrel or box of sand with oil poured into it to prevent the tool from rusting. The sand acts as an abrasive. Make sure the oil you use is environmentally safe, preferably vegetable oil. Do not use too much oil, as it will make the tools too greasy and hard to handle. Tools will stay sharp much longer if not allowed to rust. With a light film of oil upon them, they are easily cleaned after use.

Do not plunge tools with moving parts, such as shears, into the sand above the pivot. Keep the pivot area well oiled and remember to wipe sand from the tools prior to using.

Tools should be cleaned with a wire brush and lightly sanded with an emery cloth prior to placing in the oily sand.

When cleaning your lawn mower for the winter, remove all grass from the blade and underside of the mower with a wire brush. Oil blade and moving parts and wipe underside with an oiled cloth. One of the easily available spray lubricants is useful to have around to give moving parts an occasional spray. If needed, give the mower a fresh coat of paint.

Garden hoses should not be left out in cold weather. Many types of reels are now available for winding the hose loosely. Homemade ones are also convenient and serve their purpose. For a couple of dollars, an old tire rim can be picked up at a used parts place and painted, then mounted by bolting to a garage or house wall. When storing the garden hose over the winter, drain all water from the hose first.

TREES, SHRUBS & VINES

This is a good time to plant some of the cuttings started last year or earlier this spring. If it is rainy and wet, it would be best to wait for a better time, since working in wet soil can pack it down. I have had good results in the fall planting long hedges of laurel cuttings, forsythia plants and well-rooted Himrod grapevine cuttings, all taken from the previous fall or spring propagations.

Build a temporary fence of chicken wire around your tender trees such as fig and persimmon, and fill with leaves to protect during the winter.

Mid-November is a busy time on the islands, as commercial kiwi, holly and Christmas-tree growers begin to harvest their crops to get them to market for the upcoming Christmas season. If possible, take the opportunity to visit one of these operations. The knowledge and expertise needed to run a single-crop farm and make a success of it is often overlooked. Many think the work of a holly farmer or Christmas-tree plantation owner is very seasonal. The truth is just the opposite. Sales are seasonal, but the work goes on day after day, year after year. Daily work, including pest and weed control, pruning, fertilizing and marketing, plays an important role in making a living from producing a crop for just one season.

Holly

Holly (*Ilex*) is very popular worldwide at Christmastime, and with Christmas only a month away, it is in peak production right now. The bush or tree is an evergreen, with the English variety being the most widely known, although all hollies are not spiny. Some are smooth-leaved, similar to a laurel, boxwood or camellia leaf. There are varieties with purple and green stems, some with no spines, some with spines on the surface of the leaf as well as the edge, and varieties with only one or three spines per leaf. Some varieties of holly never produce berries, some are self-pollinating, while others require male and female varieties planted in close proximity to each other to produce berries.

The leaf is one way of determining what variety of holly you have. Holly comes not only in a deep rich green, but in blue-green and variegated leaf colours as well. Another way of telling the variety is by the colour and shape of the berries, which vary in colour. The typical red we all know about, but there are different shades of yellow, orange, black and a reddish-pink. The shape of the berry differs from small pea-sized to larger marble size; some are perfectly round, others more oblong.

Fertilizing is an important part of any commercial farm, whether they are growing daffodils, wheat, alfalfa or holly. In March, commercial holly trees are fertilized with a pure nitrogen fertilizer (48-0-0) and then in June given a high phosphorus fertilizer (16-20-4). Nitrogen is to promote quick growth, weight and bulk and give a rich green colour to the leaves, while phosphorus promotes fruits and flowers, ensuring strong roots and crop maturity. Phosphorus is essential to cell division. Improper phosphorus content can cause chlorosis. Holly enjoys a slightly acid soil (see pH Scale, page 176).

The middle of November is when you will find the commercial holly farm preparing to ship holly all over Canada. In order for the berries to stay on the holly sprigs and for the holly branches to arrive fresh, they are dipped in a fruit fix prior to packaging. Otherwise, in transit, the berries would fall off and leaves would start to dry up.

Hollies grow well on Vancouver Island and quite a few commercial orchards exist here. An easy grower for the home gardener since it enjoys a rich, slightly acid soil and can be pruned readily, the holly makes an attractive specimen plant or can be used as a hedge, espalier, ornamental tree or screen.

Holly

The holly bush can be easily confused with the Osmanthus. Although there are other differences, the main difference is the fact that holly leaves alternate on the stems, whereas Osmanthus leaves are across from each other. Some varieties of holly available for the home gardener are:

WILSON HOLLY (*Ilex altaciarensis* 'Wilsonii') — Reaches heights of 6 m (20 ft). It is easily grown, with evenly spined leaves and red berries.

ENGLISH or CHRISTMAS HOLLY (*Ilex aquifolium*) — Grows to 12 m (40 ft), depending upon variety. This is the true Christmas holly native to Europe and the British Isles. It is the parent to many varieties both male and female, smooth-leaved, extremely spiny, and variegated. Most varieties of Ilex aquifolium have red berries, but the variety I*lex aquifolium* 'Pyramidalis Fructuluteo' is a yellow-berried form. *Ilex aquifolium* 'Ferox' is a ferocious male with spines on the edge of the leaves and on the surface.

ILEX AQUIPERNYI—This holly grows to 6 m (20 ft), with few spines on the leaves and a heavy crop of red berries without a pollinator.

CHINESE HOLLY (*Ilex cornuta*) —A smaller tree or shrub with growth to 3 m (10 ft) and spines at the four corners of its nearly rectangular leaves and tip. The *Ilex cornuta* variety 'Burfordii' has one spine at the tip of its leaves. Most varieties of Chinese holly bear fruit without a pollinator and the majority have leaves with very few spines and large red berries. Includes the dwarf varieties, which may not exceed 45 cm (18 in) in height, some without berries and a few very spiny varieties.

JAPANESE HOLLY (*Ilex crenata*) —Growth to 6 m (20 ft) with narrow finely toothed leaves and black berries. Various Japanese hollies related to *Ilex crenata* are much shorter, ranging from 20 cm (8 in) to 120 cm (48 in), and are usually much broader than they are tall.

ILEX LATIFOLIA —Large tree with finely spined long leaves up to 20 cm (8 in) long. Berries are a dull red.

(*Ilex meserveae*) —Bushy plants to 2 m (7 ft), with purple stems, spiny blue-green leaves and heavy red berries.

AMERICAN HOLLY (*Ilex opaca*) —Slow-growing tree to 15 m (50 ft) with all varieties having spiny leaves and red berries.

ILEX PERNYI —Slow growing to 9 m (30 ft) with one to three spines on each leaf. Berries are red and set close to the branch.

Christmas Trees

Christmas-tree plantations around Vancouver Island start cutting in the middle of November in preparation for Christmas. A Christmas tree can be any upright conifer, but the most popular varieties used for Christmas are:

PINE (*Pinus*):

AUSTRIAN (*Pinus nigra*) —Growing to 12 m (40 ft) in height, it is not the favourite of most small-yard gardeners. A beautiful pine with two-needle growth, the tree is naturally dense and dark green in colour. A natural Christmas tree which takes pruning well.

WHITE (*Pinus strobus*) —This pine, widely used in the lumber industry, grows to a majestic 30 m (100 ft). The white pine has blue-green needles in bunches of five. Although needles are longer than the Austrian and Scotch pine, this makes a beautiful Christmas tree when young if properly pruned.

SCOTCH *(Pinus sylvestris)* — A medium-sized conifer with an ultimate height of 30 m (100 ft). Pruning thickens the tree up nicely with medium-length needles and it makes a nice Christmas tree.

FIR *(Abies)*:
Many species of this conifer are quite majestic in the forest or woodland scene. Quite large as a tree in a small city lot, they are still grown and appreciated by many. There are varieties of fir that are quite small and suitable for the home garden. Fir trees carry their cones in an upright position on their branches instead of hanging down like the spruce or Douglas fir.

GRAND *(Abies grandis)* — A giant forest tree with a mature height of 90 m (300 ft). The large fir is known for its rapid growth and is at home in our damp forests. Pruned when young, this tree fills out to an excellent Christmas tree. The grand fir has glossy green foliage with white bands beneath the leaves.

KOREAN *(Abies koreana)* — Glossy green on top of the needles and white beneath, the Korean fir is more suited to home gardens, with an ultimate height of approximately 15 m (50 ft). The attractive tree prunes well and suits the purpose of a Christmas tree, especially with the striking purple cones.

NOBLE *(Abies procera* or *Abies nobilis)* — Large as a garden tree, it is popular in the eastern part of Canada as a Christmas tree. Noble fir is not common to our forests but is becoming more popular. A beautiful tree with large cones, the trunk and larger part of the stems appear black against the bluish-green needles, especially when wet. This is a beautiful tree and requires very little pruning with a close growing habit.

WHITE *(Abies concolour)* — With a mature height of 50 m (160 ft), this tree holds its lower branches longer than other species of fir, which is a plus in many home gardens. Although quite tall, it is a beautiful specimen plant. The white fir has large cones which turn from green to a purple colour.

DOUGLAS FIR *(Pseudotsuga)*:
Similar to the fir *(Abies)* but with smaller buds and cones hanging down rather than standing upright on branches.

DOUGLAS FIR *(Pseudotsuga menziesii* or *Pseudotsuga taxifolia)* — This giant is a native of the western coast area of British Columbia. Although massive for yard culture, growing to 90 m (300 ft), this tree is popular in island gardens. The most common conifer on the west coast, this tree is mainly used for its timber. The *P. menziesii* takes to pruning, grows in abundance wherever a parent tree scatters its seed and therefore is an ideal Christmas tree for commercial growers.

SPRUCE *(Picea)*:
Spruce have short needles and come in blue, silver, green or grey with pendulous cones. Spruce are the largest variety of conifers and not only have the tall upright but many varieties of small spreading cultivars.

SITKA SPRUCE *(Picea sitchensis)* — This large tree, 70 m (230 ft), makes up most of the coastal rainforest. This specimen requires abundant rainfall and likes wet, undrained growing conditions.

NORWAY SPRUCE *(Picea abies* or *Picea excelsa)* — A popular tree for forestry purposes, this 40-m (120-ft) tree serves well as a Christmas tree when it is younger. The Norway spruce has beautiful dark green foliage with brown winter buds, and prunes well, making it a favourite Christmas tree in many countries.

WHITE SPRUCE *(Picea glauca)* — A popular Christmas tree growing to 25 m (70 ft) in colder climates, this beautiful spruce with its slightly pendulous branches and silver-green foliage responds well to pruning and is quite dense when young.

Pruning at the Sahtlam Tree Farm in Duncan, B.C., is done with a machete-like long-bladed shearing knife. It starts with the Scotch pine from mid-June through July, then to the grand fir in August, and ending with the Douglas fir from September through April.

Fertilizing is done in the spring with 21-0-0 with chemical sprays only being used to control weeds. Trees with insect or fungal problems are destroyed rather than sprayed with insecticides or fungicides.

Raising Kiwi

Kiwi *(Actinidia)* was quite rare not many years ago and quite costly. Now (since 1985) the kiwi is commercially grown on Vancouver Island and the plants are sold in numerous garden centres on the island.

Being a rampant grower, kiwi can take up a lot of space on a fence or trellis system. The kiwi likes a slightly acid soil with a pH between 6 and 6.5. Most varieties require a male and female be in close proximity and in bloom at the same time for the necessary pollination to produce fruit. Leaves are large, 15 to 20 cm (6 to 8 in)

Kiwi

long, depending upon the variety, and are either round or heart-shaped with a rich green on top and white below. New growth is noticeable by the fine red hairs. Distinguishing between male and female varieties is not possible until the plant blooms. The yellow or white blossoms are approximately 3 cm (1.5 in) in size. The commercial variety of the green fruit is egg-shaped and covered with a brown, fuzzy skin.

Pruning of the kiwi is similar to the grape. Maintain a strong trunk with two cordons trained overhead on a trellis system. Fruit is produced on this year's growth springing from last year's wood. Some of the more popular varieties include:

ACTINIDIA DELICIOSA 'HAYWARD' – The variety used mainly for commercial cultivation requires both a male and female for pollination. A trellis or arbour is required in a commercial growing situation to protect both the vine and the fruit. The trellis system is usually just high enough to walk under and pick the fruit hanging down. A 'Hayward' will not produce until it is approximately five years old and then not reach full production until it is seven or eight years old. The fruit ripens in the last few weeks of October or the first part of November (depending upon the season). Fruit is larger than other varieties and found in grocery stores across the country.

ACTINIDIA ARGUTA – Known as the hardy kiwi fruit, it is usually available in local garden centres. This variety is withstands colder climates than the 'Hayward'. The smooth-skinned fruit is smaller and produces more to the vine than the commercial varieties. The 'Arguta' kiwi will produce within a few years of planting and usually earlier in the year (August). This variety, like 'Hayward', also requires male and female vines to produce fruit.

ACTINIDIA ARGUTA 'ISSAI' – A self-pollinating variety of the 'Arguta' family adapted to home culture, as two vines will not be needed to ensure fruit. I have not seen this plant available in garden centres yet, but hopefully it will be soon. The convenience and space saved by being able to grow just one vine would increase the popularity of this wonderful fruit.

FLOWERS

Roses are dug in late summer to be shipped to nurseries for fall planting. Fall is the ideal time to plant roses, giving them a chance to develop a strong foothold before spring, when they will be expected to bloom. This is a good way of ensuring your rose is also freshly dug, since large rose growers dig their plants in the summer and ship them out to the nurseries. This means that you won't be buying plants that were held over the winter in a nursery setting.

Roses will require mulching, but not as much as is necessary in colder climates. Hill up with mulch or topsoil approximately 20 cm (8 in) high around the base. Many roses are still blooming in November because of the mild temperatures, although the quality, due to the lack of sun and high amount of rainfall, is less than perfect. Do not prune your rose bushes severely in the fall as this promotes growth. Any growth your rose bushes produce now will be too tender to withstand the winter frost sure to come in January or February, and it will die, possibly damaging your entire bush. Leave pruning until new growth starts in early spring. You can, however, reduce the size of the taller rose bush down to approximately 90 cm (36 in).

With a bit of luck, and no frost, some of the hardier annuals and perennials are still in bloom in November. Some of these are: cosmos, geranium, petunia, chrysanthemum, marguerite, rose and winter pansy.

Perennials can still be planted. Bulbs, such as the tulip, daffodil, hyacinth and crocus, can be planted as late as December in our climate and still bloom in the spring.

LAWNS

Keep the lawn short during the winter months. Rake and clean up the lawn when the weather is good. This will save time in the spring and will help the lawn get a healthy start for next year.

Dolomite lime can be added to the lawn at the rate prescribed on the package. Dolomite lime is not expensive and an application of lime on your lawn will definitely make a difference. Because the climate on the islands is extremely wet during the winter months, all fertilizer and lime you put on during the summer will be leached out by the rains. This is fine for growing plants such as arbutus, cedar, dogwood and fir, but if you want to grow a lawn, it will require a sweeter soil *(see pH Scale, page 176)*. If it hasn't rained and none is predicted soon, water lime into the lawn with a light sprinkling.

Low spots in the lawn or irregularities in the surface can be top-dressed now. Use good soil and when not more than 5 cm (2 in) of it is applied, the grass has a chance of coming through again. Be sure to keep all leaves and other heavy matter off the grass, as it smothers very easily during cold weather.

GARDENS

If you have an excess of leaves and don't have a compost bin going, place the leaves over root crops still growing in the garden. Next spring, they will be excellent compost to work into the garden. Vegetables left to use up during the winter are carrots, beets, turnips, parsnips, Brussels sprouts, cabbage and broccoli. Leeks and garlic may still be in the garden, but won't be used until later next year. Many gardeners plant these two members of the onion family in the fall for harvest the next fall. The top will freeze and die down in cold winters but will come up again in the spring.

PESTS

Lime sulphur and dormant oil can be sprayed on ornamentals now, until buds start to appear in the spring, to keep down scale and other insects not killed by the cold weather. Spray with lime sulphur and dormant oil mixes when temperatures are below 4°C (40°F), and when there is little or no wind. Lime sulphur and dormant oil are not chemicals, so organic gardeners can use them. Read directions carefully and use properly.

HOUSEPLANTS

There is no longer need to feed your houseplants with fertilizers such as 20-20-20. A very low-intensity fertilizer will be sufficient. A fish fertilizer (5-1-1) or alternative is adequate for a slow-growth period. Plants will slow down in response to less light.

DECEMBER
Merry Christmas!

DECEMBER IS HERE and so are the rains. The islands off the west coast record the yearly highs for rainfall in December. Rainfall *(see Weather Statistics, page 153)* can be as low as 41 mm (2 in) in areas such as Duncan Lake Dam or as high as 677 mm (40 in) in the Port Renfrew area during the month of December. With so much rain, there is very little we can do outside, so let's go inside. This is a good time to reflect upon what changes you want to make to your yard next year. The catalogues you have ordered or plan to order will come soon *(see Garden Catalogues, page 169)*. You will have made mistakes, misjudged the weather or been disappointed with some of your gardening decisions. But if you don't make mistakes, you don't learn, and I find I am learning all the time! This is one of the glories of gardening; there are no real experts and we all make mistakes. Just think of the successes of the year and the extreme pride and joy of picking your first tomato or strawberry.

Do you have a person on your Christmas list who enjoys gardening? This is the easiest person to shop for. There are numerous gardening magazines on the market chock-full of ideas and information. A subscription to one of these magazines would be enjoyable for them. Other suggestions are: garden tools, flower vases, a cold frame, bird fountains, bird feeders, a special tree or a special flower. The list is endless. The best present I ever received for

Christmas one year was a large chip truck full of hog fuel (cedar bark mulch). By spring I had beautiful paths winding through my gardens. Another year I received a set of stainless steel hand tools. I still have them and still enjoy using them.

TREES, SHRUBS & VINES

When you look over last year's garden or lawn and make plans for next year, consider the plants' sizes at maturity before purchasing new ones. A small 120-cm (4-ft) conifer looks beautiful beside your door or below your picture window, but for how long? All of a sudden you can't get out your front door or see out your picture window! Worse yet, the tree has dwarfed your house and is shading the plants growing around it to the point of suffocating them. When a professional landscaper plants a new area, the first thing you notice is the large area between plants. This is to allow for the horizontal and vertical spread of the plants. Within a year or two, your garden can change dramatically.

Trees and shrubs that have outgrown their original spaces may force you to do something quite drastic. Some shrubs require sizable space in order to show to good advantage. These kinds of trees or shrubs look miserable when hedged in between other crowding plants. You may have to remove a plant here or there to make expansion possible and improve the eye appeal of shrubs remaining. If you can save these removed plants for some other part of your yard or garden, fine! If any holes are left, perhaps you can introduce plants more restrained in their growing habits.

Upright corner shrubs are notorious for outgrowing their location and growing up into the eaves of the house, possibly causing damage. Check for height at maturity prior to purchasing a plant. If you are not familiar with the plant, check with your local nursery. Removing these plants after four or five years can be expensive, and when a plant is removed, you have to start over.

Another eyesore can be the old shrub that was growing beautifully for many years, and all of a sudden you notice that last year's snow bent some branches, and they are now sticking out like a sore thumb. Attempt to tie the out-of-place branches back into location, and leave them tied for a season. If you cut them off, you'll leave a big gap in a well-formed shrub. If it has partially or completely died for some unknown reason, you may have to remove the entire bush. This may be painful, but if you are able to get fifteen or twenty years out of your foundation plants before they become an eyesore, consider yourself lucky. I know many landscapers who automatically replace any plant when it reaches this age. To prevent the weight of snow or strong winds from damaging these sentinels, it would be wise to wrap a cord (preferably green, for camouflage purposes) around the shrub, to hold all its limbs in place. The cord can be removed in the spring after danger of heavy snows has passed.

There are many varieties of juniper, thuja, chamaecyparis and yew which are slow growing and ideal for growing under the eaves of your home, with an ultimate height, after ten years, never exceeding 6 m (18 ft). A hint when looking for plants is to look for the word *japonica* or *formosana* in the name. These plants are bred and perfected in the Orient especially because of their ability to stay compact. (Remember, the art of bonsai originated in the Orient.) These plants are available in a wide range of colours.

It is time to start thinking of pruning. The best and most effective time to prune most species is when they become dormant in the winter *(see Pruning, page 16)*. Fruit trees do not produce on the branches growing straight up or down, and branches growing across another branch will either shade or be shaded, interfering with the growth and possibly rubbing against another producing branch.

Christmas Trees in the Home

When purchasing live plants at Christmastime, ask about their care. I will touch on two of the most popular.

LIVE CHRISTMAS TREE — The live Christmas tree purchased at the nursery comes with the rootball wrapped in burlap to keep the soil around the roots and hold in moisture. The trees are dug by a mechanical digger severing all roots outside the rootball's circumference.

You will notice that all of the trees in the nursery have the same size ball of earth. These are outdoor trees, and their chances of survival aren't good when you consider that they will have their roots severed and will be kept in a warm dry environment for two or three weeks, not to mention being hung with electric lights and ornaments. This is not a very natural environment for any plant, so we must take extra-special care of these trees.

The roots must be kept quite damp and the tree should be planted out in either a movable patio planter or in the ground as

Live Christmas tree

soon as possible. They have gone through an extreme amount of stress and although, in theory, the idea of a live Christmas tree is a good one, they do not often survive the shock. A more successful idea is to plant a small evergreen spruce, fir or other conifer in a large patio pot in the spring, let it become established, tip prune if you like during the summer, and bring it into the house, pot and all, to be decorated for Christmas. Once Christmas is over, the plant can then be undecorated and returned to the outside. A small square of heavy plywood with four casters attached to the underside would assist in bringing the tree in and out without much trouble.

MINIATURE ALBERTA SPRUCE *(Picea glauca 'Albertiana Conica')* – The miniature Alberta spruce is sold in many garden centres for indoor use at Christmastime. This beautiful spruce is an outdoor tree. If you have it in your home or apartment decorated for Christmas, and continue growing it indoors because it makes a cute little houseplant, it will die. Confined to the warmth of a house or apartment, it will start to lose its needles or shoot out spindly growth. As soon as you have used it for your Christmas tree indoors, place it outside and either plant it in a larger pot, or wait for a nice day and plant it in your yard. The miniature Alberta spruce will never grow much taller than 3 m (10 ft) and is excellent for a foundation planting.

Perennials

Polyanthus or primrose *(primula)* plants are on the market and in bloom from December until spring. This is a fragrant and colourful cool-weather plant that enjoys an acid soil. Once the warm weather starts, the primrose will die back or become very nondescript until late summer, when it will again start growing and multiplying into large clumps. These can be divided during the spring and look very special when planted en masse. During December the selection is small, but as spring nears the selection will become enormous.

Polyanthus/primrose makes an excellent winter pot plant for an entrance, patio or winter hanging basket. Being highly scented, it is nice planted near the front entrance or in window boxes.

Perennials in bloom this month are:

Algerian iris	gentian
Lily turf	knapweed
winter pansy	polyanthus
Christmas rose	flowering kale/cabbage

Annuals

Deadhead winter pansies as blossoms die. This will prevent their going to seed and enable them to last through the winter. Most winter pansies will keep blooming throughout the year and can be treated as either perennials or hardy annuals.

Bulbs, Tubers & Corms

If you haven't planted your tulips, daffodils or other spring-flowering bulbs, you should plant them this month. There is a good possibility that they will still bloom even if you plant them in January but they will deteriorate rapidly if you are keeping them in a warm house. They are better planted in the ground, even if it is not the perfect location for them.

It's not too late to start a bowl of daffodils to bloom in a few months time *(see Paper whites, page 120).*

LAWNS

Dolomite lime can be added at any time over the winter except when snow is on the ground or the ground is frozen.

Walking on frozen lawns can break them down. Especially avoid walking on thinly planted or new lawns, as this will not only break the crowns of the grasses, it will also create holes where you have walked if it is muddy. Try to keep children and dogs off lawns in the wintertime.

GARDENS

Whether you still have vegetables growing in the garden or you stopped gardening upon the arrival of fall, the garden should be kept as clean as possible. Are there half-frozen squash and tomato plants lying on top of the soil? Is the row of green beans that produced so well during the summer months still in a row looking rather shabby at this time of year? Do yourself a favour and compost these plants. The easiest way is to dig a trench the width of your garden and a spade (25 cm/10 in) deep, place the expired vegetable plants in the trench then, cover with soil.

I know a woman who recycles religiously. Cans in one container, plastic in another, newspaper in another and so on. Vegetable scraps are taken to the garden or flower bed every evening after dinner and out comes the shovel. She makes a small hole, puts in the vegetable scraps, puts the dirt back over it, and the rains provide water through the winter and all scraps are composted by Mother Nature. An excellent idea for anyone, but especially so for the person who does not have a compost bin or does not want to bother with one.

The whole idea of gardening is to take ideas from other people, books, magazines, etc., and use what fits your lifestyle and works for you.

HOUSEPLANTS

Christmas plants can be cared for and most will be planted outside once the warmer weather appears. All plants you receive will appreciate full winter sun during the day and cooler temperatures at night (see Christmas Plant Care, page 8).

The Norfolk Island pine makes an excellent Christmas tree for indoors. Placing electric bulbs on the tree can be damaging to the tree, since needles will burn, but decorating with bright bows and ornaments will bring the holiday spirit to a room and the tree can be enjoyed afterwards as a wonderful addition to your home. Decorated with bows, bulbs, popcorn, cranberries, etc., this would be a marvellous gift for a shut-in.

Climate Zones/Weather Statistics — Vancouver Island

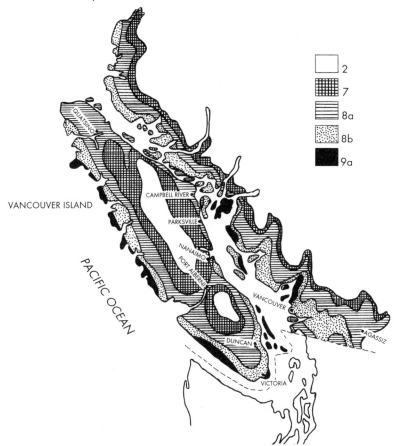

Vancouver Island, like everywhere else in the world, has climate (hardiness) zones, and it is important to know which zone you are in. Climate zones are essential for the survival of plants.

The map above shows climate zones of the coastal area of the Lower Mainland and the islands (including Vancouver Island) off the West Coast of Canada. Climate zones are based on factors such as wind, rain, sun, snow, humidity and temperature. Trial and error on your part, as well as talking with local gardeners and garden centre employees can help you in your plant selection.

The map is to be used only as a guide as there are many variations in each area. Chances are, your plant has a chance of surviving if it has the zone number indicated for your area or a lower one.

Compiled and organized by the Cartography Section, Soil Research Institute, Research Branch, Canada, Department of Agriculture. From information approved by the Plant Research Institute of Ottawa and the Meterological Branch of Energy, Mines and Resources, 1967. Department of Transport, Toronto. Printed by the Surveys and Mapping Branch department.

WEATHER STATISTICS
DAILY MAXIMUM TEMPERATURE

TOWN	JAN	FEB	MAR	APR	MAY	JUN	JUL	AUG	SEP	OCT	NOV	DEC	YR
CAMPBELL RIVER	3.8	6.5	8.4	12.3	16.6	19.5	22.8	22.1	18.4	12.5	7.4	5.0	12.9
CAPE SCOTT	5.9	7.3	7.6	9.7	12.0	13.9	15.4	16.1	14.7	12.3	8.8	6.8	10.9
COURTENAY*	—	—	—	—	—	—	—	—	—	—	—	—	—
COWICHAN BAY	4.8	7.5	9.3	12.7	16.3	19.0	22.2	21.9	19.1	13.8	8.4	5.7	13.4
DENMAN ISLAND	4.4	7.5	9.2	12.9	17.2	20.2	23.4	22.9	19.3	13.7	8.4	6.1	13.8
DUNCAN LAKE DAM	−1.5	2.4	6.2	13.0	18.7	21.9	25.8	25.0	18.9	11.5	4.2	0.3	12.2
GABRIOLA ISLAND*	—	—	—	—	—	—	—	—	—	—	—	—	—
GALIANO ISLAND*	—	—	—	—	—	—	—	—	—	—	—	—	—
JAMES ISLAND	5.6	7.6	9.1	12.5	16.3	18.9	21.7	21.2	18.3	13.1	8.7	6.6	13.3
METCHOSIN HAPPY VALLEY*	—	—	—	—	—	—	—	—	—	—	—	—	—
NANAIMO	5.4	7.9	10.0	13.8	18.0	20.5	23.5	23.2	20.0	14.3	8.9	6.7	14.4
PORT ALBERNI	3.7	6.5	9.9	14.2	18.6	21.3	25.2	24.9	21.5	14.5	8.1	4.9	14.5
PORT HARDY	4.8	6.7	7.7	10.5	13.5	15.5	17.3	17.4	15.5	11.8	7.8	5.8	11.2
PORT RENFREW	6.3	8.2	9.4	12.0	14.7	16.6	18.5	18.4	18.0	14.2	9.7	7.3	12.8
SALT SPRING ISLAND	5.6	7.9	9.2	12.9	16.8	19.3	22.3	21.9	19.5	13.9	9.0	6.5	13.7
SANDSPIT (Queen Charlotte Island)	4.5	6.0	6.8	9.0	11.8	14.3	16.7	17.6	15.8	11.8	8.1	5.8	10.7
SOUTH PENDER ISLAND	5.9	8.5	9.6	12.9	16.5	19.1	21.9	21.4	18.8	13.8	9.3	7.1	13.7
TOFINO	6.7	8.5	9.0	10.9	13.7	16.1	18.3	18.1	17.2	13.4	9.8	7.7	12.5
UCLUELET KENNEDY CAMP*	—	—	—	—	—	—	—	—	—	—	—	—	—
VICTORIA AIRPORT	6.0	8.2	9.6	12.9	16.5	19.2	21.7	21.4	19.0	14.1	9.4	7.1	13.8
YOUBOU	5.2	7.9	9.4	12.6	17.4	21.0	24.9	24.0	20.4	15.1	9.2	7.0	14.5

* Figures not available
All statistics shown are in metric

WEATHER STATISTICS
DAILY MINIMUM TEMPERATURE

TOWN	JAN	FEB	MAR	APR	MAY	JUN	JUL	AUG	SEP	OCT	NOV	DEC	YR
CAMPBELL RIVER	−1.6	0.3	0.5	2.5	5.9	8.9	11.0	11.1	8.6	5.0	1.8	0.0	4.5
CAPE SCOTT	2.0	2.8	2.8	4.4	6.4	8.8	10.6	11.3	10.3	7.8	4.8	3.1	6.3
COURTENAY*	—	—	—	—	—	—	—	—	—	—	—	—	—
COWICHAN BAY	−0.1	1.4	1.7	3.8	6.8	9.7	11.7	11.8	9.8	6.3	2.8	1.3	5.6
DENMAN ISLAND	−0.6	0.1	0.6	2.8	5.6	8.7	11.0	10.7	7.5	4.7	1.6	0.3	4.4
DUNCAN LAKE DAM	−8.1	−5.5	−3.7	−0.2	4.1	7.7	9.4	9.1	5.6	1.7	−2.1	−4.9	1.1
GABRIOLA ISLAND*	—	—	—	—	—	—	—	—	—	—	—	—	—
GALIANO ISLAND*	—	—	—	—	—	—	—	—	—	—	—	—	—
JAMES ISLAND	1.9	2.9	3.1	5.0	7.6	10.0	11.5	11.7	10.4	7.6	4.6	2.9	6.6
METCHOSIN HAPPY VALLEY*	—	—	—	—	—	—	—	—	—	—	—	—	—
NANAIMO	−0.4	0.8	1.4	3.7	6.9	10.3	12.2	12.1	9.6	5.7	2.4	1.0	5.5
PORT ALBERNI	−1.8	−0.3	0.1	1.8	5.2	8.4	10.5	10.7	8.0	5.8	1.4	0.0	4.2
PORT HARDY	−0.1	1.1	1.1	2.7	5.1	8.1	9.8	10.1	8.2	5.5	2.7	1.2	4.6
PORT RENFREW	0.1	1.0	1.1	3.0	5.6	8.7	10.4	10.4	8.8	5.8	2.8	1.3	4.9
SALT SPRING ISLAND	0.2	1.6	2.0	4.2	7.2	9.6	11.7	11.7	10.1	6.6	3.3	1.5	5.8
SANDSPIT (Queen Charlotte Island)	−0.4	1.0	1.0	2.9	5.7	8.8	11.3	11.9	9.9	6.2	2.9	1.0	5.2
SOUTH PENDER ISLAND	0.7	2.2	2.5	4.3	6.6	9.0	10.4	10.6	9.2	6.5	3.3	2.0	5.6
TOFINO	0.8	2.0	1.9	3.5	5.9	8.5	10.2	10.7	9.0	6.4	3.4	2.1	5.4
UCLUELET KENNEDY CAMP*	—	—	—	—	—	—	—	—	—	—	—	—	—
VICTORIA AIRPORT	0.1	1.3	1.7	3.9	6.7	9.4	10.8	10.7	8.7	5.6	2.5	1.3	5.2
YOUBOU	−0.3	1.1	1.3	3.2	6.4	9.5	11.9	12.0	8.8	5.7	2.5	1.2	5.3

* Figures not available
All statistics shown are in metric

Information from "Canadian Climate Normals 1951 -1980 Temperature and Precipitation British Columbia", Environment Canada, Atmospheric Environment Service UDC:551.582 (711)

WEATHER STATISTICS
EXTREME MAXIMUM TEMPERATURE

TOWN	JAN	FEB	MAR	APR	MAY	JUN	JUL	AUG	SEP	OCT	NOV	DEC	YR
CAMPBELL RIVER	14.4	17.8	21.1	20.1	29.4	31.7	37.2	22.9	27.2	21.7	15.0	14.4	37.2
CAPE SCOTT	12.2	17.2	15.0	18.3	21.7	21.7	20.6	23.9	26.7	19.2	21.1	12.0	26.7
COURTENAY*	—	—	—	—	—	—	—	—	—	—	—	—	—
COWICHAN BAY	15.0	17.8	20.0	23.9	29.4	32.8	35.6	34.4	31.7	24.0	17.2	15.5	35.6
DENMAN ISLAND	12.8	15.6	19.4	20.6	28.3	30.0	35.6	33.3	28.3	20.6	15.6	15.0	35.6
DUNCAN LAKE DAM	8.9	10.0	16.7	29.4	30.6	33.3	36.5	35.0	32.2	21.7	18.3	9.5	36.5
GABRIOLA ISLAND*	—	—	—	—	—	—	—	—	—	—	—	—	—
GALIANO ISLAND*	—	—	—	—	—	—	—	—	—	—	—	—	—
JAMES ISLAND	13.9	15.6	18.9	25.6	30.0	33.9	35.0	34.4	31.1	25.6	17.2	13.9	35.0
METCHOSIN HAPPY VALLEY*	—	—	—	—	—	—	—	—	—	—	—	—	—
NANAIMO	16.1	18.3	21.7	27.8	31.7	33.3	40.6	35.6	30.6	25.0	17.8	15.0	40.6
PORT ALBERNI	15.6	17.8	23.3	30.6	33.3	37.2	41.1	39.4	35.6	27.8	20.6	16.7	41.1
PORT HARDY	12.8	16.7	18.3	22.2	28.3	31.7	26.7	28.3	25.6	22.8	19.4	14.8	31.7
PORT RENFREW	13.9	15.0	17.8	22.2	27.2	28.3	31.7	31.7	28.9	24.0	17.2	14.0	31.7
SALT SPRING ISLAND	14.4	17.2	20.6	27.8	31.7	35.0	38.3	35.6	31.7	26.1	18.9	14.4	38.3
SANDSPIT (Queen Charlotte Island)	12.2	13.4	13.9	18.9	21.7	25.0	27.8	26.7	24.1	18.9	15.6	13.4	27.8
SOUTH PENDER ISLAND	12.8	15.0	17.2	24.4	29.4	29.4	31.1	32.2	29.4	24.5	17.5	14.0	32.2
TOFINO	14.4	18.9	18.3	21.7	25.6	32.2	32.8	31.3	29.4	23.9	21.1	15.6	32.8
UCLUELET KENNEDY CAMP*	—	—	—	—	—	—	—	—	—	—	—	—	—
VICTORIA AIRPORT	15.0	18.3	20.0	24.4	29.4	33.3	36.1	34.4	31.1	25.6	18.3	16.1	36.1
YOUBOU	15.0	19.4	19.4	22.2	30.6	32.8	37.2	36.7	31.7	22.8	17.2	14.4	37.2

* Figures not available
All statistics shown are in metric

WEATHER STATISTICS
EXTREME MINIMUM TEMPERATURE

TOWN	JAN	FEB	MAR	APR	MAY	JUN	JUL	AUG	SEP	OCT	NOV	DEC	YR
CAMPBELL RIVER	-17.2	-7.2	-8.9	-2.8	-1.7	2.8	4.4	4.4	2.2	-1.7	-8.3	-17.8	-17.8
CAPE SCOTT	-8.3	-4.7	-2.8	-1.1	2.2	4.4	7.2	7.8	5.0	0.6	-4.4	-11.1	-11.1
COURTENAY*	—	—	—	—	—	—	—	—	—	—	—	—	—
COWICHAN BAY	-16.1	-11.7	-9.4	-3.9	-1.1	0.6	4.4	4.4	0.0	-4.4	-13.3	-15.0	-16.1
DENMAN ISLAND	-12.2	-7.8	-9.4	-3.3	-2.8	1.7	3.9	3.9	0.0	-2.8	-5.6	-12.8	-12.8
DUNCAN LAKE DAM	-29.0	-25.0	-20.0	-12.2	-3.3	-1.1	2.2	1.7	-5.0	-9.4	-18.3	-31.7	-31.7
GABRIOLA ISLAND*	—	—	—	—	—	—	—	—	—	—	—	—	—
GALIANO ISLAND*	—	—	—	—	—	—	—	—	—	—	—	—	—
JAMES ISLAND	-13.9	-13.3	-7.8	-2.2	0.6	3.3	4.4	4.4	2.2	-1.7	-10.0	-13.9	-13.9
METCHOSIN HAPPY VALLEY*	—	—	—	—	—	—	—	—	—	—	—	—	—
NANAIMO	-17.2	-17.2	-11.1	-3.9	-2.8	0.6	4.4	3.3	-1.1	-6.7	-11.7	-12.2	-17.2
PORT ALBERNI	-21.7	-15.6	-13.9	-7.8	-5.6	0.0	3.3	2.8	-3.9	-7.8	-12.8	-15.6	-21.7
PORT HARDY	-14.4	-8.9	-12.8	-3.3	-1.1	1.7	2.8	3.3	-0.6	-3.9	-10.0	-12.2	-14.4
PORT RENFREW	-9.4	-7.2	-6.7	-2.2	0.0	1.7	5.6	2.2	-0.6	-2.8	-6.1	-11.1	-11.1
SALT SPRING ISLAND	-15.0	-15.0	-10.0	-5.6	-0.6	0.6	3.9	3.9	-0.6	-6.7	-13.3	-14.4	-15.0
SANDSPIT (Queen Charlotte Island)	-13.9	-12.2	-12.2	-2.8	-1.1	2.2	5.0	5.6	-0.6	-2.2	-6.7	-12.8	-13.9
SOUTH PENDER ISLAND	-9.4	-5.6	-4.4	-2.8	-0.6	2.8	4.4	3.9	1.7	-2.2	-5.0	-9.4	-9.4
TOFINO	-15.0	-7.2	-5.0	-1.7	0.0	2.2	3.9	4.4	-0.6	-2.2	-7.0	-12.2	-15.0
UCLUELET KENNEDY CAMP*	—	—	—	—	—	—	—	—	—	—	—	—	—
VICTORIA AIRPORT	-15.6	-15.0	-8.9	-3.9	-1.1	2.2	4.1	4.4	-1.1	-4.4	-13.3	-14.4	-15.6
YOUBOU	-9.4	-7.2	-5.6	-1.7	-0.6	3.3	6.7	5.6	0.6	-1.1	-4.4	-13.9	-13.9

* Figures not available
All statistics shown are in metric

Information from "Canadian Climate Normals 1951 - 1980 Temperature and Precipitation British Columbia", Environment Canada, Atmospheric Environment Service UDC:551.582 (711)

WEATHER STATISTICS
RAINFALL

TOWN	JAN	FEB	MAR	APR	MAY	JUN	JUL	AUG	SEP	OCT	NOV	DEC	YR
CAMPBELL RIVER	169.4	158.1	143.8	76.5	53.0	49.1	40.0	55.0	77.1	162.5	228.6	245.7	1458.8
CAPE SCOTT	285.4	243.3	222.5	184.9	135.3	103.2	83.1	106.5	191.5	351.4	326.7	332.3	2566.1
COURTENAY	179.4	145.2	130.1	75.1	46.9	48.2	33.7	45.8	63.5	155.7	227.0	231.2	1381.8
COWICHAN BAY	142.1	99.9	84.4	47.9	35.5	33.4	21.4	29.0	43.8	90.5	144.5	162.4	934.8
DENMAN ISLAND	168.6	141.3	118.0	72.3	36.7	38.8	26.0	39.6	46.8	145.6	205.1	230.3	1269.2
DUNCAN LAKE DAM	22.9	30.4	31.7	35.2	48.0	54.4	42.5	47.6	53.1	54.3	56.2	41.6	517.9
GABRIOLA ISLAND	118.3	87.1	72.5	43.2	34.5	29.9	22.3	29.8	49.1	79.1	119.6	129.2	814.6
GALIANO ISLAND	125.8	78.1	71.5	39.7	29.9	34.5	23.2	30.2	45.6	87.1	114.3	139.5	819.4
JAMES ISLAND	123.5	76.1	52.4	32.8	23.6	22.9	16.7	24.8	34.2	73.5	110.7	124.0	715.2
METCHOSIN HAPPY VALLEY	199.0	131.2	97.7	57.3	30.9	24.7	17.4	25.5	49.3	111.5	158.0	204.7	1107.2
NANAIMO	143.2	106.4	94.2	59.5	41.9	42.5	24.3	45.0	48.9	106.5	162.3	168.9	1043.6
PORT ALBERNI	248.6	215.6	206.9	122.9	72.4	47.9	38.4	43.1	88.7	216.4	287.2	326.5	1914.6
PORT HARDY	181.6	148.3	128.5	106.2	68.6	70.7	52.0	69.0	136.2	244.6	239.8	260.3	1705.8
PORT RENFREW	579.7	441.0	391.8	215.8	143.5	122.6	80.1	87.6	201.1	420.5	522.2	677.3	3883.2
SALT SPRING ISLAND	159.0	99.9	94.8	49.4	36.8	34.2	23.5	33.3	44.1	97.9	146.4	170.9	990.2
SANDSPIT (Queen Charlotte Island)	113.3	98.0	88.5	82.1	52.1	51.7	43.2	49.5	89.9	194.3	175.6	161.5	1199.7
SOUTH PENDER ISLAND	112.1	71.8	55.7	38.7	31.4	32.6	20.7	34.7	42.2	78.5	107.9	116.7	743.0
TOFINO	382.7	357.3	361.2	231.4	143.0	101.7	86.1	114.1	163.2	391.8	429.3	464.2	3226.0
UCLUELET KENNEDY CAMP	420.5	374.0	336.9	222.9	130.4	115.3	82.8	112.9	188.8	384.6	452.4	480.3	3301.8
VICTORIA AIRPORT	134.0	91.1	65.5	38.9	28.5	29.0	18.1	26.7	39.6	78.4	128.4	144.4	822.6
YOUBOU	236.9	209.1	156.9	124.5	62.3	46.0	39.4	57.9	89.8	194.9	253.3	286.2	1757.2

All statistics shown are in metric

WEATHER STATISTICS
SNOWFALL

TOWN	JAN	FEB	MAR	APR	MAY	JUN	JUL	AUG	SEP	OCT	NOV	DEC	YR
CAMPBELL RIVER	43.6	14.9	9.4	0.5	0.0	0.0	0.0	0.0	0.0	0.1	11.9	34.9	115.3
CAPE SCOTT	23.0	9.6	11.6	3.5	0.0	0.0	0.0	0.0	0.0	0.2	4.1	11.9	63.9
COURTENAY	43.7	18.4	8.7	0.9	0.0	0.0	0.0	0.0	0.0	0.4	11.2	36.1	112.0
COWICHAN BAY	27.3	10.4	11.5	0.1	0.0	0.0	0.0	0.0	0.0	0.1	10.7	27.8	112.3
DENMAN ISLAND	38.8	13.2	10.8	0.4	0.0	0.0	0.0	0.0	0.0	0.1	6.8	22.6	92.7
DUNCAN LAKE DAM	88.2	35.8	17.3	1.2	0.0	0.0	0.0	0.0	0.0	0.4	26.3	72.5	241.7
GABRIOLA ISLAND	16.2	6.6	1.1	0.0	0.0	0.0	0.0	0.0	0.0	0.0	1.1	13.4	38.4
GALIANO ISLAND	15.1	5.5	4.3	0.1	0.0	0.0	0.0	0.0	0.0	0.0	0.6	10.3	35.9
JAMES ISLAND	12.7	5.6	4.2	T	0.0	0.0	0.0	0.0	0.0	0.0	1.7	8.7	32.9
METCHOSIN HAPPY VALLEY	15.4	3.1	6.0	0.3	0.0	0.0	0.0	0.0	0.0	0.0	2.1	13.2	40.1
NANAIMO	28.8	10.2	6.0	0.3	0.0	0.0	0.0	0.0	0.0	0.0	3.8	22.6	71.7
PORT ALBERNI	65.0	10.8	9.3	2.0	0.0	0.0	0.0	0.0	0.0	0.2	6.7	43.6	137.6
PORT HARDY	29.6	10.5	11.0	1.3	T	0.0	0.0	0.0	0.0	0.2	4.0	15.5	72.1
PORT RENFREW	15.4	10.9	18.7	0.6	0.0	0.0	0.0	0.0	0.0	0.0	0.8	15.3	61.7
SALT SPRING ISLAND	31.8	9.7	7.1	0.3	0.0	0.0	0.0	0.0	0.0	0.0	3.2	22.9	75.0
SANDSPIT (Queen Charlotte Island)	34.0	15.5	11.2	2.1	0.1	0.0	0.0	0.0	0.0	T	5.4	17.1	85.4
SOUTH PENDER ISLAND	9.0	3.4	1.2	0.2	0.0	0.0	0.0	0.0	0.0	0.1	1.3	7.5	22.7
TOFINO	20.5	6.0	8.6	2.0	0.0	0.0	0.0	0.0	0.0	0.0	2.7	13.2	53.0
UCLUELET KENNEDY CAMP	10.9	3.9	8.4	0.2	0.0	0.0	0.0	0.0	0.0	0.0	1.3	10.3	35.0
VICTORIA AIRPORT	20.0	8.1	6.1	0.3	0.0	0.0	0.0	0.0	0.0	0.0	2.3	13.1	49.9
YOUBOU	29.4	3.7	6.2	0.3	0.0	0.0	0.0	0.0	0.0	0.0	1.7	31.9	73.2

All statistics shown are in metric

Information from "Canadian Climate Normals 1951 -1980 Temperature and Precipitation British Columbia", Environment Canada, Atmospheric Environment Service UDC:551.582 (711)

WEATHER STATISTICS
TOTAL PRECIPITATION

TOWN	JAN	FEB	MAR	APR	MAY	JUN	JUL	AUG	SEP	OCT	NOV	DEC	YR
CAMPBELL RIVER	222.6	172.5	154.8	77.4	53.0	49.1	40.0	55.0	77.1	162.8	239.7	276.5	1580.5
CAPE SCOTT	307.6	252.7	234.5	187.5	135.3	103.2	83.1	106.4	191.5	351.5	331.3	344.0	2628.6
COURTENAY	225.4	166.9	142.3	75.3	47.0	48.2	33.7	45.8	63.5	155.9	238.8	259.8	1502.6
COWICHAN BAY	169.3	110.3	91.7	48.2	35.5	33.4	21.4	29.0	43.8	90.5	147.0	181.2	1001.3
DENMAN ISLAND	210.3	158.7	129.1	72.5	36.8	38.8	26.0	39.6	46.8	145.9	215.1	251.9	1371.5
DUNCAN LAKE DAM	112.0	66.3	46.8	36.2	48.0	54.4	42.5	47.6	53.1	54.7	81.7	114.1	757.4
GABRIOLA ISLAND	133.2	89.5	78.1	43.2	34.5	29.9	22.3	29.8	49.1	79.1	118.7	140.4	847.8
GALIANO ISLAND	141.7	83.6	75.6	39.9	29.9	34.5	23.2	30.2	45.6	87.1	114.9	149.5	855.7
JAMES ISLAND	136.2	81.7	56.5	32.8	23.6	22.9	16.7	24.8	34.2	73.5	112.4	132.7	748.0
METCHOSIN HAPPY VALLEY	216.4	135.0	106.0	57.8	30.9	24.7	17.4	25.5	49.3	111.5	159.5	216.7	1150.7
NANAIMO	173.5	122.7	99.6	60.0	41.9	42.5	24.3	45.0	48.9	106.5	168.2	193.2	1126.3
PORT ALBERNI	294.3	236.8	213.8	123.4	72.4	47.9	38.4	43.1	88.7	216.6	291.9	351.7	2019.0
PORT HARDY	211.2	159.4	141.8	107.5	68.6	70.7	52.0	69.0	136.2	244.8	244.7	276.9	1782.8
PORT RENFREW	599.7	451.1	415.6	212.6	143.5	122.6	80.1	87.6	201.1	420.5	521.8	687.0	3943.2
SALT SPRING ISLAND	190.8	109.6	101.9	49.7	36.8	34.2	23.5	33.3	44.1	97.9	149.6	193.8	1065.2
SANDSPIT (Queen Charlotte Island)	144.0	113.2	99.6	84.4	52.2	51.7	43.2	49.5	89.9	194.4	180.9	178.0	1281.0
SOUTH PENDER ISLAND	119.9	75.7	59.3	38.9	31.4	32.6	20.7	34.7	42.2	78.6	109.5	124.3	767.8
TOFINO	404.3	366.4	372.4	233.8	143.0	101.7	86.1	114.1	163.2	291.8	432.3	479.2	3288.3
UCLUELET KENNEDY CAMP	427.8	378.0	345.2	222.7	130.4	115.3	82.8	112.9	188.8	384.6	453.7	492.5	3334.7
VICTORIA AIRPORT	154.3	99.2	71.7	39.3	28.5	29.0	18.1	26.7	39.6	78.4	130.8	157.3	872.9
YOUBOU	295.6	222.6	169.3	126.3	62.3	46.0	39.4	57.9	89.8	194.9	256.6	313.2	1873.9

All statistics shown are in metric

WEATHER STATISTICS
GREATEST PRECIPITATION IN 24 HOURS

TOWN	JAN	FEB	MAR	APR	MAY	JUN	JUL	AUG	SEP	OCT	NOV	DEC	YR
CAMPBELL RIVER	76.7	95.3	71.4	79.8	38.9	50.8	39.4	42.2	36.1	89.2	91.9	104.9	104.9
CAPE SCOTT	145.8	73.4	77.5	80.8	68.8	37.1	44.5	46.2	130.7	109.4	129.0	94.5	145.8
COURTENAY	102.1	89.9	76.7	74.9	35.1	34.5	37.1	51.3	51.8	61.0	85.1	102.9	102.9
COWICHAN BAY	96.5	56.1	48.3	36.1	39.9	37.6	26.7	57.2	56.6	54.9	63.0	63.8	96.5
DENMAN ISLAND	99.6	72.9	73.2	68.6	55.9	44.2	44.5	37.3	54.1	74.9	78.7	80.3	99.6
DUNCAN LAKE DAM	34.0	27.2	19.6	26.7	25.4	29.7	23.6	34.8	31.2	25.1	38.1	56.9	56.9
GABRIOLA ISLAND	49.0	38.6	35.1	24.9	24.4	21.3	22.4	40.6	37.3	35.6	43.1	46.6	49.0
GALIANO ISLAND	65.3	44.2	30.2	33.3	25.1	37.3	20.6	33.0	25.4	51.1	46.2	45.0	65.3
JAMES ISLAND	101.9	51.8	45.5	33.3	41.1	33.8	29.5	49.0	30.5	48.5	76.5	65.0	101.9
METCHOSIN HAPPY VALLEY	61.7	68.8	90.2	33.8	26.4	26.4	15.7	47.0	32.5	51.3	68.4	104.4	104.4
NANAIMO	71.6	76.2	43.4	35.6	43.2	31.8	31.8	51.3	47.0	69.6	69.9	65.0	76.2
PORT ALBERNI	105.7	123.4	105.2	76.2	63.0	47.8	70.4	38.9	57.7	91.2	139.7	125.7	139.7
PORT HARDY	98.3	55.1	65.8	48.5	37.8	42.2	35.8	54.6	96.3	113.7	86.6	153.8	153.8
PORT RENFREW	166.4	192.8	121.9	94.7	91.7	91.4	106.7	54.6	88.9	216.4	142.2	234.6	234.6
SALT SPRING ISLAND	93.2	57.2	40.1	50.8	46.5	40.1	40.1	78.5	59.9	53.6	85.1	79.8	93.2
SANDSPIT (Queen Charlotte Island)	57.2	35.1	47.5	79.5	48.3	39.1	22.1	38.6	48.5	58.6	61.7	55.6	79.5
SOUTH PENDER ISLAND	46.7	39.9	35.6	24.4	19.3	24.9	17.5	52.6	19.8	52.1	52.0	55.4	55.4
TOFINO	174.2	128.5	169.7	106.2	95.5	51.3	98.3	131.3	105.9	154.2	155.4	166.4	174.2
UCLUELET KENNEDY CAMP	153.9	168.9	157.5	75.9	91.2	62.5	135.4	100.8	114.6	168.1	185.1	159.0	185.1
VICTORIA AIRPORT	64.3	55.9	54.1	31.2	38.1	40.9	19.6	32.5	27.4	57.4	68.3	72.9	72.9
YOUBOU	144.0	63.0	41.4	53.1	38.9	26.4	19.1	49.5	34.8	104.9	54.4	63.5	144.0

All statistics shown are in metric

Information from "Canadian Climate Normals 1951 - 1980 Temperature and Precipitation British Columbia", Environment Canada, Atmospheric Environment Service UDC:551.582 (711)

TREES

Common Name	Botanical Name	*Height (metres)	*Zone	Decid.	Brdlf. Everg.	Conif.	Bloss.	* Fruit/ Berries	Fall Colour
Almond, flowering	Prunus	5 to 8	7	x			x		
Apple, crab	Malus	5 to 12	2 to 5	x			x	x	x
Apricot, flowering	Prunus	6 to 9	7	x			x	x	x
Arborvitae	Thuja	5 to 60	3			x		cones	
Arborvitae, false	Thujopsis	15 to 30	7			x			
Ash	Fraxinus	12 to 18	2 to 7	x				x	x
Aspen	see Poplar								
Avocado		6 to 9	9		x			x	x
Beech	Fagus	12 to 24	4 to 6	x					x
Birch	Betula	5 to 21	2 to 4	x					x
Buckeye	see Chestnut, horse								
Catalpa		5 to 18	5	x			x	pods	
Cedar	Cedrus	15 to 30	6 to 8			x		cones	
Cedar, incense	Calocedrus	18 to 30	8			x			
Cherry, flowering	Prunus	5 to 15	4 to 7	x			x		
Cherry, Cornelian	Cornus	5 to 8	5	x			x		
Chestnut, Chinese	Castanea	12 to 18	6	x			x	nuts	
Chestnut, horse	Aesculus	6 to 23	2 to 8	x			x	nuts	x
Chinese scholar tree	Sophora	9 to 23	6	x			x		
Cork tree	Phellodendron	9 to 15	3	x				x	
Cottonwood	see Poplar								
Cryptomeria		9 to 30	6			x			
Cypress	Cupressus	12 to 24	8			x		cones	
Cypress, bald	Taxodium	12 to 36	5 to 9			x		cones	
Cypress, false	Chamaecyparis	5 to 23	4 to 7			x			
Cypress, Leyland	Cupressocyparis	12 to 18	7			x			
Dogwood	Cornus	3 to 12	6 to 8	x			x	x	
Dove tree	Davidia	8 to 12	7	x			x		
Empress tree	Paulownia	12 to 15	7	x			x	pods	
Eucalyptus		6 to 23	7 to 8		x				
Fig	Ficus	5 to 9	4 to 9	x			x	x	
Filbert	Corylus	5	2 to 7	x			x	nuts	
Fir	Abies	9 to 27	1 to 5			x		cones	
Fir, Douglas	Pseudotsuga	21 to 30	3 to 7			x		cones	
Franklin tree	Franklinia	6 to 9	7	x			x		x
Fringe tree	Chionanthus	4 to 9	5 to 6	x			x	x	x
Ginkgo biloba	see Maidenhair tree								
Golden chain	Laburnum	5 to 6	6	x			x		
Goldenrain tree	Koelreuteria	6 to 9	6	x			x	pods	
Gum, American sweet	Liquidambar	6 to 8	5	x			x		x
Hackberry	Celtis	9 to 18	2 to 7	x				x	
Hawthorn	Crataegus	4 to 11	2 to 6	x			x	x	x
Hemlock	Tsuga	14 to 36	4 to 8			x			
Hickory	Carya	18 to 24	4 to 5	x				nuts	
Holly	Ilex	6 to 12	7		x		x	x	
Honey locust	Gleditsia	9 to 36	4	x				pods	
Hornbeam	Carpinus	6 to 18	3 to 6	x			x		x
Hornbeam, Hop	Ostrya	8 to 18	3	x				x	

TREES

Common Name	Botanical Name	*Height (metres)	*Zone	Decid.	Brdlf. Everg.	Conif.	Bloss.	*Fruit/ Berries	Fall Colour
Ironwood	see Hornbeam, Hop								
Japanese Angelica	Aralia elata	8 to 9	4	x			x	x	
Japanese Pagoda tree	see Chinese scholar								
Japanese Snowdrop	Styrax	6 to 9	5	x			x		x
Juneberry	see Serviceberry								
Juniper	Juniperus	6 to 23	2 to 7			x		x	
Katsura tree	Cercidiphyllum	8 to 12	5	x					x
Kentucky coffee tree	Gymnocladus	12 to 27	5	x				pods	x
Larch	Larix	12 to 18	2 to 3			x		cones	
Larch, golden	Pseudolarix	6 to 15	7			x		cones	x
Laurel	Prunus	6 to 9	8		x		x	x	
Linden	Tilia	8 to 18	2 to 6	x					
Locust	Robinia	11 to 18	4	x			x	pods	
Loquat	Eriobotrya	5 to 8	7		x		x	x	
Magnolia		5 to 21	5 to 9	x	x		x		
Maidenhair tree	Ginkgo biloba	11 to 36	4	x					x
Maple	Acer	5 to 27	2 to 7	x					x
Mimosa	see Silk tree								
Monkey puzzle	Araucaria	16 to 18	8			x		cones	
Mountain ash	Sorbus	6 to 18	3 to 4	x			x	x	x
Mulberry	Morus	6 to 14	3	x			x	x	
Mulberry, paper	Broussonetia	11 to 15	6	x			x	x	
Oak	Quercus	9 to 36	3 to 8	x				nuts	x
Oleaster	see Russian olive								
Oriental Arborvitae	see Arborvitae								
Palm (various)		1 to 24	8 to 9		x				
Parrotia		5 to 6	7	x			x		x
Peach, flowering	Prunus	6 to 8	6	x			x		
Pear, ornamental	Pyrus	5 to 8	5	x			x	x	x
Pecan	see Hickory								
Persimmon	Diospyros	5 to 9	7 to 9	x			x	x	x
Pine	Pinus	15 to 45	1 to 6			x		cones	
Pine, umbrella	Sciadopitys	18 to 24	7			x		cones	
Pineapple, Guava	Feijoa	6 to 8	9		x		x	x	
Pistachio, ornamental	Pistacia	14 to 15	8	x					x
Plum, flowering	Prunus	6 to 9	5 to 6	x			x	x	x
Poplar	Populus	9 to 41	1 to 5	x					x
Redbud	Cercis	3 to 15	6 to 9	x			x		x
Redwood	Sequoia	25 to 110	8			x		cones	
Redwood, dawn	Metasequoia	24 to 35	5			x			x
Russian olive	Elaeagnus	3 to 6	2	x			x	x	
Sassafras		12 to 18	6	x			x	x	x
Sequoia, giant	Sequoiadendron	30 to 90	7			x		cones	
Serviceberry	Amelanchier	6 to 14	3 to 4	x			x	x	
Shadblow	see Serviceberry								
Silk tree	Albizia	6 to 12	8	x			x		
Silver bell	Halesia	6 to 18	6 to 8	x			x		x
Spruce	Picea	18 to 50	1 to 5			x		cones	
Strawberry tree	Arbutus	3 to 8	8		x		x	x	

TREES

Common Name	Botanical Name	*Height (metres)	*Zone	Decid.	Brdlf. Everg.	Conif.	Bloss.	* Fruit/ Berries	Fall Colour
Sumac	Rhus	5 to 9	2 to 3	x			x		x
Sycamore	Platanus	6 to 9	5 to 6	x				x	
Torreya		15 to 23	8 to 9			x		x	
Tulip tree	Liriodendron	18 to 24	4	x			x		x
Walnut	Juglans	14 to 18	2 to 9	x			x	nuts	
Willow	Salix	9 to 15	All	x					
Willow, corkscrew	see Willow								
Yew, Plum	Cephalotaxus	5 to 6	9			x		x	
Yew	Taxus	6 to 12	4 to 7			x		x	

* Individual varieties may be different

SHRUBS / BUSHES

Common Name	Botanical Name	*Zone	*Decid.	*Brdlf. Everg.	Conif.	Blossom	Hedge	Fall Colour
Abelia		7	x	x		sum./fall		
Acacia	Robinia	4 to 5	x			spring		
Almond	Prunus	2 to 7	x	x		spring	x	
Anemone, bush	Carpenteria	9		x		summer		
Angelica tree	Aralia	5	x			summer		
Aralia, five-leaved	Acanthopanax	4 to 5	x			fall		
Aralia, Japanese	Fatsia	8		x		fall/win.		
Arborvitae	Thuja	3 to 7			x		x	
Arborvitae, false	Thujopsis	8			x		x	
Aucuba		8		x		spring		
Azalea	see Rhododendron							
Azara		9		x		win./spr.		
Bamboo		7 to 8		x				
Bamboo, heavenly	Nandina	8		x				x
Barberry	Berberis	5 to 7	x	x		spring	x	x
Bayberry	Myrica	2	x					
Beauty-berry	Callicarpa	6 to 7	x			summer		x
Beauty bush	Kolkwitzia	5	x			summer		x
Beech	Fagus	6	x				x	x
Bluebeard	Caryopteris	6 to 8	x			sum./fall		x
Boxwood	Buxus	5 to 7		x		spring	x	
Bridal wreath	see Spirea							
Broom	Cytissus	5 to 7	x			spring		
Broom, Spanish	Spartium	8	x			spring		
Buckeye, bottlebrush	Aesculus	4	x			summer		
Buckthorn, sea	Hippophae	2	x			summer	x	
Buddleia		5	x			sum./fall		
Buffaloberry	Sherpherdia	1	x					
Camellia		8		x		win./spr.	x	
Cedar	Cedrus	7 to 8			x		x	x
Cherry	Prunus	2 to 7	x	x		spring	x	
Coralberry	Symphoricarpos	2 to 5	x			summer		x
Cotoneaster		2 to 5	x	x		spr./sum.	x	x
Cranberry, high-bush	Viburnum	2 to 7	x	x		spr./sum.	x	x

SHRUBS / BUSHES

Common Name	Botanical Name	*Zone	*Decid.	*Brdlf. Everg.	Conif.	Blossom	Hedge	Fall Colour
Creambush	Holodiscus	5	x			summer		
Cryptomeria					x			x
Currant, flowering	Ribes	2 to 7	x			spring	x	
Currant, Indian	Symphoricarpos	2 to 5	x			summer		x
Cypress, false	Chamaecyparis	4 to 7			x		x	
Daphne		2 to 8	x			spr./sum.		
Deutzia		5 to 6	x			spring		
Dogwood	Cornus	2 to 6	x			summer		x
Elder	Sambucus	3	x			spr./sum.		x
Elderberry	see Elder							
Enkianthus		5 to 9	x			spring		x
Escallonia		8		x		sum./fall	x	
Euonymous		2 to 6		x		spring	x	x
Filbert	Corylus	2 to 5	x			spring		
Fir	Abies	1 to 8			x		x	
Fir, Douglas	Pseudotsuga	7			x		x	
Firethorn	Pyracantha	6 to 8		x		spring	x	x
Forsythia		4 to 6	x			spring	x	
Forsythia, white	Abeliophyllum	5	x			spring		
Fothergilla		6	x			spring		x
Fuchsia		8		x		summer	x	
Genista		3 to 7	x			spr./sum.		
Glory-bower	Clerodendrum	8	x			summer		x
Goldflame Spirea	see Spirea							
Grape holly	see Mahonia							
Hawthorne	Crataegus	2 to 6	x			spring	x	x
Hazel, winter	Corylopsis	7	x			win./spr.		
Hazel, witch	Hamamelis	4 to 6	x			win./spr.		x
Hazelnut	see Filbert							
Heath	Erica	5 to 8		x		win./spr.		x
Heath, Irish	Daboecia	7		x		sum./fall		
Heather, Scotch	Calluna	6		x		sum./fall		
Hemlock	Tsuga	4			x		x	
Hibiscus		6	x			summer		
Holly	Ilex	6 to 7		x		spring		x
Honeysuckle	Lonicera	2 to 8	x	x		spr./sum.		x
Hornbeam	Carpinus	3	x			spring	x	
Hydrangea		3 to 6	x			summer		x
Indigo	Indigofera	5	x			summer		
Jasmine	Jasminum	6	x			spring		
Juniper	Juniperus	2			x		x	
Kerria		5	x			spring		x
Laurel	Purnus	2 to 7	x	x		spring	x	
Laurel, mountain	Kalmia	1 to 5		x		summer		
Leadplant	Amorpha	2	x			summer		
Leucothoe		6 to 9		x		spr./sum.		x
Lilac	Syringa	2 to 6	x			spr./sum.	x	
Lilac, California	Ceanothus	7	x			spring		

SHRUBS / BUSHES

Common Name	Botanical Name	*Zone	*Decid.	*Brdlf. Everg.	Conif.	Blossom	Hedge	Fall Colour
Linden	Viburnum	2 to 7	x	x		spr./sum.	x	x
Magnolia		5 to 6	x			spring		
Mahonia		5		x		spring	x	x
Manzanita	Arctostaphylos	1 to 7		x		spring		x
Mock orange	Philadelphus	2 to 5	x			summer	x	
Ninebark	Physocarpus	2	x			summer		x
Ocean spray	see Creambush							
Orange, Mexican	Choisya	8		x		spring		
Oregon snowball	Viburnum	2 to 7	x	x		spr./sum.	x	
Osmanthus		7 to 8		x		spring	x	
Otto Luykens	Prunus	2 to 7	x	x		spring	x	
Pea tree	Caragana	2	x			summer	x	
Pearlbush	Exochorda	5	x			spring		
Photinia		8	x	x		spr./sum.		x
Pieris	Andromeda	5		x		win./spr.		
Pine	Pinus	1 to 5			x		x	
Pittosporum		9		x		spring	x	
Potentilla		2 to 3	x			sum./fall	x	
Privet	Ligustrum	5 to 9	x	x		summer	x	
Quince	Chaenomeles	5	x			spring	x	
Raphiolepsis		8		x		fall/win./spr.		
Redwood	Sequoia	8			x			
Rhododendron		4 to 6	x	x		win./spr.		x
Rose	Rosa	4	x			spr./sum.	x	
Rubus		8	x			spring		
Russian olive	Elaeagnus	2 to 7	x	x		spr./sum.	x	
Salal	Gaultheria	4 to 7		x		summer		
Santolina		9		x			x	
Siberian Pea tree	see Pea tree							
Silk tassel	Garrya	8		x		spring		x
Skimmia		7 to 8		x		spring		x
Smoke tree	Cotinus	5	x			summer		x
Snowberry	Symphoricarpos	2 to 5	x			summer		x
Spirea	Spiraea	2 to 5	x			spr./sum.		x
Spirea, false	Sorbaria	2 to 4	x			summer		
Spruce	Picea	2 to 4			x		x	
St. John's wort	Hypericum	7		x		sum./fall		x
Stephandra		5 to 7	x			summer		x
Sumac	Rhus	3 to 5	x			sum./fall		x
Sweet pepper bush	Clethra	5	x			summer		x
Tamarix		3 to 9	x			spr./sum./fall		
Vaccinium		1 to 7	x	x		spr./sum.		x
Veronica	Hebe	8		x		summer	x	
Viburnum		2 to 7	x	x		spr./sum.	x	x
Vitex		5 to 8	x			summer		
Wayfaring tree	Viburnum	2 to 7	x	x		spr./sum.	x	
Weigela		4 to 5	x			spr./sum.		
Willow	Salix	2 to 5	x			spring	x	x
Yew	Taxus	4 to 7			x		x	

* Individual varieties may be different

VINES

Common Name	Botanical Name	*Zone	*Decid.	*Brdlf. Everg.	Blossom	Feature	Fall Colour
Akebia		6 to 7	x	x	spring	leaves/pods	
Bittersweet	Celastrus	All	x		summer	berries	
Blueberry climber	Ampelopsis	8	x		summer	berries	x
Clematis		4 to 6	x	x	spr./sum.	flowers	
Dutchman's pipe	Aristolochia	All	x		summer	flowers	
Fatshedera		8		x	fall/win.	leaves	
Gooseberry, Chinese	see Kiwi vine						
Honeysuckle	Lonicera	2 to 6	x	x	spring	flowers	
Hydrangea, climbing		5	x		summer	flowers	
Ivy	Hedera	6 to 8		x	summer	leaves	
Ivy, Boston	Parthenocissus	5	x	x	summer	leaves	x
Jasmine	Jasminum	8 to 9		x	summer	flowers	
Kiwi vine	Actinidia	8	x		spring	fruit	
Rose	Rosa	4	x		summer	flowers	
Silver-lace vine	Polygonum	6	x		summer	flowers	
Trumpet creeper	Campsis	6 to 8	x		summer	flowers	
Virginia creeper	Parthenocissus	2	x		summer	leaves	x
Wisteria		6	x		spring	flowers	

* Individual varieties may be different

GROUND COVERS

Common Name	Botanical Name	*Zone	Blossom Period	Special Features	Location Shade	Sun	Fall Colour	Decid.	Everg.
Ajuga		4	May/June	foliage	x	x	x		x
Bishop's weed	Aegopodium	1		foliage	x			x	
Broom, Vanc. gold	Genista	5	May	blossom		x		x	
Bugleweed	Ajuga	4	May/June	foliage	x	x	x		x
Bunchberry	Cornus	8	May/June	blossom	x	x		x	
Buttons, brass	Cotula	8		bloss./fol.					
Catmint	Nepita	2				x			
Checkerberry	Gaultheria	4	summer	all	x			x	x
Cinquefoil	Potentilla	2	summer	blossom		x		x	
Cornus		8	May/June	blossom	x	x		x	
Cotoneaster		1 to 7	spring	berries	x	x		x	x
Cranberry, mountain	Vaccinium	1	spring	all	x			x	
Creeper, Taiwan	Rubus	7							x
Dogwood, creeping	Cornus	1	May/June	blossom	x	x		x	
Euonymous		1		foliage	x	x	x	x	x
Ginger, wild	Asarum	6	spring	foliage					
Goutweed	see Bishop's weed								
Grape, Oregon	Mahonia	7	spring	berr./blos.	x				x
Houttuynia		6	June/July	foliage	x	x		x	
Hypericum		7	summer	blossom		x		x	
Ivy	Hedera			foliage	x	x			x
Juniper, various	Juniperus			foliage	x	x			x
Kinnikinnick	Arctostaphylos	4	spring	all	x	x			x
Lily turf	Liriope	6	summer	blossom	x	x			
Lingonberry	Vaccinium	5	May	all					x

GROUND COVERS

Common Name	Botanical Name	*Zone	Blossom Period	Special Features	Location Shade	Sun	Fall Colour	Decid.	Everg.
Moss, Irish	Arenaria	3		foliage	x	x			
Pachystima	Paxistima	1	spring	foliage	x	x	x		x
Periwinkle	Vinca	5	April/June	all	x				x
Rosemary, bog	Andromeda	3	spring	fol./bloss.		x			x
Salal	Gaultheria	5	March/June	foliage	x				x
Spurge, Japanese	Pachysandra	3	summer	foliage	x				x
St. John's wort	Hypericum	7	summer	blossom	x	x			x
Strawberry, wild	Fragaria	1	spring	fruit	x	x			x
Strawberry, coastal	Fragaria	4	spring	fruit	x	x			x
Twinflower	Linnaea	2		fol./bloss.	x	x			x
Thyme	Thymus	2	June/Sept	foliage					x
Uva Ursi	see Kinnikinnick								
Vinca minor	see Periwinkle								

* Individual varieties may be different

PERENNIALS

Common Name	Botanical Name	Height (cm)	Blossom Period	Use Dry	Use Cut	Location Sun	Location Shade
Adam's Needle	Yucca	90 to 180	summer		x	x	
African lily	Agapanthus	45 to 120	summer			x	partial
Alkanet	Anchusa	30 to 150	summer			x	
Anemone		20 to 90	fall				partial
Artemesia		15 to 150	summer			x	
Aster, Stokes	Stokesia	30 to 45	summer		x	x	
Aubretia		8 to 15	spring			x	partial
Baby's breath	Gypsophila	90 to 120	summer	x	x	x	
Balloonflower	Platycodon	45 to 60	summer		x	x	partial
Boneberry	Actaea	25 to 60	spr./sum.			x	x
Basket of gold	Alyssum	15 to 20	spring			x	
Bearberry	Arctostaphylos	30 to 45	spring			x	partial
Beardtongue	Pentstemon	30 to 60	summer		x	x	
Bear's breech	Acanthus	60 to 90	summer			x	x
Bellflower	Campanula	60 to 90	summer		x	x	partial
Bergenia		25 to 45	spring			x	x
Blanketflower	Gaillardia	15 to 90	summer		x	x	
Bleeding heart	Dicentra	30 to 75	spring		x	x	partial
Bluebell	Mertensia	45	spring		x		partial
Bluestar	Amsonia	60 to 90	spring			x	
Boltonia		120 to 180	summer			x	
Broom	Cytissus	25 to 120	spring			x	
Bugbane	Cimicifuga	90 to 240	fall		x	x	x
Bugle weed	Ajuga	15 to 23	spr./sum			x	partial
Bunchberry	Cornus	15 to 23	spr./sum				partial
Burning bush	see Gas plant						
Buttercup	Ranunculus	45	spring		x	x	partial
Butterfly weed	Asclepeas	60	summer			x	
Candytuft	Iberis	15 to 60	spring			x	
Carnation	see Pinks						

PERENNIALS

Common Name	Botanical Name	Height (cm)	Blossom Period	Use		Location	
				Dry	Cut	Sun	Shade
Catmint	Nepita	23	summer			x	
Centaurea		60 to 120	summer			x	
Centranthus		60 to 90	summer			x	
Chamomile	Anthemis	30 to 90	summer	x	x	x	
Chinese lantern	Physalis	20 to 75	summer	x	x	x	partial
Chinese forget-me-not	Cynoglossum	60 to 90	summer			x	partial
Cinquefoil	Potentilla	15 to 60	summer			x	partial
Clematis		60 to 120	summer			x	partial
Columbine	Aquilegia	38 to 90	spring		x	x	partial
Coneflower	Echinacea	75 to 90	summer	x	x	x	
Coral bells	Heuchera	30 to 60	summer		x	x	
Corydalis		20 to 30	spr./sum.				x
Cranesbill	Geranium	30 to 90	summer			x	partial
Cupid's dart	Catananche	60	summer			x	
Daisy, gloriosa	see Coneflower						
Daisy, painted	Pyrethrum	60 to 90	spr./sum.		x	x	
Daisy, Shasta	Chrysanthemum	30 to 60	sum./fall		x	x	partial
Daphne		15 to 90	spring			x	partial
Daylily	Hemerocallis	38 to 120	summer		x	x	partial
Delphinium		75 to 180	summer		x	x	
Dianthus	see Pink	8 to 30	spring			x	
Draba		8 to 30	spring			x	
Dryas		3 to 23	summer			x	
Dusty miller	see Senecio						
Edelweiss	Leontopodium	20	summer			x	
Epimedium		15 to 23	summer			x	partial
Fairy bells	Disporum	25 to 30	spring				partial
False dragonhead	Physostegia	60 to 90	sum./fall		x	x	partial
False spirea	Astilbe	38 to 105	summer			x	partial
Feverfew	Matricaria	15 to 60			x	x	partial
Flax	Linum	30 to 60	summer			x	
Fleabane	Erigeron	25 to 60	summer			x	
Foam flower	Tiarella	20 to 30	spring				partial
Four o'clock	Mirabilis	45 to 120				x	
Foxglove	Digitalis	90 to 150			x	x	
Fuchsia, cape	Phygelius	90 to 120	sum./fall		x	x	
Galax		15 to 30	spring				partial
Gas plant	Dictamanus	60 to 90	summer	x		x	partial
Gayfeather	Liatris	60 to 150	summer	x	x	x	partial
Gentian	Gentiana	8 to 30	spring			x	partial
Geum		30 to 60	spring		x	x	partial
Ginger, wild	Asarum	12 to 20	spring			x	partial
Globe thistle	Echinops	90 to 150	summer	x	x	x	
Globeflower	Trollius	60 to 90	spring		x	x	partial
Goat's rue	Galega	90	summer	x	x	x	partial
Goatsbeard	Aruncus	120 to 150	summer			x	x
Goldenrod	Solidago	75 to 90	summer		x	x	
Goldthread	Coptis	9 to 15	summer				partial

PERENNIALS

Common Name	Botanical Name	Height (cm)	Blossom Period	Use Dry	Use Cut	Location Sun	Location Shade
Gypsophila, creeping		9 to 12	summer			x	
Haberlea		8 to 15	spring				x
Heath, spike	Bruckenthalia	23 to 60	summer			x	partial
Hens & chicks	Sempervivum	30	summer			x	
Heucherilla		30 to 45	summer			x	partial
Hollyhock	Althaea	90 to 120	summer			x	
Hosta		20 to 45	summer				x
Hypericum	see St. John's wort						
Incarvillea		45 to 60	spring			x	partial
Inula		25 to 60	summer		x	x	
Iris, bearded		20 to 90	spring		x	x	
Jacob's ladder	Polemonium	20 to 90	summer			x	partial
Jeffersonia		15 to 25	spring				x
Kinnikinnick	see Bearberry						
Lady's mantle	Alchemilla	15 to 45	summer			x	partial
Lamb's ear	Stachys	30 to 60	summer		x	x	partial
Lamium		90	spring				x
Lavender, sea	Limonium	45 to 60	summer	x	x	x	
Lavender	Lavendula	30 to 120	summer	x	x	x	
Lenten	see Rose, Christmas						
Leopard's-bane	Doronicum	30 to 45	spring		x	x	partial
Lily, plantain	see Hosta						
Lily of the valley	Convallaria	15 to 20	spring		x		x
Lily turf	Liriope	30 to 45	summer		x	x	partial
Lithospermum		15 to 30	spring			x	
Loosestrife	Lythrum	45 to 180	summer		x	x	partial
Lungwort	Pulmonaria	20 to 25	spring				x
Lupine	Lupinus	15 to 45	summer		x	x	
Lychnis		15 to 30	summer			x	
Mayapple	Podophyllum	45	spring				x
Michaelmas daisy	Aster	25 to 120	fall			x	
Monarda		60 to 90	summer		x	x	partial
Monkshood	Aconitum	75 to 290	summer			x	
Mullein	Verbascum	60 to 120	summer			x	
Oenothera		20 to 30	summer			x	
Omphalodes		20	spring				partial
Pampas grass	Cortaderia selloana	240 to 300	sum./fall	x		x	
Pansy	Viola	15 to 20	yearly		x		
Pea	Lathyrus	180 to 270	summer		x	x	
Peony	Paeonia	60 to 120	spring		x	x	
Phlox		12 to 105	sum./fall		x	x	
Pincushion flower	Scabiosa	75	summer		x	x	
Pinks	Dianthus	30 to 60	summer		x	x	
Polyanthus	Primula	15 to 20	win./spr.			x	x
Poppy, Oriental	Papaver	60 to 90	summer		x	x	
Poppy, plume	Bocconia	150 to 240	summer	x	x	x	
Poppy, Matilija	Romneya	240	summer		x	x	
Ramonda		9 to 15	summer				x

PERENNIALS — Bulbs, Corms & Tubers

Common Name	Botanical Name	Height (cm)	Blossom Period	Use Dry	Use Cut	Location Sun	Location Shade
Red-hot poker	Tritoma	60 to 120	sum./fall		x	x	
Rock cress	Arabis	15 to 25	spring			x	
Rose, Christmas	Helleborus	30 to 45	win./spr.		x	x	x
Rue	Ruta	60 to 90	summer	x	x	x	
Sage, meadow	Salvia	45 to 120	summer		x	x	
Sage, Russian	Perovskia	60 to 90	summer	x		x	
Sea holly	Eryngium	45 to 90	summer	x		x	
Senecio	Ligularia	75 to 180	summer				partial
Shooting star	Dodecatheon	10 to 45	spring			x	x
Shortia		15 to 20	summer			x	
Siberian bugloss	Brunnera	30 to 45	spring				partial
Sidalcea		45 to 90	summer			x	
Silene		8 to 38	summer			x	
Snapdragon	Antirrhinum	15 to 90	summer		x	x	
Sneezeweed	Helenium	45 to 120	summer			x	
Snow-in-summer	Cerastium	8 to 15	summer			x	partial
Solomon's seal	Polygonatum	45 to 120	spring				x
Speedwell	Vernonica	38 to 60	summer		x	x	partial
Spiderwort	Tradescantia	45 to 60	sum./fall				x
Spurge	Euphorbia	45 to 60	summer		x	x	partial
St. John's wort	Helianthemum	8 to 30	summer			x	
Stokesia		30 to 45	summer		x	x	
Stonecrop	Sedum	38 to 40	sum./fall			x	
Sunflower, golden	Heliopsis	12 to 150	summer		x	x	
Sunflower	Helianthus	120	summer		x	x	
Thrift	Armeria	8 to 15	summer			x	
Thyme, Mother of	Thymus	5	summer	x		x	
Tickseed	Coreopsis	30 to 90	summer		x	x	
Turtlehead	Chelone	60 to 120	summer				partial
Twinflower	Linnaea	8 to 10	spring				partial
Uva-ursi	see Bearberry						
Valerian	Valeriana	120	summer		x	x	partial
Vancouveria		20 to 30	summer				partial
Violet	Viola	15 to 20	yearly		x		
Wild senna	Cassia	90 to 150	summer			x	
Wintergreen	Gaultheria	8 to 15	spring				partial
Woodruff, sweet	Asperula	15 to 20	spring			x	partial
Yarrow	Achillea	45 to 90	summer	x		x	

PERENNIALS — Bulbs, Corms & Tubers

Common Name	Botanical Name	Height (cm)	Blossom Period	Use Dry	Use Cut	Location Sun	Location Shade
Aconite, winter	Eranthis	10	win./spr.			x	partial
Allium	Allium aflatunense	10 to 90	summer			x	
Buttercup	Ranunculus	30 to 45	spr./sum./win.		x	x	partial
Crinum		90	summer		x	x	
Crocus, autumn	Colchicum	15	fall			x	partial

PERENNIALS — Bulbs, Corms & Tubers

Common Name	Botanical Name	Height (cm)	Blossom Period	Use Dry	Use Cut	Location Sun	Location Shade
Crocus		15	spr./fall			x	partial
Cyclamen, hardy		15	spr./sum./win.			x	partial
Daffodil	Narcissus	20 to 45	spring		x	x	partial
Fritillaria		20 to 90	spring		x	x	partial
Glory-of-the-snow	Chiondoxa lucilae	20	spring			x	
Harlequin flower	Sparaxis	30 to 45	spring			x	partial
Hyacinth	Hyacinthus	20 to 25	spring		x	x	partial
Hyacinth, grape	Muscari						
Hyacinth, wood	Endymion	30	spring	x		x	
Iris, bulb	Hymenocallis	30 to 45	spring	x		x	partial
Lily	Lilium	45 to 120		x		x	
Lily, African corn	Ixia	45	spri.sum.	x		x	
Lily, trout	Erythronium	15	spring				x
Lily, spider	Lycoris	25 to 60	sum./fall			x	
Lily, calla	Zantedeschia	45 to 60	summer	x		x	partial
Onion, ornamental	see Allium						
Oxalis		5 to 10	spring			x	partial
Scilla		10 to 15	spring			x	partial
Snowdrop	Galanthus	15	spring			x	partial
Snowflake	Leucojum	15 to 30	spr./sum.			x	partial
Star of Bethlehem	Ornithogalum	15 to 30	spring			x	partial
Sternbergia		15 to 25	spring			x	
Tulip		20 to 45	spring		x	x	partial

Canadian Garden Catalogues

A. J. WOODWARD & SONS – 635 Fort St., Victoria, BC, V8W 1G1 – (Sutton Seeds from England) $1.00

AIMERS – 81 Temperance St., Aurora, ON , L4G 2R1 – (Wildflowers) $1.00

ALBERTA NURSERIES AND SEEDS LTD. – Box 20, Bowden, AB, T0M 0K0

ALEX CARON – RR #3, King City, ON, L0G 1K0 – (Potatoes) $1.00

ALPENFLORA GARDENS – 17985 - 40th Ave., Surrey, BC, V3S 4N8 – (Perennials) $2.00

AUBIN NURSERIES LTD. – Box 1089, Carman, MB, R0G 0J0

BC CERTIFIED BUDWOOD ASSN., Agri. Can. Res. Stn., Summerland, BC, V0H 1Z0

BECKER'S SEED POTATOES – RR #1, Trout Creek, ON, P0H 2L0

BERRY HILL LTD. – 75 Burwell Rd., St. Thomas, ON, N5P 3R5 – (Equipment)

BISHOP SEEDS LTD. – Box 338, Belleville, ON, K8N 5A5

BLUEBERRY HILL – RR #1, Maynooth, ON, K0L 2S0 – (Blueberries)

BOUGHEN NURSERIES – PO Box 12, Valley River, MB, R0L 2B0

BRACKENSTONE HERBS – Box 752, Nelson, BC, V1L 5R7 – $3.00

BRADNER BULB CO. – 6775 Bradner Rd., RR #1, Mt. Lehman, BC, V0X 1V0

BRICKMAN'S BOTANICAL GARDENS – Wartburg, RR #1, Sebringville, ON, N0K 1X0 – $3.00

BUMPER CROP SOIL-LESS GARDEN CENTRE – 1316 Centre St. N.W., Calgary, AB, T2E 2A7 – $2.00

CAMPBERRY FARM – RR #1, Niagara-on-the-Lake, ON, L0S 1J0 – (Hardy nuts, fruits) $1.00

CANADIAN HYDROPONICS – #104, 8318 120th St., Surrey, BC, V3W 3N4

CANADIAN ORGANIC GROWERS – 46 Lorindale, Toronto, ON, M5M 3C2 – $1.00

CARL PALLEK & SON – Box 137, Virgil, ON, L0S 1T0 – (Roses)

CENTRE HORTICOLE J. GUY CHARBONNEAU LTEE.– 223 St-Andre C.P. 418, St. Remi, PQ, J0L 2L0

CLARGREEN GARDENS LTD. – 814 Southdown Rd., Mississauga, ON, L5J 2Y4 – (Aquatic plants, orchids, bonsai)

CORN HILL NURSERY LTD. – RR #5, Petitcodiac, NB, E0A 2H0 – $2.00

CRUICKSHANK'S INC. – 1015 Mount Pleasant Rd., Toronto, ON, M4P 2M1 – (Bulbs, garden products) $3.00

DACHA BARINKA – 46232 Strathcona Rd., Chilliwack, BC, V2P 3T2 – (Seeds for drying plants)

DILL'S GARDEN GIANT – 400 College Rd., Windsor, NS, B0N 2T0 – (Giant pumpkins)

DOMINION SEED HOUSE – 115 Guelph St., Georgetown, ON, L7G 4A2

DONNA BARKER – Box 474, Vilna, AB, T0A 3L0 – (Potatoes)

EARLY'S FARM & GARDEN CENTRE– Box 3024, Saskatoon, SK, S7K 3S9 – $1.00

ENVIRONS – 7065 Twiss Rd. RR #3, Campbellville, ON, L0P 1B0 – (Nursery trees)

EXOTIC TROPICAL SEEDS – Box 51057, 234 Tyndall Ave., Winnipeg, MB, R2R 2S6 – $2.00

FERNCLIFF GARDENS – 8394 McTaggart St., Mission, BC, V2V 6S6 – (Dahlia, gladiolus, iris, peony)

FISH LAKE GARLIC MAN – RR #2, Demorestville, ON, K0K 1W0 – $1.00

FOREST MUSHROOMS – Box 658, Smoky Lake, AB, T0A 3C0

FOXFIRE HERBS – Ste 391, 1215 Davie St., Vancouver, BC, V6E 1N4 – $1.00

GARDEN IMPORT INC. – P.O. Box 760, Thornhill, ON, L3T 4A5 – (Unusual and hard-to-find items) $3.00

GAZE SEED – Box 640, 9 Buchanan St., St. John's, NF, A1C 5K8 – (vegetables)

GILBERT'S PEONY GARDENS – Box 67, Clora, ON, N0B 1S0 – $1.00

GOLDEN BOUGH TREE FARM – Marlbank, ON, K0K 2L0 – $1.00

GREGORY A. PECK – Bear River, NS, B0S 1B0 – (Giant pumpkin seeds) $5.95

GRIMO NUT NURSERY – RR #3 Lakeshore Rd., Niagara-on-the-Lake, ON, L0S 1J0 – $1.00

HALIFAX SEED CO. INC. – Box 8026, 5860 Kane St., Halifax, NS, B3K 5L8

HAPPY HERBS – General Delivery, Sandford, ON, L0C 1E0 – $1.00

HARMONY GARDENS – RR #3, Merrick-ville, ON, K0G 1N0 – (Garlic)

HARRISON'S GARDEN CENTRE – Box 460, Carnduff, SK, S0C 0S0 – $2.00

HAZELGROVE GARDENS – S-11 C11 RR 5, Kelowna, BC, V1X 4K4 – (Herbs, perennials)

HERITAGE SEED PROGRAM – RR #3, Uxbridge, ON, L0C 1K0

HONEYWOOD LILLIES – Box 63, Parkside, SK, S0J 2A0 – (Lilies, iris, peonies) $1.00

HORTICO INC. – 723 Robson Rd., Waterdown, ON, L0R 2H1 – (Roses, perennials, shrubs/vines) $2.00

HUMBER NURSERIES – RR #8, Highway 50, Brampton, ON, L6T 3Y7

HURONVIEW NURSERIES – 1811 Brigoen Side Rd., Bright's Grove, ON, N0N 1C0

ISLAND SEED MAIL ORDER – Box 4278, Station A, Victoria, BC, V8X 3X8

LAKESHORE TREE FARMS LTD. – RR #3, Saskatoon, SK, S7K 3J6 – $2.00

LEONARD W. BUTT – Huttonville, ON, L0J 1B0 – (Gladiolus) $1.00

LES JARDINS OSIRIS – CP 336, Repentigny, PQ, J6A 7C6 – (Daylilies, hosta, Siberian iris) $1.00

LES VIOLETTES NATALIA – 124 ch. Grapes, Sawyerville, PQ, J0B 3A0 – (African violets, gesneriads) $2.00

LINDEL LILIES – 5510 - 239th St., Langley, BC, V3A 7N6 – $1.00

LINDENBERG SEEDS LTD. – 803 Princess Ave., Brandon, MB, R7A 0P5 – (Northern seeds)

M. WILLIAMS–THE BERRY PATCH – 103 Broadview Ave., Pointe Claire, PQ, H9R 3Z3 – $2.00

MCCONNELL NURSERIES INC. – RR #1, Port Burwell, ON, N0J 1T0

MCFAYDEN SEED CO. LTD. – P.O. Box 1800, Brandon, MB, R7A 6N4 – $1.00

MCMATH'S DAFFODILS – 6340 Francis Rd., Richmond, BC, V7C 1K5

MOCHIAS ENT. – 12343 - 216 St., Maple Ridge, BC, V2X 5K2 – (Flowering bulbs)

MONASHEE PERENNIALS – RR #7, Site 6, Box 9, Vernon, BC, V1T 7Z3

MOORE WATER GARDENS – P.O. Box 340, Hwy #4, Port Stanley, ON, N0L 2A0

MORDEN NURSERIES LTD. – Box 1270, Morden, MB, R0G 1J0

NATURAL LEGACY SEEDS – RR #2, C-1 Laird, Armstrong, BC, V0E 1B0

NON-TOXIC PEST CONTROL – 492 Camden Pl., Winnipeg, MB, R3G 2V7

NORTHERN KIWI NURSERY – RR #3, Niven Rd., Niagara-on-the-Lake, ON, L0S 1J0

NORTHERN STAR PLANTS & HERBS – Box 2262, Stn A, London, ON, N6A 4E3 – $1.00

ONTARIO SEED CO. LTD. – Box 2262, Stn A, London, ON, N6A 4E3 – $1.00

ORCHIBEC ENR. – 200 Jean Gauvin, Ste-Foy, PQ, G2E 3L9 – (Orchids) $2.00

ORCHID HAVEN – 900 Rossland Rd. E., Whitby, ON, L1N 5R5

ORCHIDS FOR EVERYONE – 7 Wagner St., Glenbourne, ON, K0H 1S0

PACIFIC NORTHWEST SEED CO. – Box 460, Vernon, BC, V1T 6M4 – $1.00

PHIPPS AFRICAN VIOLETS – RR #1, Paris, ON, N3L 3E1 – $2.00

PICKERING NURSERIES INC. – 670 Kingston Rd., Pickering, ON, L1V 1A6 – $2.00

PLANTS 'N' THINGS – Pollock Rd., RR #2, Keswick, ON, L4P 3E9 – (African violets, begonias, etc.) $2.00

PRAIRIE GROWN GARDEN SEEDS – Box 118, Cochin, SK, S0M 0L0

PRAIRIE ORCHID CO. – 515 Elmhurst Rd., Winnipeg, MB, R3R 0V2 – $1.00

PRISM PERENNIALS – C45 S25 RR #1, Castlegar, BC, V1N 3H7 – $2.00

RAINFOREST GARDENS – RR#1, S-2, C-22, Port Moody, BC, V3H 3C8 – (Shade perennials) $2.00

RAINFOREST MUSHROOM SPAWN – Box 1793, Gibsons, BC, V0N 1V0 – $2.00

RANDALL PRUE PLANT DOCTOR – 2916 Bellerive, Carignan, PQ, J3L 4K2 – (Natural products) $2.50

RAWLINSON GARDEN SEED – 269 College Rd., Truro, NS, B2N 2P6 – $1.00

REIMER WATERSCAPES – Box 34, Tillonsburg, ON, N4G 4H3

RICHTER'S – Goodwood, ON, L0C 1A0 – (Herbs) $2.50

RIVER VIEW FARM – Box 92, Maitland, NS, B0N 1T0 – (Herbs)

RIVERLAND GARDENS – 8595 Darnley Rd., Mont Royal, PQ, H4T 2A4 –

(Tayberries, etc.) $1.00

ROBLYN ERIE FARM & NURSERY –
Perth, ON, K7H 3C5 – $3.50

ROCKY MOUNTAIN SEED SERVICE –Box 215,
Golden, BC, V0A 1H0 –(Flower seeds) $1.00

ROSEBERRY GARDENS – Box 933, Thunder Bay, ON, P7C 4X8 – (Roses, azaleas, lilies, etc.) $2.00

RYERSE GLAD GARDENS – RR #1,
Waterford, ON, N0E 1Y0 – (Gladiolus)

SALLY & CO. – P.O. Box 24121, 300 Eagleson Rd., Kanata, ON, K2M 2C3 –
(Exotic tropical seeds)

SALT SPRING SEEDS – Box 33, Ganges,
BC, V0S 1E0 – (Northern climate seeds)

SAM AIKENS – RR #4, Blenheim, ON,
N0P 1A0 – (English walnut trees)

SANCTUARY SEEDS – 2388 West 4th Ave.,
Vancouver, BC, V6K 1P1 – (Vegetables, herbs) $1.00

SCARAMOUCHE GALLERY –635 Fort St.,
Victoria, BC, V8W 1G1 –(Tomatoes) $1.00

SCHRIENER'S IRIS GARDENS CRESCENT
NURSERY – RR #4, Rockwood, ON,
N0B 2K0 – $4.00

SEDONA GARDENS – Box 5430, Victoria,
BC, V8R 6S4 – (Rare plants) $0.50

SEED CENTRE LTD. – Box 3867, Stn D,
Edmonton, AB, T5L 4K1 – (Vegetables)

SELECT ROSES – 22771 - 38 Ave., Langley,
BC, V3A 6H5

SHADES OF HARMONY – Box 598, Kingston,
NS, B0P 1R0 – (Untreated seeds) $2.00

SIBERIA SEEDS – Box 3000, Olds, AB,
T0M 1P0 – (Tomatoes)

SOC. OF ONTARIO NUT GROWERS – RR #1,
Niagara-on-the-Lake, ON, L0S 1J0 – $8.00

SOUTH BAY VINEYARDS – RR #2, Milford,
ON, K0K 2P0

SPEYSIDE HEATHER CANADA – 218 Oakland Ave., London, ON, N5W 4J3

SPRINGWOOD MINIATURE ROSES – RR
#3, Caledon East, ON, L0N 1E0 – $1.00

SPROUT FARMS FRUIT TREE NURSERy – Box
538, Bon Accord, AB, T0A OK0 – $2.00

STANLEY ZUBROWSKI – Box 26, Prairie
River, SK, S0E 1J0 – (Tomatoes) SASE

STIRLING PERENNIALS – RR #1, Morpeth,
ON, N0P 1X0 – $2.00

STOKES SEEDS – 39 James St., Box 10, St.
Catharines, ON, L2R 6R6

SURSUM CORDA – RR #3, Scotstown, PQ,
J0B 3B0 – (Fruit trees) $2.00

T & T SEEDS LTD.– Box 1710, Winnipeg,
MB, R3C 3P6 – $1.00

TERRITORIAL SEEDS LTD. – Box 46225,
Stn G, Vancouver, BC, V6R 4G5 – $1.00

THE BUTCHART GARDENS – Box 4010,
Stn. A, Victoria, BC, V8X 3X4 – $1.00

THE GARLIC CO. – Box 367, Markdale,
ON, N0C 1H0 – $8.00

THE HERB FARM – RR #4, Norton, NB,
E0G 2N0 – $2.00

THE LIVING PRAIRIE MUSEUM – 2795
Ness Ave., Winnipeg, MB, R3J 3S4 –
(Prairie grasses, shrubs)

TREGUNNO SEEDS LTD. – 126 Catherine
St. N., Hamilton, ON, L8R 1J4

TROPICAL AIR PLANTS – 4150 S. Service
Rd., Burlington, ON, L7L 4X5 – $1.00

TSOLUM RIVER FRUIT TREES – Box 68,
Merville, BC, V0R 2M0 – $3.50

V. KRAUS NURSERIES LTD. – Carlisle, ON,
L0R 1H0

VALLEY ORCHID PARTNERS – 12621
Woolridge Rd., Pitt Meadows, BC, V3Y 1Z1

VANNOORT BULB CO. LTD. – 417 Winona Rd. N., Winona, ON, L0R 2L0

VESEY'S SEEDS LTD. – York, PE, C0A 1P0

VINELAND NURSERIES – Box 98, Vineland
Station, ON, L0R 2E0 – $1.00

W.H. PERRON & CO. – 515 Labelle Blvd.,
Chomedey Laval, PQ, H7V 2T3 – $3.00

W. RICHARDSON FARMS LTD. – Pontypool, ON, L0A 1K0 – (Trees, shrubs)

WEST COAST VIOLETS – 2692 East 45th
Ave., Vancouver, BC, V5R 3C1 – $1.00

WEST KOOTENAY HERB NURSERY – RR
#2, Nelson, BC, V1L 5P5

WESTERN BIOLOGICALS LTD. –
Box 283, Aldergrove, BC, V0X 1A0 –
(Mushrooms) $2.00

WILLIAM DAM SEEDS – Box 8400,
Dundas, ON, L9H 6M1 – $1.00

WINDMILL POINT FARM & NURSERIES –
2103 Perrot Blvd., N.D. de L'Ile Perrot,
PQ, J7V 5V6 – (Fruit & nut trees)

WOODLAND NURSERIES – 2151 Camilla
Rd., Mississauga, ON, L5A 2K1 –
(Rhododendrons) $3.50

WOODWINDS NURSERY – Gen. Del., Bluevale,
ON, N0G 1G0 – (Fruit trees) $1.00

Latin Glossary

This glossary will help gardeners understand the names of many of the plants. Some are named after a certain person, the person who discovered or bred the plant (names will end in i or ii), or the area they are from (ending in a, us or um). The names of plants may be very confusing to many of you, but in reality can be of much assistance to you when purchasing plants or planning your landscaping because the name tells so much about the plant once a few simple terms are understood. Latin was the universal language of the scholars all over the world back in the eighteenth century and has become the international medium for the scientific naming of plants and animals.

Plants have two botanical names. The first word is the name of a GENUS, groups the plant and is a noun. The second word is the SPECIES, an adjective that describes the plant. It actually pins down which of the types of plants mentioned in the genus it is and can be found in hundreds of genera but it will occur only once with each genus. (EXAMPLE: *Acer palmatum* —This tells us that it is a maple [*Acer*] with palm-shaped leaves [*palmatum*]). Simple! What if there are several maples with palm-shaped leaves? You guessed it! A third name.

The third name refers to VARIETIES. This name, also an adjective, further describes the plant. (EXAMPLE: *Acer palmatum* 'Dissectum Atropurpureum' —tells us it is a maple [*Acer*] with palm-shaped leaves [*palmatum*] with very deeply cut and finely divided leaves [dissectum] that are deep purple in colour [atropurpureum]). Now, is it still confusing? A little more help. Suppose you wanted a maple with palm-shaped leaves that was deeply cut and finely divided with pale yellowish green leaves. You would find the name for that plant is *Acer palmatum* 'Dissectum Flavescens'. Suppose you wanted the same maple but with pale bronze leaves. The name for that plant is *Acer palmatum* 'Dissectum Ornatum'.

There are still more names added to the ones above for more detail and breeding on the plants, but this is enough to start with. Before going through the list, let's try it out with a few different plants showing all three names. Some plants will only have two names.

GENUS	SPECIES	VARIETIES
Acer [Maple]	*palmatum* [palm-shaped leaves]	'Dissectum Atropurpureum' [deeply cut, finely divided leaves; dark purple]
Hydrangea [Hydrangea]	*paniculata* [cluster]	'Grandiflora' [large]
Euonymus [Euonymus]	*japonicus* [of Japan]	[NONE]
Euonymus [Euonymus]	*japonicus* [of Japan]	'Albomarginatus' [green leaves margined white]
Ilex [Holly]	*aquifolium* [sharp leaves]	'Pyramidalis' [pyramid-shaped]

As you can see, the genus is always capitalized because it is a noun and the family name, the species starts with a lowercase letter. The variety is capitalized and in single quotes. You may see the names written A. p. 'Dissectum Atropurpureum'. Don't let it confuse you. The A. is for "Acer" and the lowercase p. is for "palmatum".

a-, an- — prefix —without, not

abies —fir

acaulis —stemless

acerifolius —maplelike leaves

acuminatus —leaves taper to a point

acutus —with sharp-pointed leaves

adpressus —pressing against, hugging

albidus, albus, alba, albo —dead-white colour

alternifolius, alternus —alternate

altus —tall

amabilis —lovely

amplxicaulis —leaves embrace the stem

angustifolius — narrow leaves

ante- — prefix — before

anti- — prefix — against

annuus — annual

aquaticus, aquatilis — of the water

aquifolius, aquifolium — sharp leaves

arboreum — treelike

arenicola — of the sand

argentatus, argentea — silvery

argyrophyllum — with silver leaves

armatus — armed

aromaticus — aromatic

arvensis — of the field

asper — rough

atropurpureus, atropurpureum — dark purple, almost black

aureus, aurea — golden

auriculatum — eared

australis, meridionalis — southern

autumnalis — flowers in autumn

azureus, azurea — azure, sky blue

baccatus — berried, berrylike

barbatum, barbatus — barbed or bearded

bi- — prefix — two, both, double

bicolour — with two colours

biennis — biennial

borealis, septentrionalis — northern

bulbosus — growing from or having a bulb

bullatus — inflated, with pimpled surface

buxifolius — leaves like boxwood

caerulea — blue

caesius — blue gray

calophytum — beautiful plant

calostrotum — with a beautiful covering

campanulatus, campanula — bell- or cup-shaped

campestris — of the field or plains

campylocarpum — with best fruit

candidus, candida — shining/glistening white

canescens — becoming white or hoary; old

canus — ashy gray, hoary (frosted)

capitatus — headlike

cardinalis — red

carneus — flesh-coloured

cedrus — cedar

centralis, medius — central

cereus — waxy

cernuus — nodding or drooping

chamaecyparis — false cypress

chryseum — golden yellow

chrysos — gold

ciliatus, cilatum — fringed

cinereus — light grey

citrinus — yellow

citriodorus — having the odor of citrus

co-, con- — prefix — together, with

coccineus — scarlet

coeruleus — dark blue

compactus — compact, dense

communis — common

concolour — one colour

confertus — crowded, pressed together

coniferous — cone-bearing

contortus — twisted

contra- — prefix — against, opposite

cordatus, cordifolius — heart-shaped

cristatus — crested

croceus — yellow

cruetus — bloody

cyaneus — blue

decidua — not permanent, to fall

decorum — ornamental

decumbens — lying down

decurrens — running down the stem

dendron — tree

depressus — pressed down

dichroanthum — with two coloured flowers

discolour — two colours, separate colours

divaricata — spreading

diversi — varying

ec- — prefix — out

ecto- — prefix — outside

edulis — edible

elata — tall

elegans — elegant; slender, willowy

elongatus — elongated

em-, en- — prefix — in

endo- — prefix — within

-ensis — suffix — to mean (of a place)

erecta, erectus — standing upright

fastigatus — branches erect, close together

fastigiatum — erect

ferrugineum — rusty-coloured

filiformis — threadlike

fimbriatus — fringed

flavus, flavulus, flavidus, flava — yellow

floridus — free-flowering

floris, flos — flower

foetida — ill-smelling

forestii — scarlet

fragrans — fragrant

frondonsus — leafy

fructus — fruit

fruticosus — shrubby

fulgens — shiny

fulvus — tawny

-genic — suffix — origin

glabrus — smooth; not having down or hairs

glauca — grey-blue

glaucus — whitish with a bloom, blue-gray-green

gracilis — slender, thin, small

grande — large

grandi — large, showy reticulatus veined

haematodes — bloodlike

heterophyllus — with leaves of different forms or colours

hippophaeoides — sea buckthorn-like (grey-green)

hirsutum, hirsutus — hairy, with coarse hairs

hirtellus — with coarse but short hairs

hispidus — bristly

horridus, horridulus — prickly

hortensis — of gardens

humifusus — sprawling on the ground

humilis — low, small, humble

-ifer, -iferous — suffix — bearing or having cones)

ilicifolius — hollylike leaves

impeditum — tangled

impressus — impressed upon

incanus — gray, hoary (frosted)

iniscus — with leaves cut into sharp teeth

insularis — of the island

intermedia — between, middle

keleticum — charming

laciniatus — fringed or with torn edges

laevigatus, laevis — smooth

lanatus, lanuginosus, lanulosus — woolly

lanceolatus — with leaves narrow, pointed

larix — larch

latifolius — with broad leaves

laurifolius — laurel-like leaves

leucaspis — white shield

lutea — — yellow

linearis — leaves narrow with parallel sides

littoralis — of the seashore

lobatus — lobed

luteus — reddish yellow

maculatus — spotted

marginatus — margin, edge

maritimus — of the sea

minor — smaller

mollis, mollearis — soft, soft hairy, tender; supple, pliable, graceful; gentle, mild, pleasant

montanus — of the mountains

monstrus — strange, wonderful; monstrosity, horrible

mucronatus — pointed

nanus, nana — dwarf

nerliflorum — flowers like oleanders (shades of pink to scarlet)

niger, nigra — black

nobilis — noble, high born

nudicaulis — with nude (leafless) stems

nutans — nodding, swaying

obtusa — blunt or flattened; not pointed

occidentalis — western

odorata — fragrant

officinalis — used commercially; medicinal

-oid — suffix — like

oides — like or resembling

orbiculare — circular

orientalis — eastern

ovalifolius — with oval leaves

ovatus — egg-shaped

pachypodus — with thick stalks

pallidus — pale

palmatus — with divided or lobed leaves

palustris — of the swamps

paniculata — clusters, panicles

parvifolius — small leaves

patens — open spreading growth

perennis — perennial

perfoliatus — with stem growing through the leaf or pair of joined leaves

picea — spruce

pilostus — with long hairs

pinnatus — constructed like a feather

pinus — pine

planta — plant

plenus — double, full

plumosus — feathery

praecox — precocious

pratensis — of the meadows

procumbens — trailing, bent down

procumbent — prostrate, lying down

prostratus — prostrate, lying on the ground

pubescens — downy

pulchellus — beautiful

pumilus — dwarfish, small

pungens — piercing

purpureus, purpurea — purple

pusilius — puny, insignificant

pygmaea — dwarf, small

pyramidalis — pyramid-shaped

racemosum — flowers in racemes

radicans — rooting, especially along the stem

ramosus — branching

renifolius — with kidney-shaped leaves

repens, reptans — creeping

reticulatus — veined

retusus — notched at blunt apex

rigidus — stiff

riparius — of river banks

rivularis, rivalis — of brooks

roseus — coloured

rotundifolius — with round leaves

rubra, ruber, rubens — red, ruddy

rubiginosum — reddish-brown

rufus — ruddy

rugosus — wrinkled, rough

russatum — reddened

saccharatus — sweet, sugary

sagittalis — arrowlike

sagittifolius — with arrowhead-shaped leaves

salicifolius — willow-like leaves

sativus — cultivated

sauveolens — sweet-smelling

saxatilis — inhabiting rocks

saxicola — of the rocks

scaber, scaberrimus, scabrus — rough,

scandens — climbing

scintillans — sparkling

scoparius — broomlike

sempervirens — evergreen

serratus — serrated

sinuatus — edges curving in and out

spectabilis — handsome, showy

spicata — spiked

stiratus — marked with lines

strictus — straight, erect

stoloniferous — having stolons

sub- — prefix — under, beneath, below

suffruticosa — shrubby

super-, supra- — prefix — beyond, superior

sylvestris, sylvaticus — of the woods

sym- — prefix — with, along, together, beside

taxus — yew

tenellus, tenuis — slender

tenuifolius — with narrow leaves

tomentosus, tomentosa — with short tangled hairs

tri- — prefix — three

triflorum — three-flowered

tsuga — hemlock

tuberosus — growing from or forming a tuber

undulatus — with wavy margins

variegata — diversity of colours

vernus — flowering in spring

villosus — shaggy with long hairs

violaceus — violet-coloured

virginianus, virginicus, viridirufus — reddish green colour

viridis, viridescens — green, becoming green

vulgaris — common

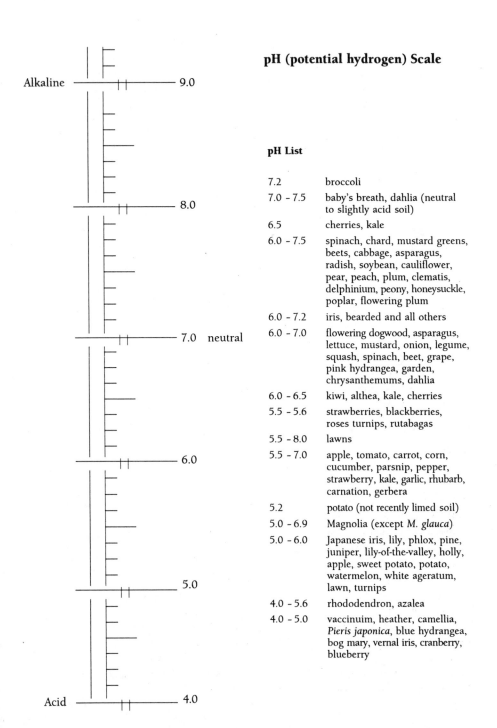

pH (potential hydrogen) Scale

Alkaline ——— 9.0

8.0

7.0 neutral

6.0

5.0

Acid ——— 4.0

pH List

pH	
7.2	broccoli
7.0 - 7.5	baby's breath, dahlia (neutral to slightly acid soil)
6.5	cherries, kale
6.0 - 7.5	spinach, chard, mustard greens, beets, cabbage, asparagus, radish, soybean, cauliflower, pear, peach, plum, clematis, delphinium, peony, honeysuckle, poplar, flowering plum
6.0 - 7.2	iris, bearded and all others
6.0 - 7.0	flowering dogwood, asparagus, lettuce, mustard, onion, legume, squash, spinach, beet, grape, pink hydrangea, garden, chrysanthemums, dahlia
6.0 - 6.5	kiwi, althea, kale, cherries
5.5 - 5.6	strawberries, blackberries, roses turnips, rutabagas
5.5 - 8.0	lawns
5.5 - 7.0	apple, tomato, carrot, corn, cucumber, parsnip, pepper, strawberry, kale, garlic, rhubarb, carnation, gerbera
5.2	potato (not recently limed soil)
5.0 - 6.9	Magnolia (except *M. glauca*)
5.0 - 6.0	Japanese iris, lily, phlox, pine, juniper, lily-of-the-valley, holly, apple, sweet potato, potato, watermelon, white ageratum, lawn, turnips
4.0 - 5.6	rhododendron, azalea
4.0 - 5.0	vaccinuim, heather, camellia, *Pieris japonica*, blue hydrangea, bog mary, vernal iris, cranberry, blueberry

Index

A

Abies (fir), 142

Abutilon, 77

Acer (maple), ix, 14, 32, 54, 71, 112 - 113, 129 - 130

Aconite, winter (Eranthis hyemalis), 124

Aconitum (monkshood), 118, 133

Actinidia (kiwi), 105, 139, 143 - 144

Ageratum (floss flower), 25, 39, 75

Ajuga (carpet bugle), 74, 163

Alchemilla mollis (lady's mantle), 73

Allium, 123, 167

Althaea (hollyhock), 73 - 74, 90, 94, 98, 107, 118

Alyssum, 38, 56, 73, 75, 78, 164

Amaryllis, 11 - 12, 72

Anemone, 4, 123, 164

Annuals, 25, 39, 56, 74, 90, 100, 108, 118, 133, 151

Antirrhinum (snapdragon), 39 - 40, 56, 75, 90, 97, 100, 100, 119

Aphids, 7, 36, 48, 68, 94, 102,

Apple, 2, 7, 52, 81, 88, 91, 130

Application to Import, 2

Apricot, 29, 52, 88

Aquilegia (columbine), 56, 72, 89, 98, 118, 165

Arborvitae (Thuja), 149, 158, 160

Arbutus (Strawberry tree), 2, 27, 43, 53 - 54, 146

Asparagus, 58, 66, 92

Aster novae-angliae (Michaelmas daisy), 73, 75, 118, 133

Aubretia, 38, 56, 164

Aucuba, 4

Azalea, 3, 11, 14, 33, 54, 87 - 88, 104, 160

B

Baby's breath (Gypsophila paniculata), 73, 108, 164 - 165

Bachelor's button (Centaurea cyranus), 74

Balloonflower (Platycodon grandiflorum), 72 - 73, 164

Barberry (Berberis), 4, 160

Beans, 27, 47, 61, 66, 92, 102, 126, 152

Beauty bush (Kolkwitzia amabilis), 4, 160

Beech (Fagus), 113, 130, 158, 160

Bees, 48, 52, 83

Beets, 47, 59, 61, 80, 92, 102, 109, 125, 135 - 136, 146

Begonia, 6, 9, 26, 41, 76 - 77, 94, 101, 117, 134

Bellflower (Campanula), 98, 108, 164

Bergenia, 38, 56, 73, 134, 164

Birch (Betula), 17, 32, 158

Birds, 2, 7, 54, 83

Black spot, 7, 35 - 36, 71, 89, 114

Black-eyed Susan (Rudbeckia hirta), 82

Bleeding heart (Dicentra), 38, 73 - 74, 98, 118, 164

Bluebell (Endymion), 40, 164

Boltonia, 118, 133, 164

Boxwood (Buxus sempervirens), 139, 160

Broccoli, 59, 61, 66, 80, 103, 125, 146

Brodiea, 123

Broom (Cytisus), 32, 54, 87, 160, 164

Brussels sprouts, 27, 61, 66, 102 - 103, 146,

Buddleia (butterfly bush), 18, 160

Bugbane (Cimicifuga), 98, 164

Bulbs,

    forcing, 3, 69, 119 - 120

    list, 6, 26, 40 - 42, 56 - 57, 72, 79, 91, 101, 108, 119 - 121, 123, 133, 145, 151

    planting, 6, 10, 26, 40, 56 - 57, 79, 91, 101, 108, 119, 121, 124, 133 - 134, 151

Butterfly flower (Schizanthus), 78

C

Cabbage, 27, 47, 59, 61, 66, 80, 100, 102 - 103, 135, 146, 151

Cabbage moth, 103

Caladium, 134

Calendula, 40, 56, 75, 100

Calluna (heather), 4, 14, 32, 53 - 54

Camass, 124

Camellia, 3 - 4, 14, 32, 54, 70, 86 - 87, 104, 113, 160

Campanula (bellflower), 98, 108, 164

Candytuft (Iberis sempervirens), 56, 164

Cane spot, 7

Canna, 41, 57, 134

Carnation (Dianthus), 55, 72, 164

Carrots, 47, 54, 59, 62, 65, 80, 92, 102, 109, 125, 135 - 136, 146

Cauliflower, 27, 59, 62, 66, 80, 92, 102 - 103, 109, 125